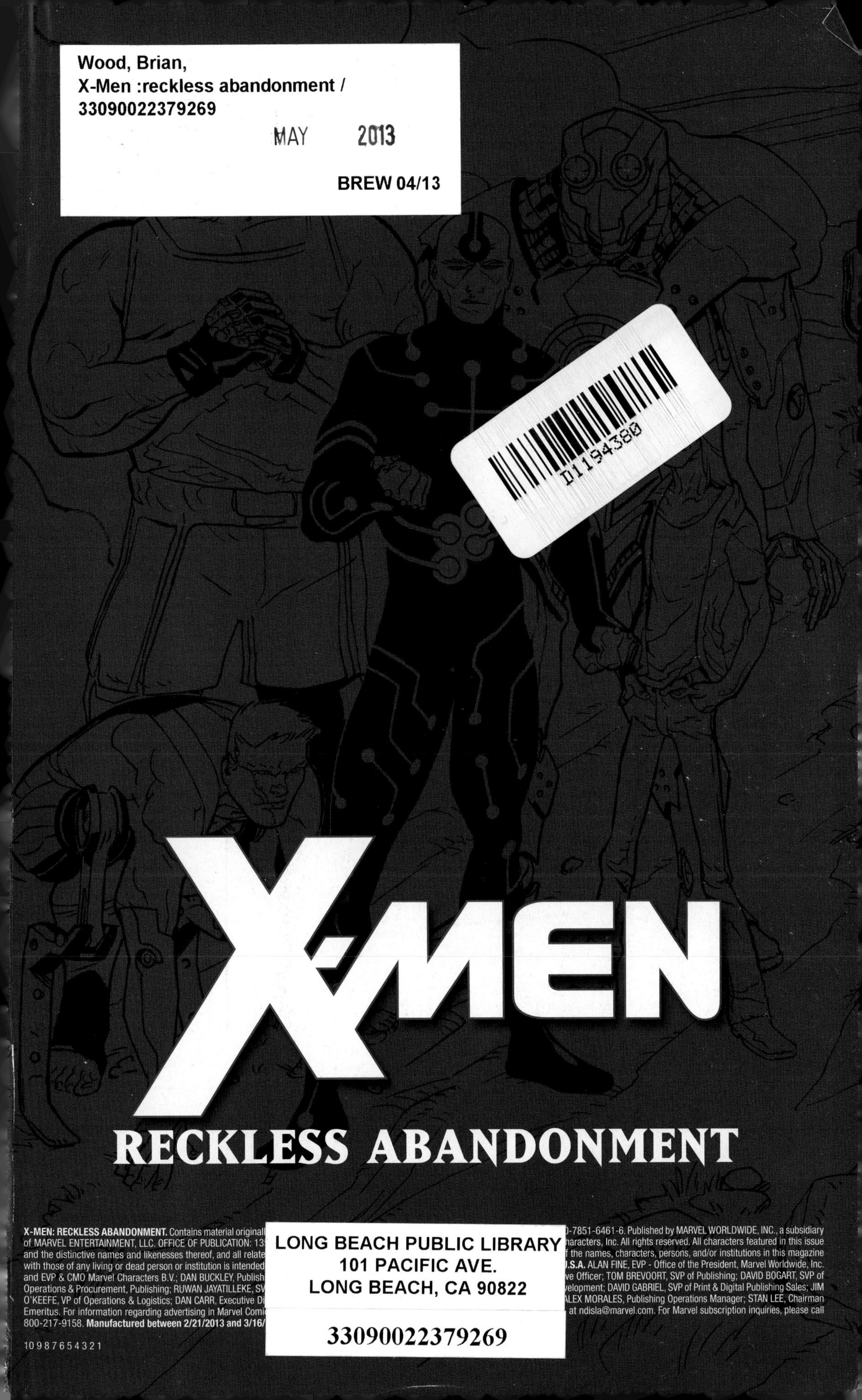

X-MEN
RECKLESS ABANDONMENT

X-MEN: RECKLESS ABANDONMENT. Contains material originall … 0-7851-6461-6. Published by MARVEL WORLDWIDE, INC., a subsidiary of MARVEL ENTERTAINMENT, LLC. OFFICE OF PUBLICATION: 13 … haracters, Inc. All rights reserved. All characters featured in this issue and the distinctive names and likenesses thereof, and all relate … f the names, characters, persons, and/or institutions in this magazine with those of any living or dead person or institution is intended … **.S.A.** ALAN FINE, EVP - Office of the President, Marvel Worldwide, Inc. and EVP & CMO Marvel Characters B.V.; DAN BUCKLEY, Publish … ve Officer; TOM BREVOORT, SVP of Publishing; DAVID BOGART, SVP of Operations & Procurement, Publishing; RUWAN JAYATILLEKE, SV … velopment; DAVID GABRIEL, SVP of Print & Digital Publishing Sales; JIM O'KEEFE, VP of Operations & Logistics; DAN CARR, Executive Di … ALEX MORALES, Publishing Operations Manager; STAN LEE, Chairman Emeritus. For information regarding advertising in Marvel Comi … at ndisla@marvel.com. For Marvel subscription inquiries, please call 800-217-9158. **Manufactured between 2/21/2013 and 3/16/**

10 9 8 7 6 5 4 3 2 1

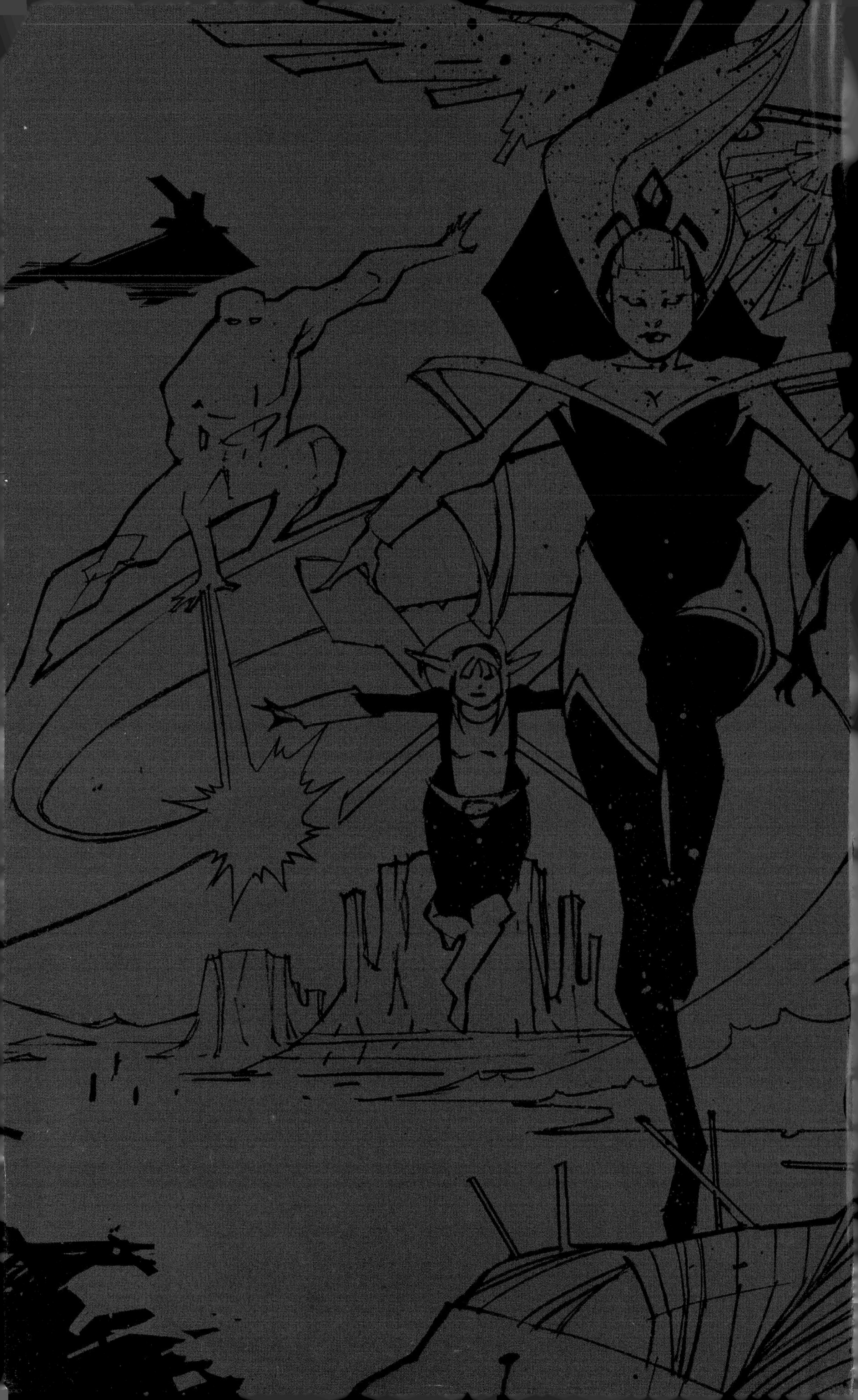

RECKLESS ABANDONMENT

WRITERS

BRIAN WOOD (#36-37) & **SETH PECK** (#38-41)

PENCILER (#36-37)

DAVID LÓPEZ

INKER (#36-37)

ÁLVARO LÓPEZ

ARTISTS (#38-39)

PAUL AZACETA
& MATTHEW SOUTHWORTH

ARTISTS (#40-41)

JEFTE PALO & GUILLERMO MOGORRON

WITH **LORENZO RUGGIERO** (INKER, #41)

COLOR ARTISTS

RACHELLE ROSENBERG (#36-37),
RICO RENZI (#38-39), **LEE LOUGHRIDGE** (#39)
& **ANDRES MOSSA** (#40-41)

LETTERER

VC'S JOE CARAMAGNA

COVER ARTISTS

DAVID LÓPEZ (#36-40)
AND **ADAM KUBERT**
& **MORRY HOLLOWELL** (#41)

ASSISTANT EDITOR

JENNIFER M. SMITH

EDITOR

JEANINE SCHAEFER

X-MEN GROUP EDITOR

NICK LOWE

COLLECTION EDITOR: CORY LEVINE
ASSISTANT EDITORS: ALEX STARBUCK & NELSON RIBEIRO
EDITORS, SPECIAL PROJECTS: JENNIFER GRÜNWALD & MARK D. BEAZLEY
SENIOR EDITOR, SPECIAL PROJECTS: JEFF YOUNGQUIST
SVP OF PRINT & DIGITAL PUBLISHING SALES: DAVID GABRIEL

EDITOR IN CHIEF: AXEL ALONSO
CHIEF CREATIVE OFFICER: JOE QUESADA
PUBLISHER: DAN BUCKLEY
EXECUTIVE PRODUCER: ALAN FINE

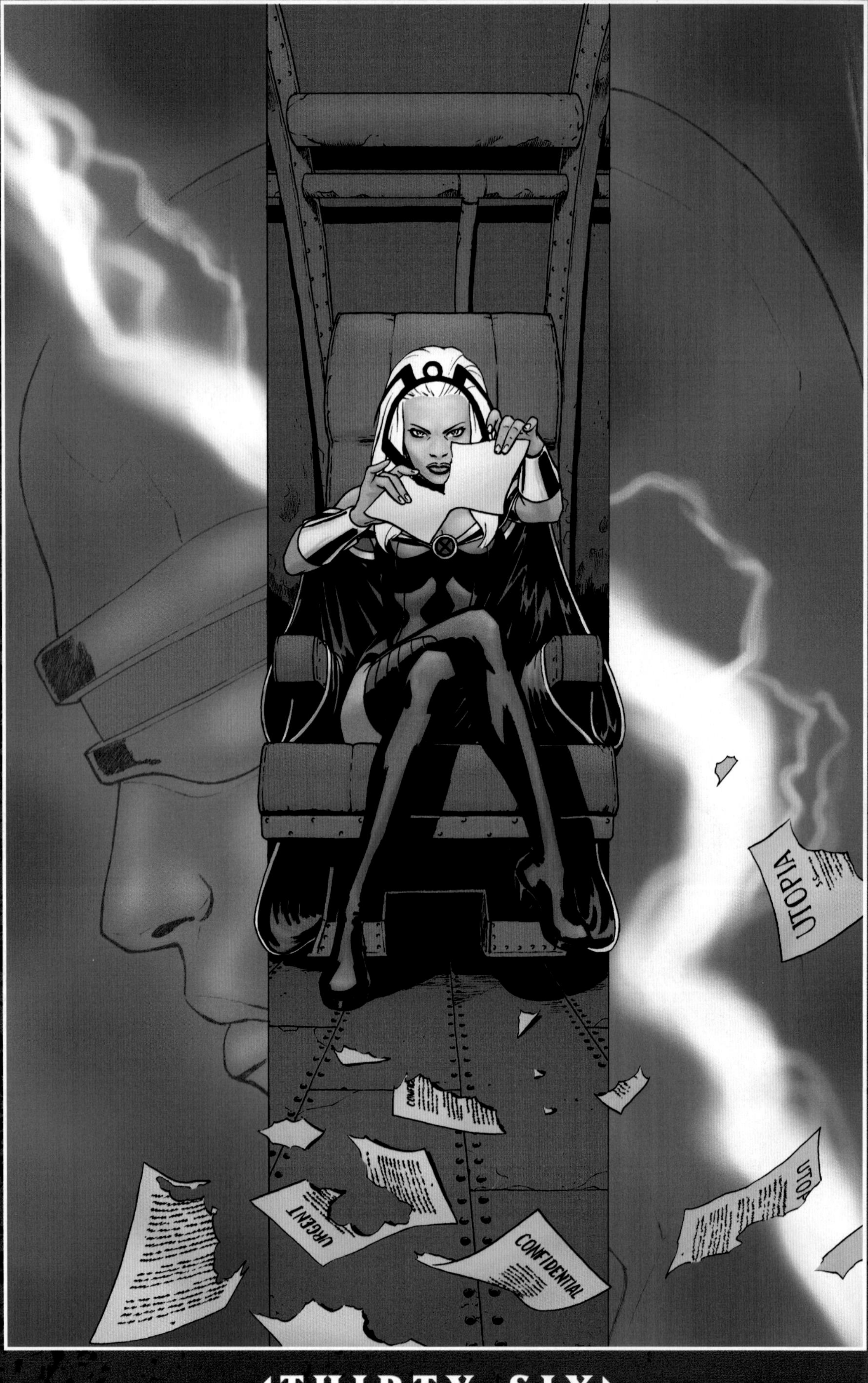
UTOPIA
URGENT
CONFIDENTIAL

THIRTY-SIX

X-MEN

Born with abilities beyond those of normal men, the mutant species has long been hated and feared by the humans around them. The mutant super heroes known as the X-Men are looking to change that, making the world safe for human and mutant alike.

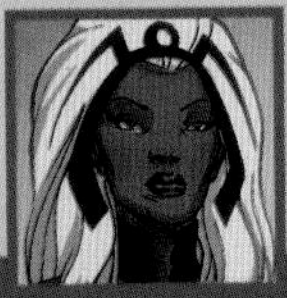

STORM
Weather control

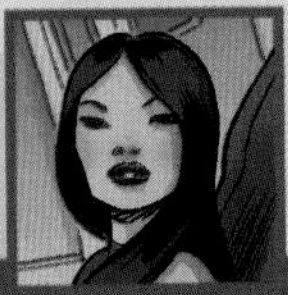

PSYLOCKE
Telepathic ninja

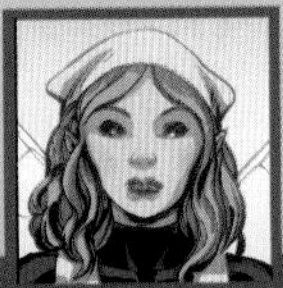

PIXIE
Winged magic-user

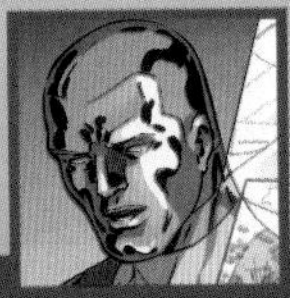

COLOSSUS
Organic steel skin

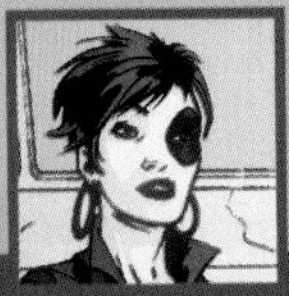

DOMINO
Luck manipulation

PREVIOUSLY

For years, the X-Men believed that the mutant species was a very recent development in the history of human evolution. Then they encountered David Michael Gray, a rogue scientist who had discovered, and cloned, the remains of a race of "proto-mutants" who lived hundreds of years ago.

When the X-Men attacked his lab, Gray killed himself and all of the cloned proto-mutants. Later, the X-Men tracked down and took possession of the last remaining sample of proto-mutant DNA. But Storm still suspected that some loose ends had not been tied up. Acting without the authorization of X-Men leader Cyclops, Storm enlisted the Israeli super hero Sabra to help her search the globe for any sign of proto-mutant activity – and Sabra may have found what she was looking for...

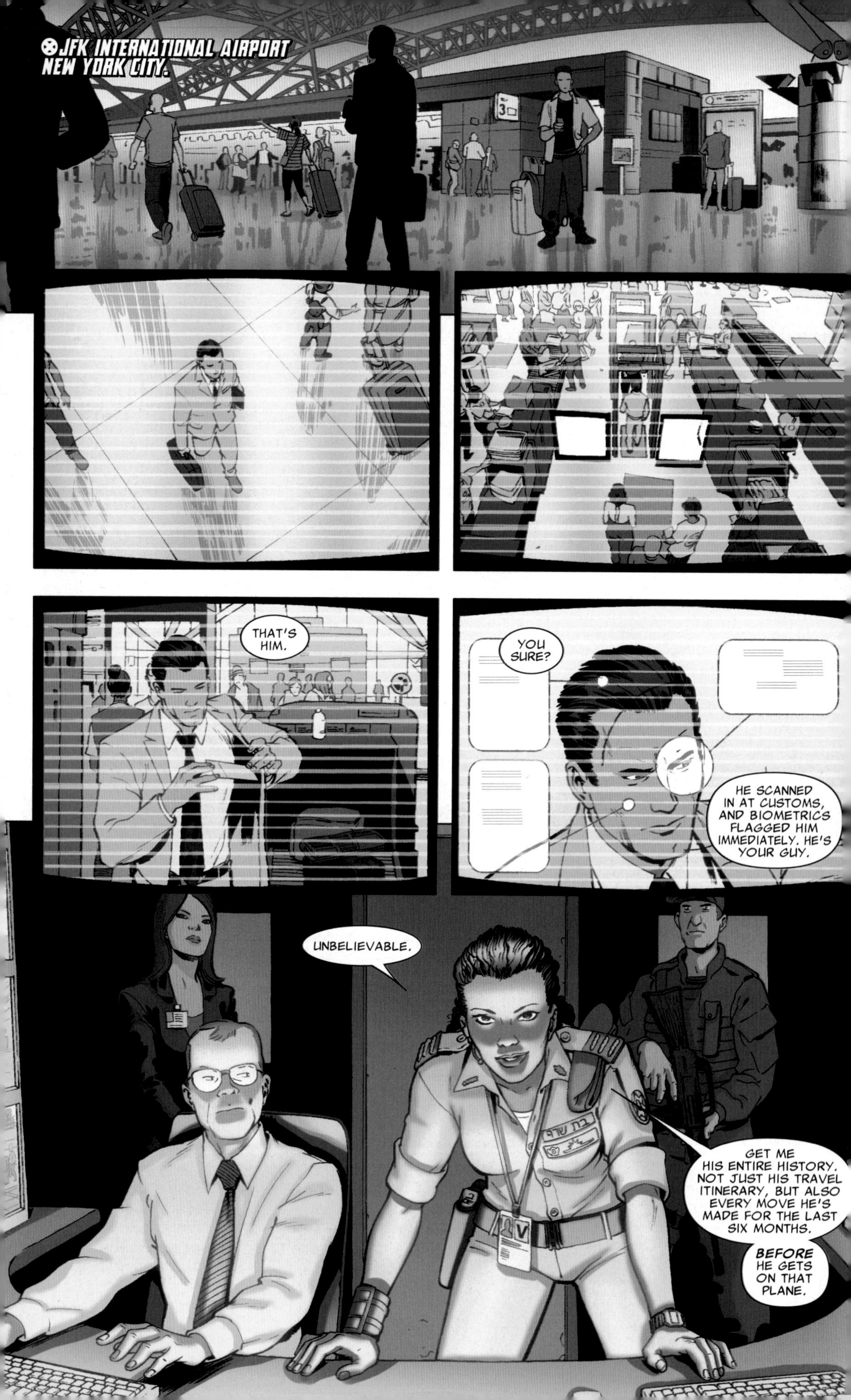
JFK INTERNATIONAL AIRPORT NEW YORK CITY.
THAT'S HIM.
YOU SURE?
HE SCANNED IN AT CUSTOMS, AND BIOMETRICS FLAGGED HIM IMMEDIATELY. HE'S YOUR GUY.
UNBELIEVABLE.
GET ME HIS ENTIRE HISTORY. NOT JUST HIS TRAVEL ITINERARY, BUT ALSO EVERY MOVE HE'S MADE FOR THE LAST SIX MONTHS.
BEFORE HE GETS ON THAT PLANE.

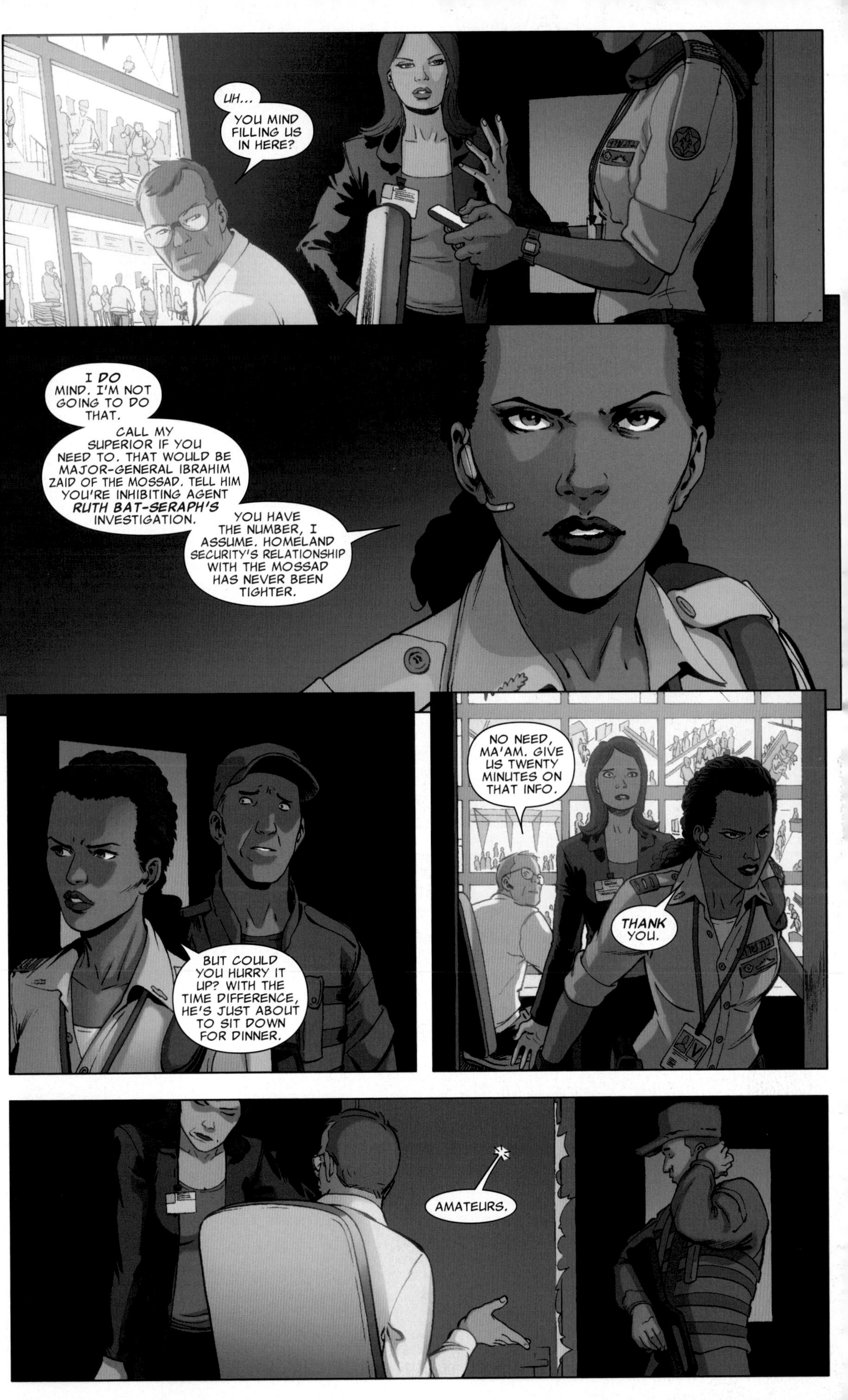
UH...
YOU MIND FILLING US IN HERE?
I DO MIND. I'M NOT GOING TO DO THAT.
CALL MY SUPERIOR IF YOU NEED TO. THAT WOULD BE MAJOR-GENERAL IBRAHIM ZAID OF THE MOSSAD. TELL HIM YOU'RE INHIBITING AGENT RUTH BAT-SERAPH'S INVESTIGATION.
YOU HAVE THE NUMBER, I ASSUME. HOMELAND SECURITY'S RELATIONSHIP WITH THE MOSSAD HAS NEVER BEEN TIGHTER.
BUT COULD YOU HURRY IT UP? WITH THE TIME DIFFERENCE, HE'S JUST ABOUT TO SIT DOWN FOR DINNER.
NO NEED, MA'AM. GIVE US TWENTY MINUTES ON THAT INFO.
THANK YOU.
AMATEURS.

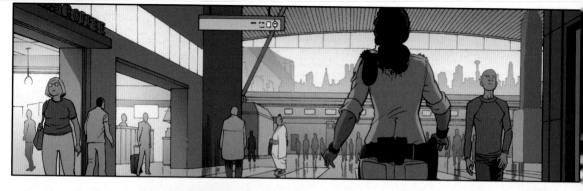

COME ON, WHERE ARE YOU...?

GOTCHA.

HOW'S THAT INFO COMING?

...

THAT'S FINE. ALSO, I WANT HIS FLIGHT DELAYED. NOTHING OBVIOUS, GIVE US THIRTY MINUTES OR SO.

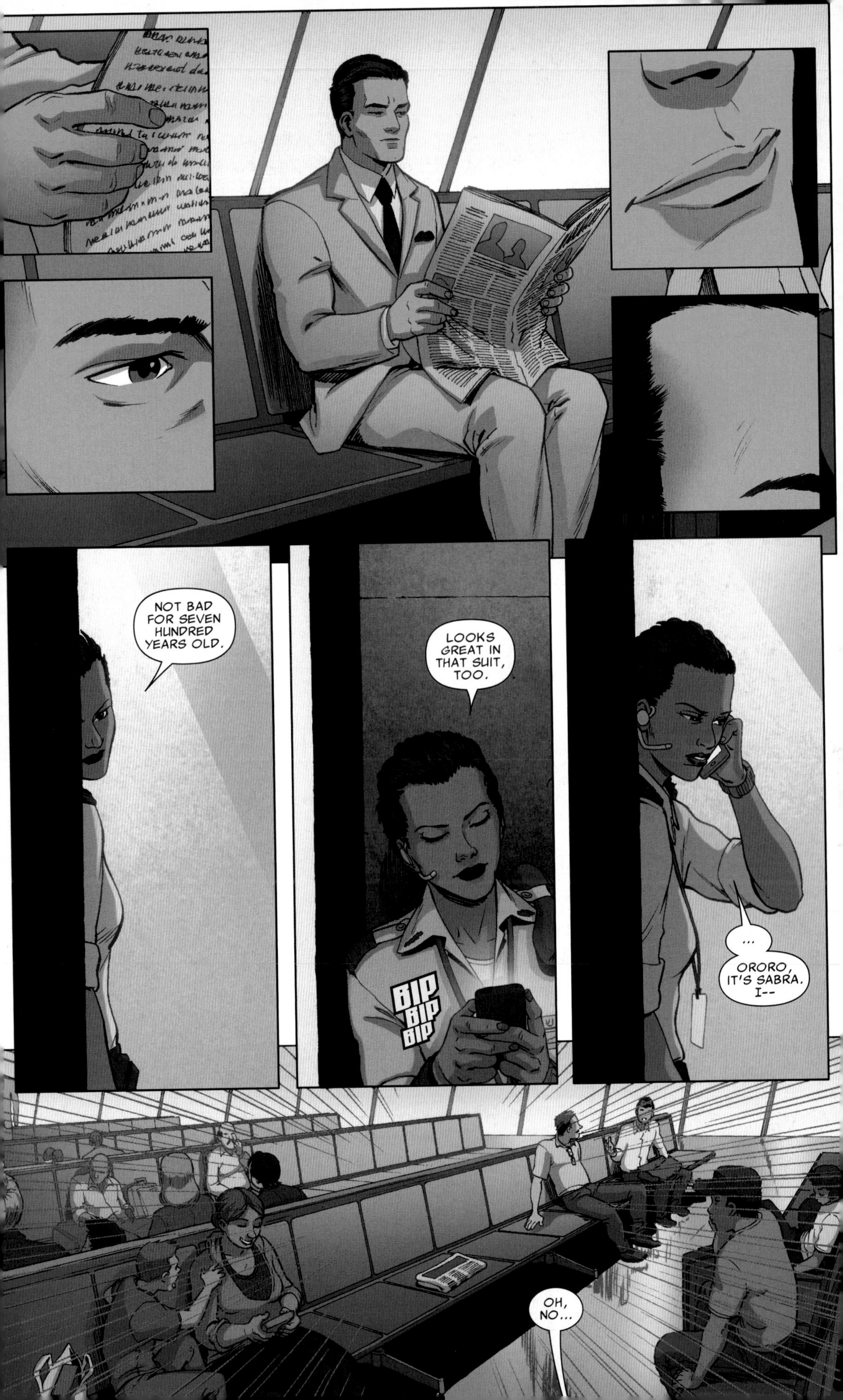
NOT BAD FOR SEVEN HUNDRED YEARS OLD.
LOOKS GREAT IN THAT SUIT, TOO.
BIP BIP BIP
...
ORORO, IT'S SABRA. I--
OH, NO...

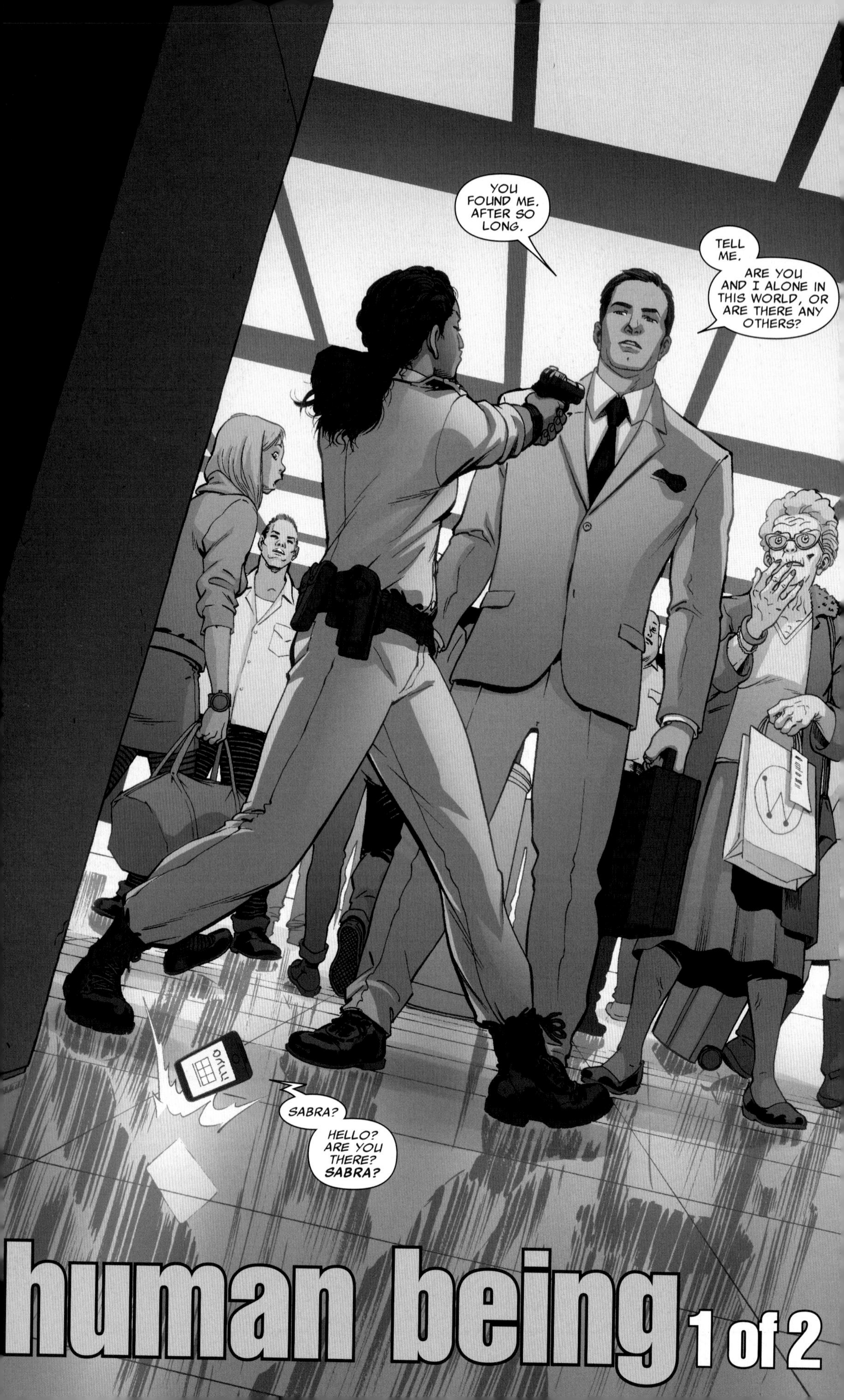

YOU FOUND ME. AFTER SO LONG.
TELL ME.
ARE YOU AND I ALONE IN THIS WORLD, OR ARE THERE ANY OTHERS?
SABRA?
HELLO? ARE YOU THERE? SABRA?
human being 1 of 2

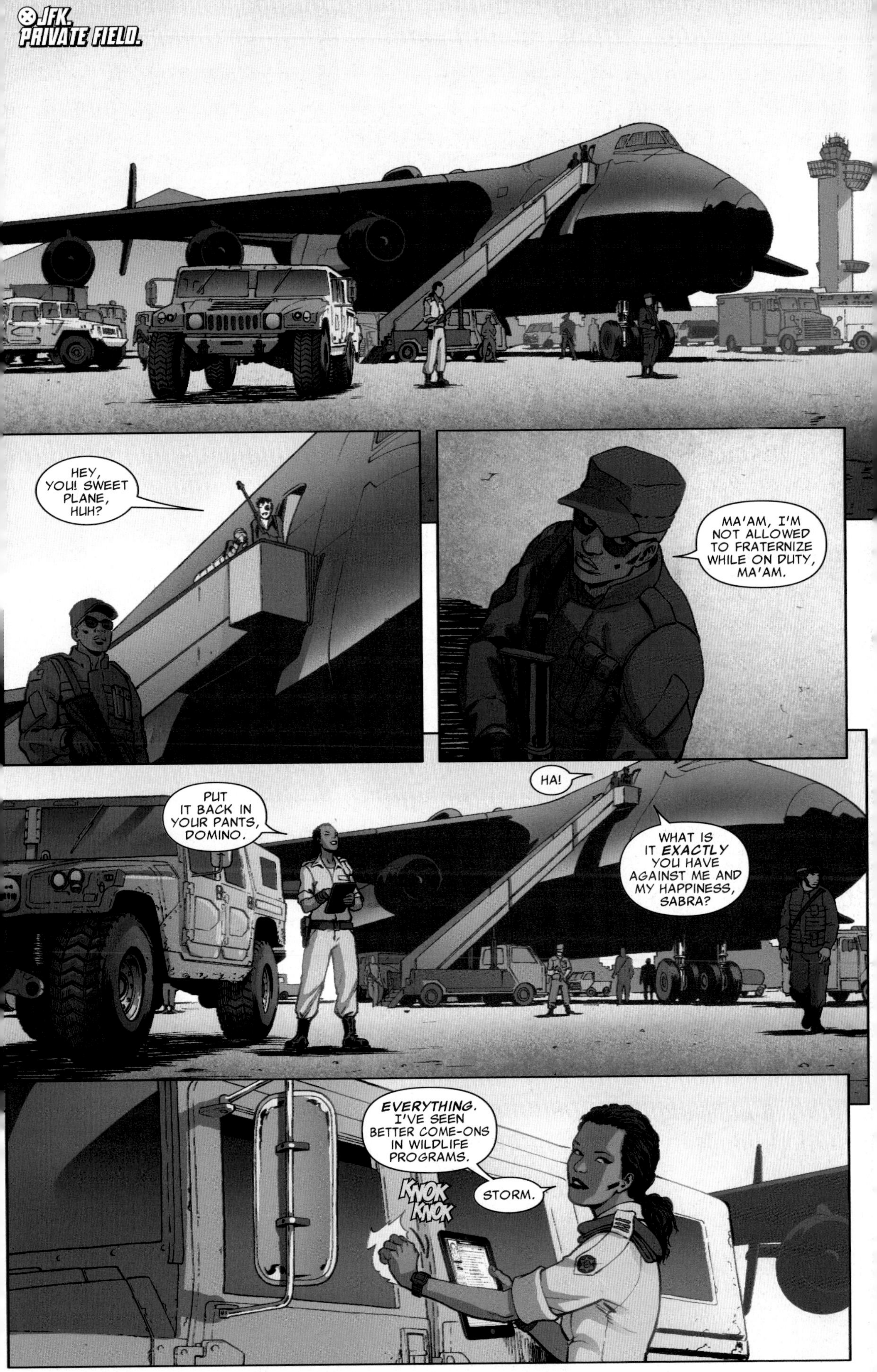
JFK.
PRIVATE FIELD.
HEY, YOU! SWEET PLANE, HUH?
MA'AM, I'M NOT ALLOWED TO FRATERNIZE WHILE ON DUTY, MA'AM.
PUT IT BACK IN YOUR PANTS, DOMINO.
HA!
WHAT IS IT EXACTLY YOU HAVE AGAINST ME AND MY HAPPINESS, SABRA?
EVERYTHING. I'VE SEEN BETTER COME-ONS IN WILDLIFE PROGRAMS.
KNOK KNOK
STORM.

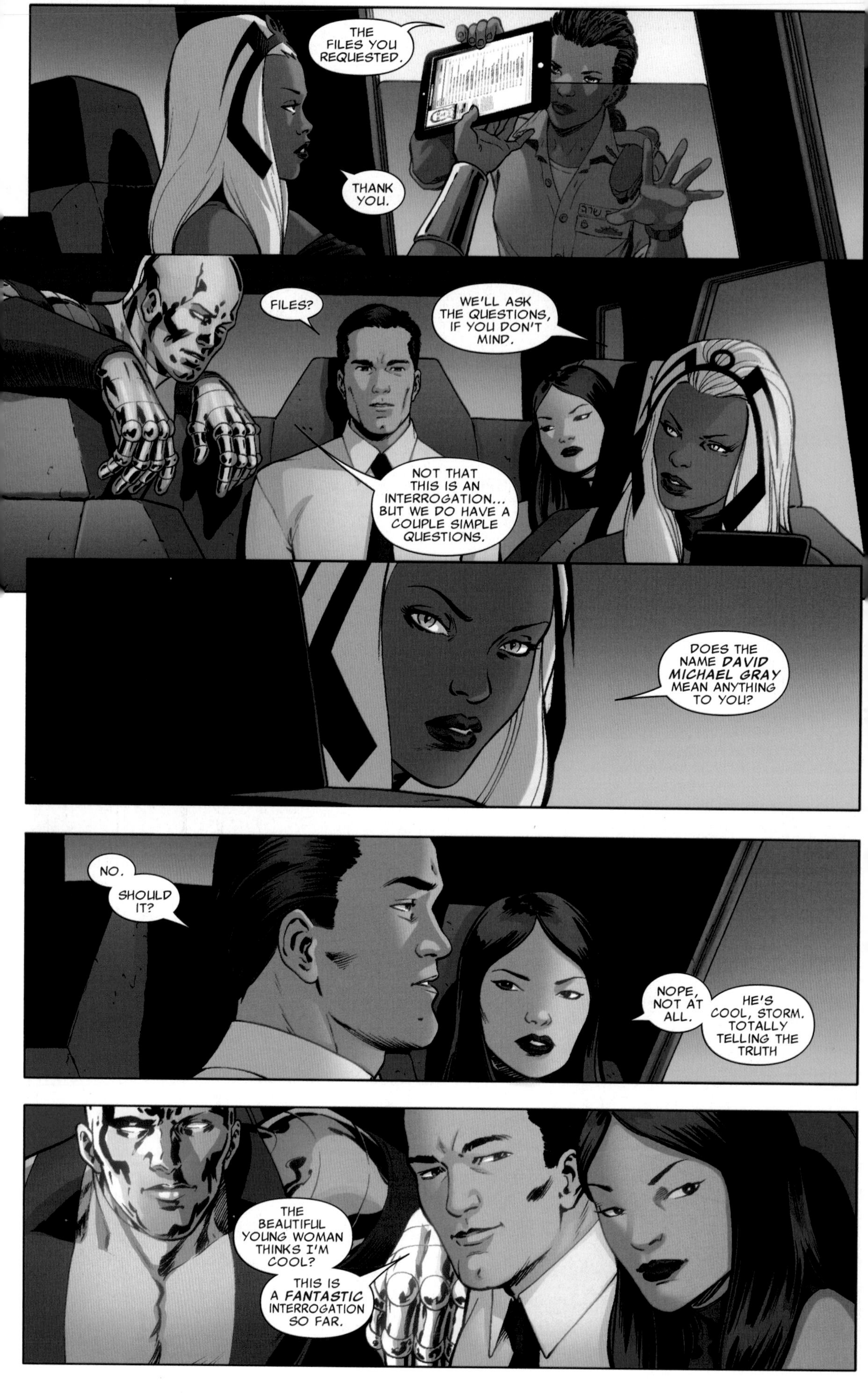
THE FILES YOU REQUESTED.
THANK YOU.
FILES?
WE'LL ASK THE QUESTIONS, IF YOU DON'T MIND.
NOT THAT THIS IS AN INTERROGATION... BUT WE DO HAVE A COUPLE SIMPLE QUESTIONS.
DOES THE NAME DAVID MICHAEL GRAY MEAN ANYTHING TO YOU?
NO.
SHOULD IT?
NOPE, NOT AT ALL.
HE'S COOL, STORM. TOTALLY TELLING THE TRUTH
THE BEAUTIFUL YOUNG WOMAN THINKS I'M COOL?
THIS IS A FANTASTIC INTERROGATION SO FAR.

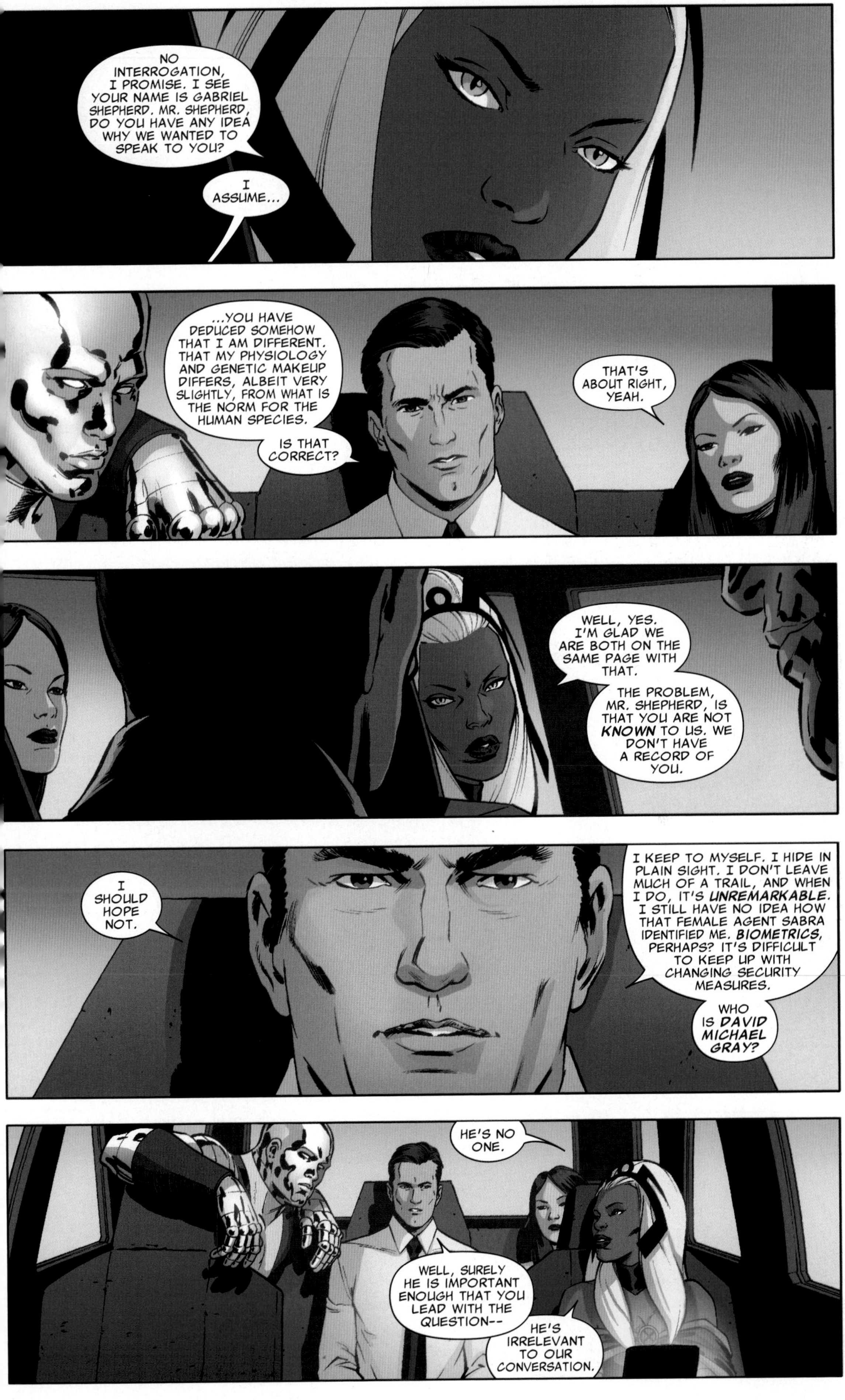
NO INTERROGATION, I PROMISE. I SEE YOUR NAME IS GABRIEL SHEPHERD. MR. SHEPHERD, DO YOU HAVE ANY IDEA WHY WE WANTED TO SPEAK TO YOU?
I ASSUME...
...YOU HAVE DEDUCED SOMEHOW THAT I AM DIFFERENT. THAT MY PHYSIOLOGY AND GENETIC MAKEUP DIFFERS, ALBEIT VERY SLIGHTLY, FROM WHAT IS THE NORM FOR THE HUMAN SPECIES.
IS THAT CORRECT?
THAT'S ABOUT RIGHT, YEAH.
WELL, YES. I'M GLAD WE ARE BOTH ON THE SAME PAGE WITH THAT.
THE PROBLEM, MR. SHEPHERD, IS THAT YOU ARE NOT KNOWN TO US. WE DON'T HAVE A RECORD OF YOU.
I SHOULD HOPE NOT.
I KEEP TO MYSELF. I HIDE IN PLAIN SIGHT. I DON'T LEAVE MUCH OF A TRAIL, AND WHEN I DO, IT'S UNREMARKABLE. I STILL HAVE NO IDEA HOW THAT FEMALE AGENT SABRA IDENTIFIED ME. BIOMETRICS, PERHAPS? IT'S DIFFICULT TO KEEP UP WITH CHANGING SECURITY MEASURES.
WHO IS DAVID MICHAEL GRAY?
HE'S NO ONE.
WELL, SURELY HE IS IMPORTANT ENOUGH THAT YOU LEAD WITH THE QUESTION--
HE'S IRRELEVANT TO OUR CONVERSATION.

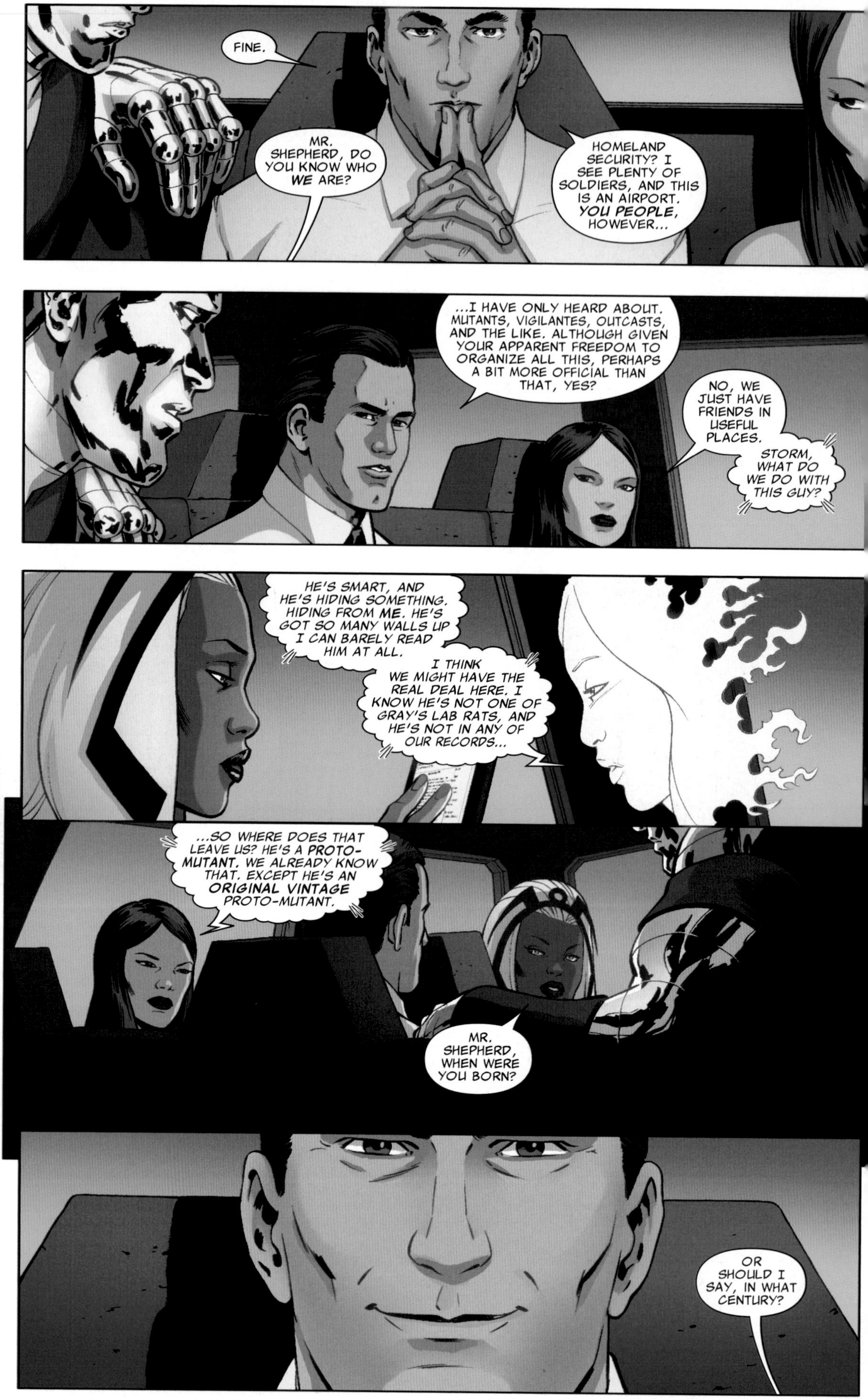
FINE.
MR. SHEPHERD, DO YOU KNOW WHO WE ARE?
HOMELAND SECURITY? I SEE PLENTY OF SOLDIERS, AND THIS IS AN AIRPORT. YOU PEOPLE, HOWEVER...
...I HAVE ONLY HEARD ABOUT. MUTANTS, VIGILANTES, OUTCASTS, AND THE LIKE. ALTHOUGH GIVEN YOUR APPARENT FREEDOM TO ORGANIZE ALL THIS, PERHAPS A BIT MORE OFFICIAL THAN THAT, YES?
NO, WE JUST HAVE FRIENDS IN USEFUL PLACES.
STORM, WHAT DO WE DO WITH THIS GUY?
HE'S SMART, AND HE'S HIDING SOMETHING. HIDING FROM ME. HE'S GOT SO MANY WALLS UP I CAN BARELY READ HIM AT ALL.
I THINK WE MIGHT HAVE THE REAL DEAL HERE. I KNOW HE'S NOT ONE OF GRAY'S LAB RATS, AND HE'S NOT IN ANY OF OUR RECORDS...
...SO WHERE DOES THAT LEAVE US? HE'S A PROTO-MUTANT. WE ALREADY KNOW THAT. EXCEPT HE'S AN ORIGINAL VINTAGE PROTO-MUTANT.
MR. SHEPHERD, WHEN WERE YOU BORN?
OR SHOULD I SAY, IN WHAT CENTURY?

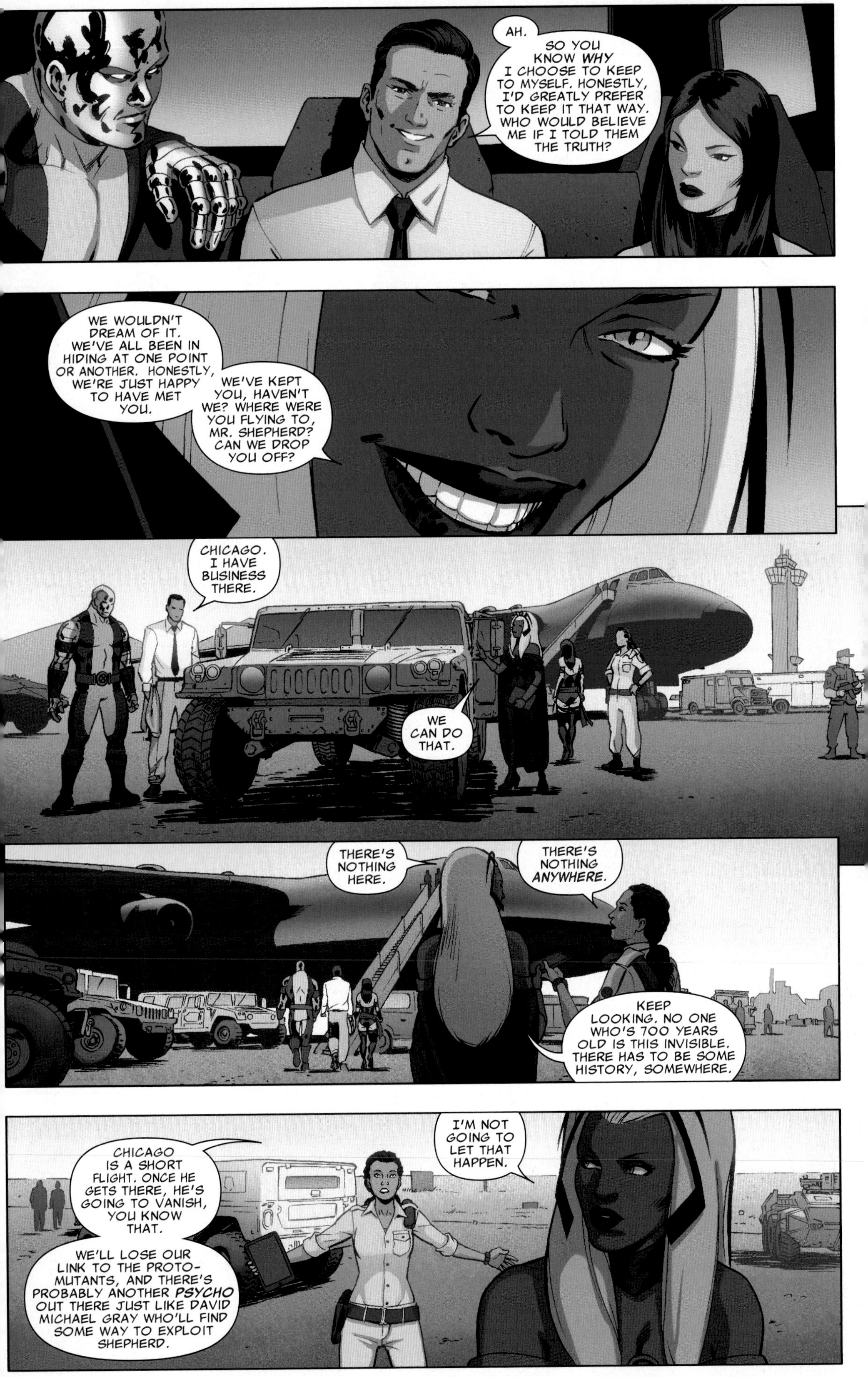
AH.
SO YOU KNOW *WHY* I CHOOSE TO KEEP TO MYSELF. HONESTLY, I'D GREATLY PREFER TO KEEP IT THAT WAY. WHO WOULD BELIEVE ME IF I TOLD THEM THE TRUTH?
WE WOULDN'T DREAM OF IT. WE'VE ALL BEEN IN HIDING AT ONE POINT OR ANOTHER. HONESTLY, WE'RE JUST HAPPY TO HAVE MET YOU.
WE'VE KEPT YOU, HAVEN'T WE? WHERE WERE YOU FLYING TO, MR. SHEPHERD? CAN WE DROP YOU OFF?
CHICAGO. I HAVE BUSINESS THERE.
WE CAN DO THAT.
THERE'S NOTHING HERE.
THERE'S NOTHING *ANYWHERE*.
KEEP LOOKING. NO ONE WHO'S 700 YEARS OLD IS THIS INVISIBLE. THERE HAS TO BE SOME HISTORY, SOMEWHERE.
CHICAGO IS A SHORT FLIGHT. ONCE HE GETS THERE, HE'S GOING TO VANISH, YOU KNOW THAT.
WE'LL LOSE OUR LINK TO THE PROTO-MUTANTS, AND THERE'S PROBABLY ANOTHER *PSYCHO* OUT THERE JUST LIKE DAVID MICHAEL GRAY WHO'LL FIND SOME WAY TO EXPLOIT SHEPHERD.
I'M NOT GOING TO LET THAT HAPPEN.

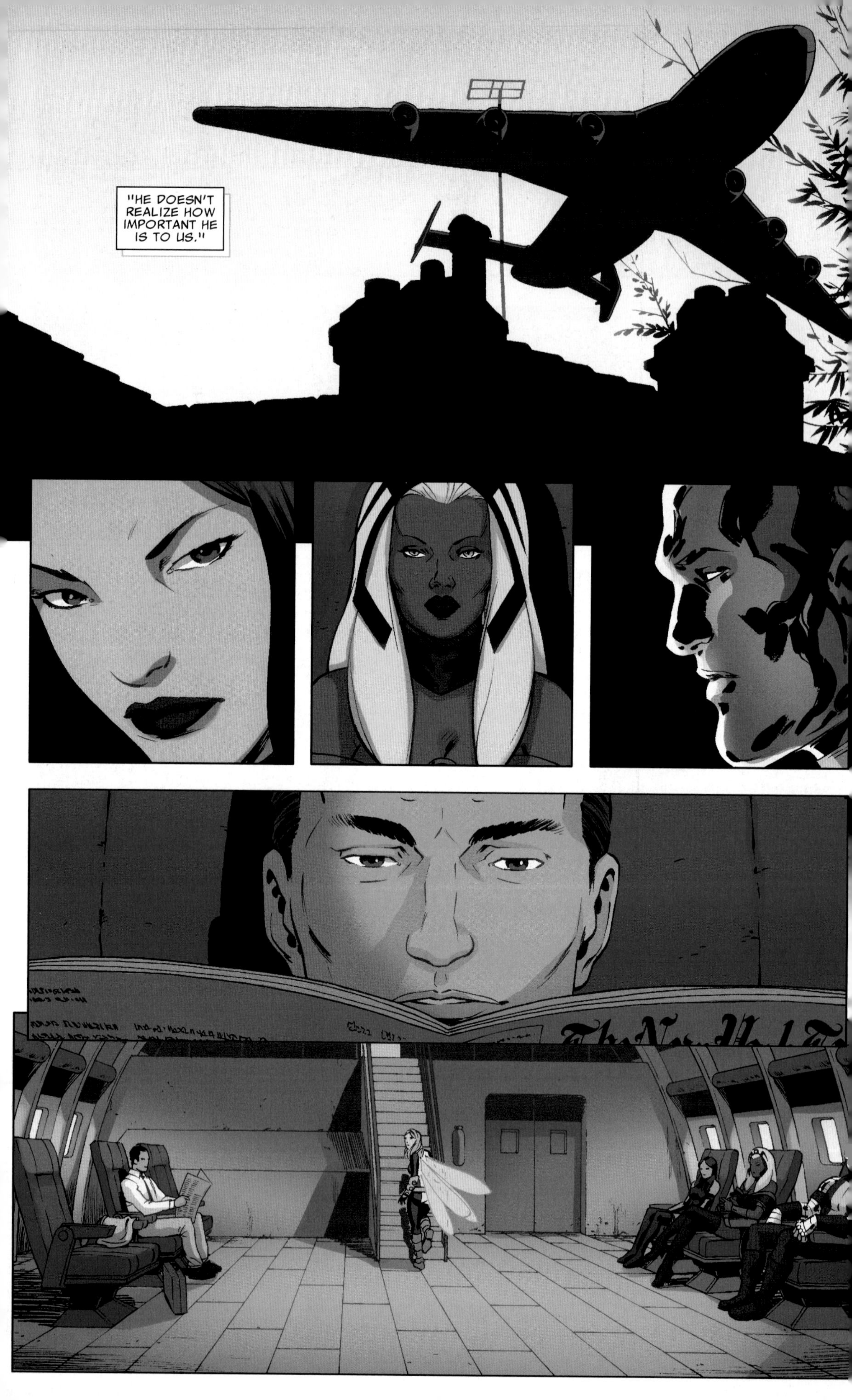
"HE DOESN'T REALIZE HOW IMPORTANT HE IS TO US."

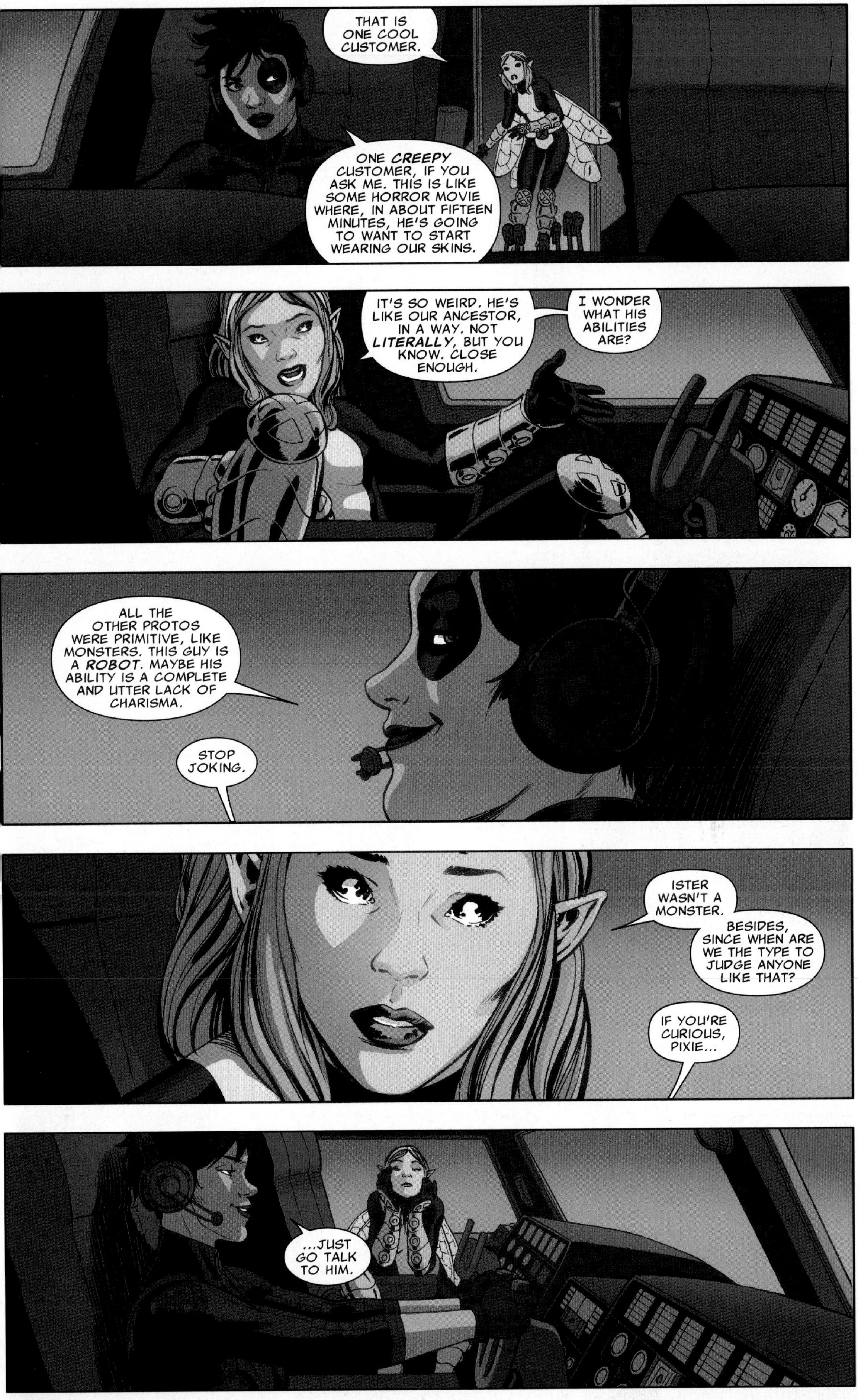
THAT IS ONE COOL CUSTOMER.
ONE CREEPY CUSTOMER, IF YOU ASK ME. THIS IS LIKE SOME HORROR MOVIE WHERE, IN ABOUT FIFTEEN MINUTES, HE'S GOING TO WANT TO START WEARING OUR SKINS.
IT'S SO WEIRD. HE'S LIKE OUR ANCESTOR, IN A WAY. NOT LITERALLY, BUT YOU KNOW. CLOSE ENOUGH.
I WONDER WHAT HIS ABILITIES ARE?
ALL THE OTHER PROTOS WERE PRIMITIVE, LIKE MONSTERS. THIS GUY IS A ROBOT. MAYBE HIS ABILITY IS A COMPLETE AND UTTER LACK OF CHARISMA.
STOP JOKING.
ISTER WASN'T A MONSTER.
BESIDES, SINCE WHEN ARE WE THE TYPE TO JUDGE ANYONE LIKE THAT?
IF YOU'RE CURIOUS, PIXIE...
...JUST GO TALK TO HIM.

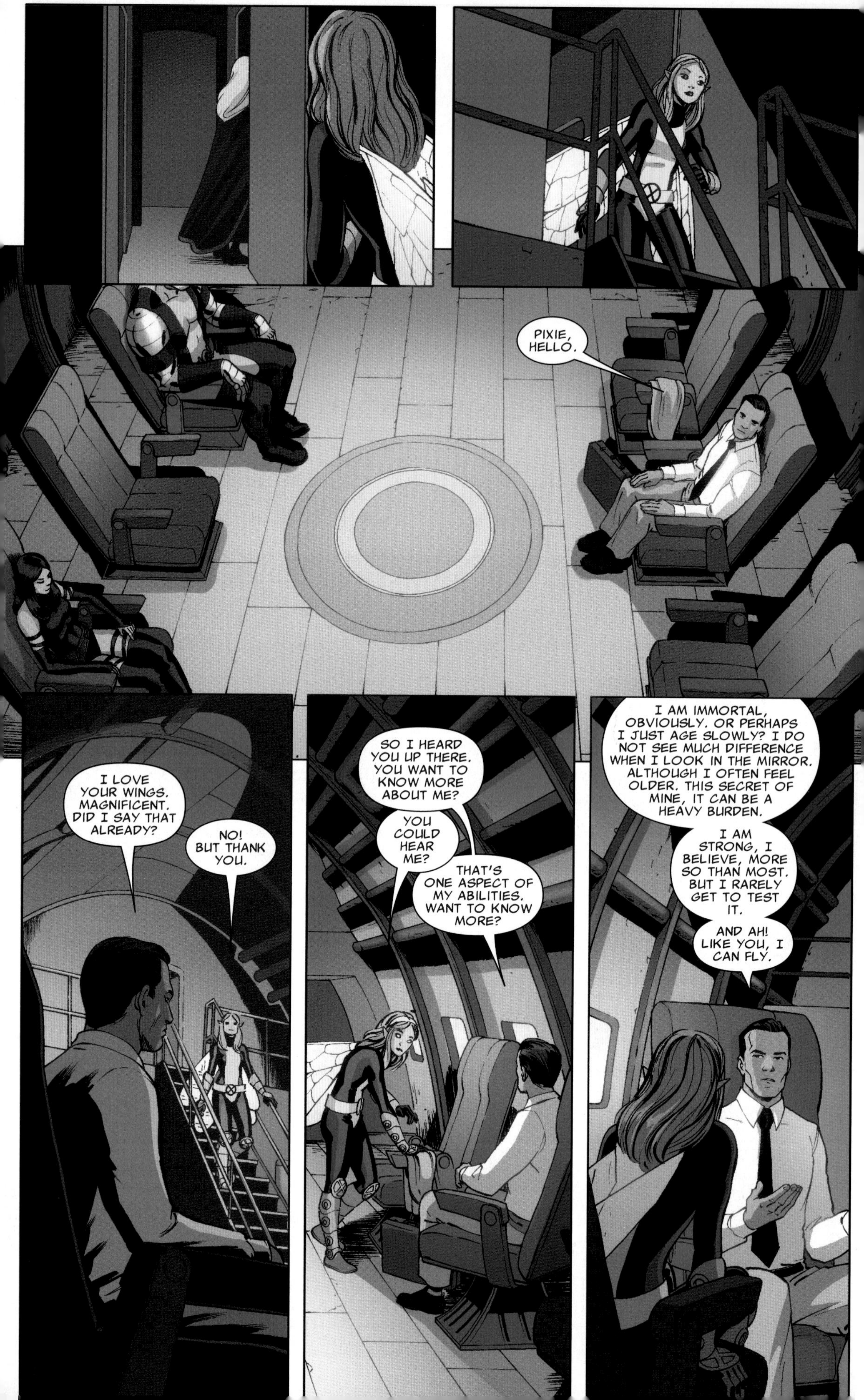
PIXIE, HELLO.
I LOVE YOUR WINGS. MAGNIFICENT. DID I SAY THAT ALREADY?
NO! BUT THANK YOU.
SO I HEARD YOU UP THERE. YOU WANT TO KNOW MORE ABOUT ME?
YOU COULD HEAR ME?
THAT'S ONE ASPECT OF MY ABILITIES. WANT TO KNOW MORE?
I AM IMMORTAL, OBVIOUSLY. OR PERHAPS I JUST AGE SLOWLY? I DO NOT SEE MUCH DIFFERENCE WHEN I LOOK IN THE MIRROR. ALTHOUGH I OFTEN FEEL OLDER. THIS SECRET OF MINE, IT CAN BE A HEAVY BURDEN.
I AM STRONG, I BELIEVE, MORE SO THAN MOST. BUT I RARELY GET TO TEST IT.
AND AH! LIKE YOU, I CAN FLY.

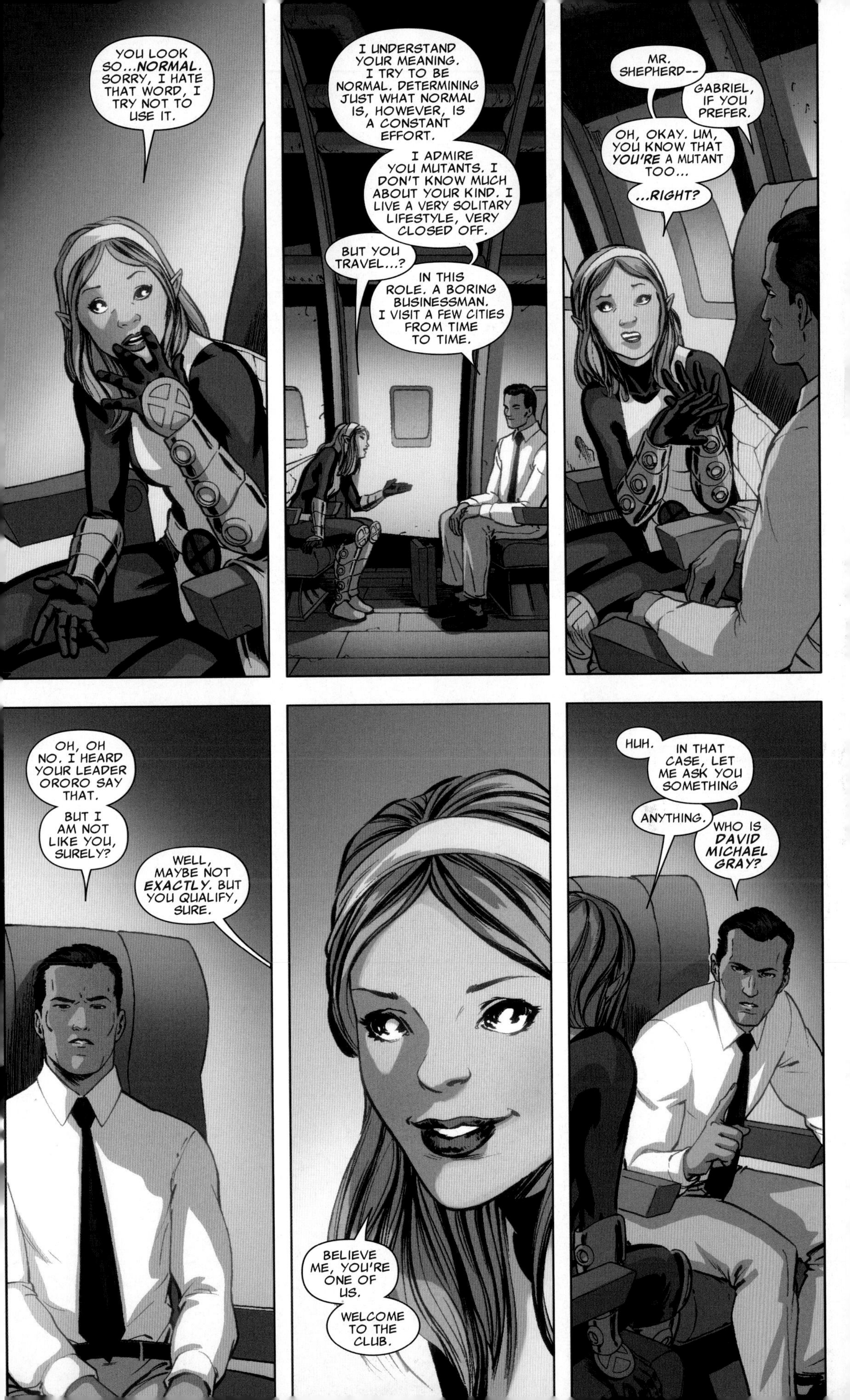
YOU LOOK SO...NORMAL. SORRY, I HATE THAT WORD, I TRY NOT TO USE IT.
I UNDERSTAND YOUR MEANING. I TRY TO BE NORMAL. DETERMINING JUST WHAT NORMAL IS, HOWEVER, IS A CONSTANT EFFORT.
I ADMIRE YOU MUTANTS. I DON'T KNOW MUCH ABOUT YOUR KIND. I LIVE A VERY SOLITARY LIFESTYLE, VERY CLOSED OFF.
BUT YOU TRAVEL...?
IN THIS ROLE. A BORING BUSINESSMAN. I VISIT A FEW CITIES FROM TIME TO TIME.
MR. SHEPHERD--
GABRIEL, IF YOU PREFER.
OH, OKAY. UM, YOU KNOW THAT YOU'RE A MUTANT TOO...
...RIGHT?
OH, OH NO. I HEARD YOUR LEADER ORORO SAY THAT.
BUT I AM NOT LIKE YOU, SURELY?
WELL, MAYBE NOT EXACTLY. BUT YOU QUALIFY, SURE.
BELIEVE ME, YOU'RE ONE OF US.
WELCOME TO THE CLUB.
HUH.
IN THAT CASE, LET ME ASK YOU SOMETHING
ANYTHING.
WHO IS DAVID MICHAEL GRAY?

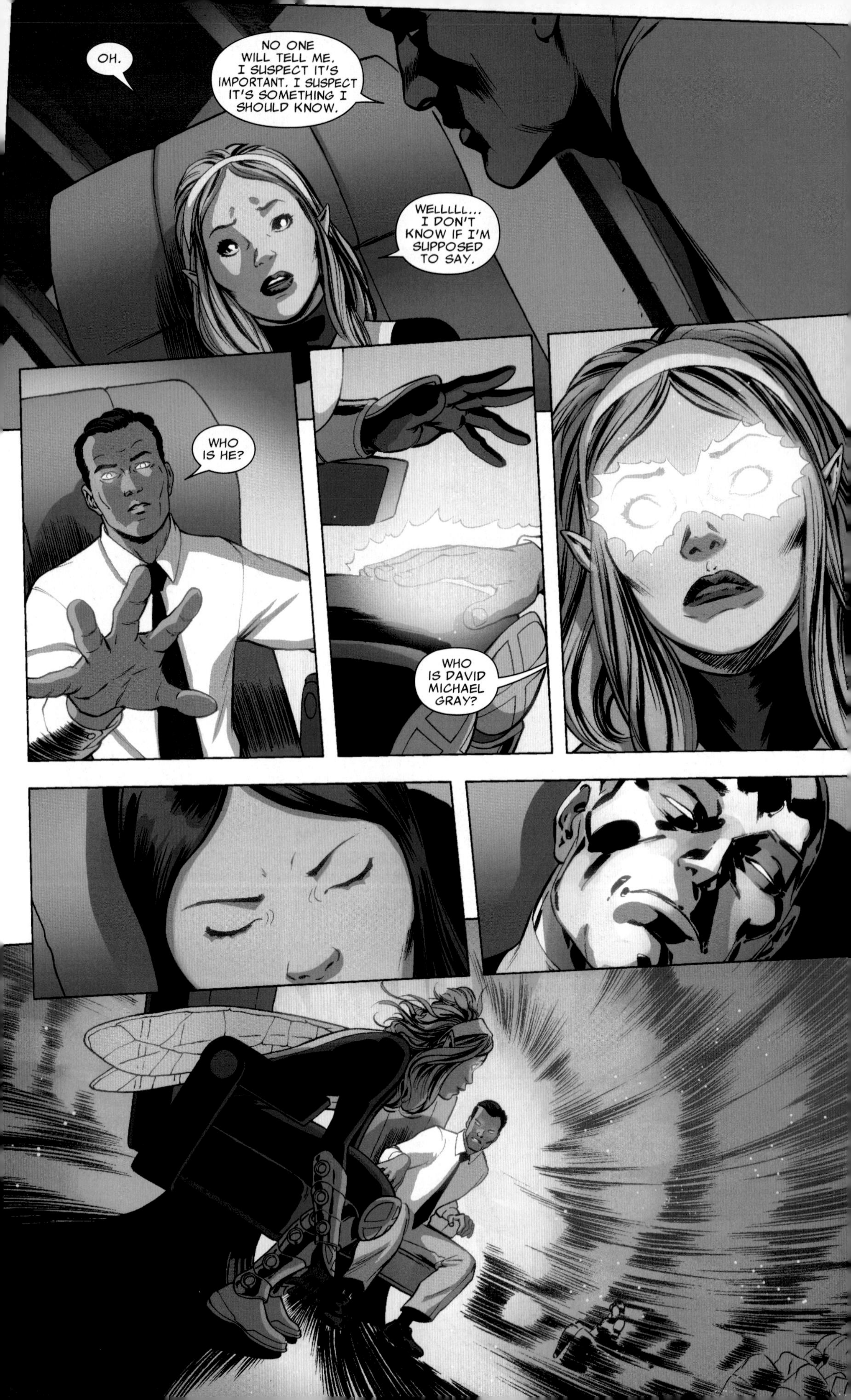
OH.
NO ONE WILL TELL ME. I SUSPECT IT'S IMPORTANT. I SUSPECT IT'S SOMETHING I SHOULD KNOW.
WELLLLL... I DON'T KNOW IF I'M SUPPOSED TO SAY.
WHO IS HE?
WHO IS DAVID MICHAEL GRAY?

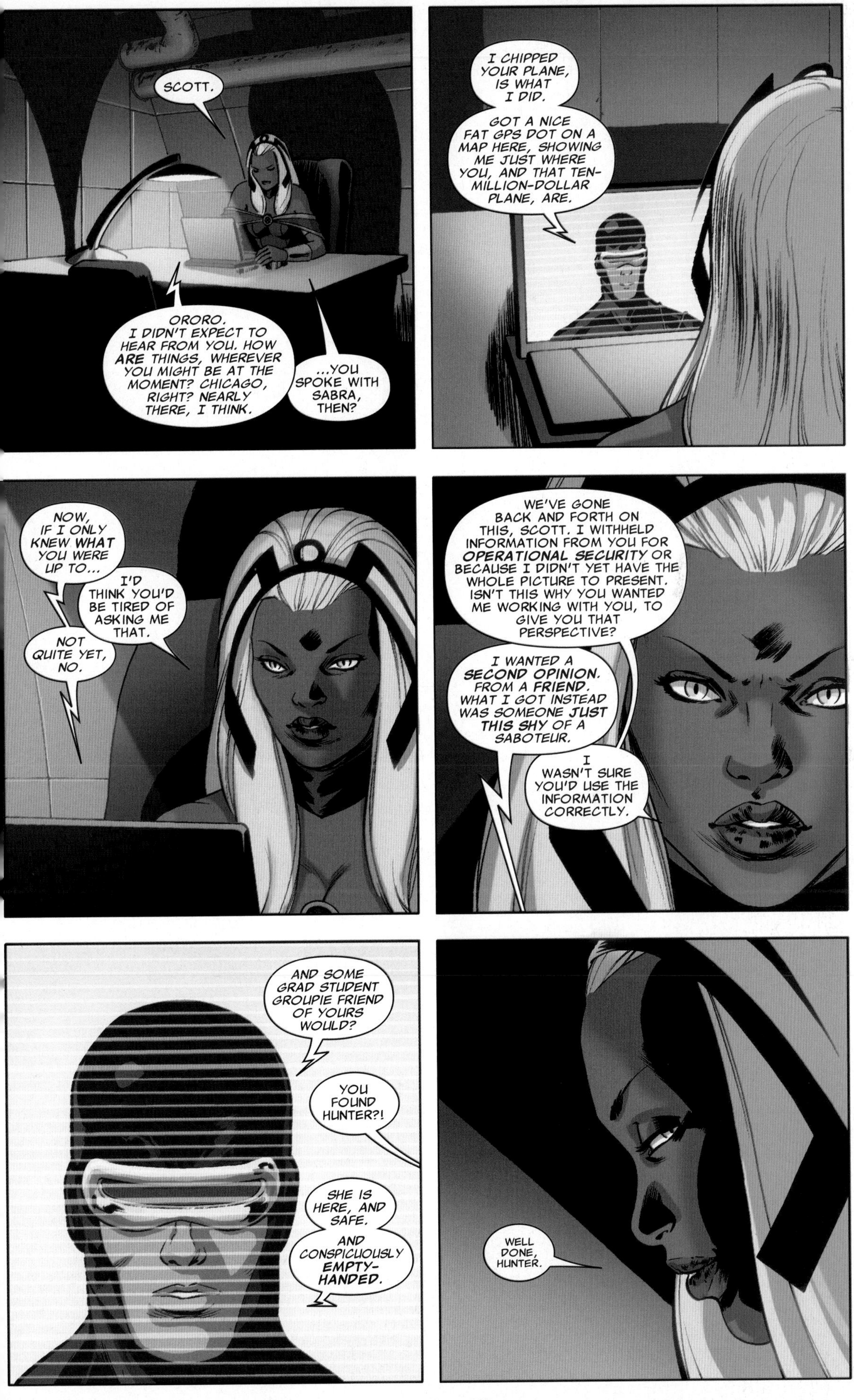
SCOTT.
ORORO. I DIDN'T EXPECT TO HEAR FROM YOU. HOW ARE THINGS, WHEREVER YOU MIGHT BE AT THE MOMENT? CHICAGO, RIGHT? NEARLY THERE, I THINK.
...YOU SPOKE WITH SABRA, THEN?
I CHIPPED YOUR PLANE, IS WHAT I DID.
GOT A NICE FAT GPS DOT ON A MAP HERE, SHOWING ME JUST WHERE YOU, AND THAT TEN-MILLION-DOLLAR PLANE, ARE.
NOW, IF I ONLY KNEW WHAT YOU WERE UP TO...
I'D THINK YOU'D BE TIRED OF ASKING ME THAT.
NOT QUITE YET, NO.
WE'VE GONE BACK AND FORTH ON THIS, SCOTT. I WITHHELD INFORMATION FROM YOU FOR OPERATIONAL SECURITY OR BECAUSE I DIDN'T YET HAVE THE WHOLE PICTURE TO PRESENT. ISN'T THIS WHY YOU WANTED ME WORKING WITH YOU, TO GIVE YOU THAT PERSPECTIVE?
I WANTED A SECOND OPINION. FROM A FRIEND. WHAT I GOT INSTEAD WAS SOMEONE JUST THIS SHY OF A SABOTEUR.
I WASN'T SURE YOU'D USE THE INFORMATION CORRECTLY.
AND SOME GRAD STUDENT GROUPIE FRIEND OF YOURS WOULD?
YOU FOUND HUNTER?!
SHE IS HERE, AND SAFE.
AND CONSPICUOUSLY EMPTY-HANDED.
WELL DONE, HUNTER.

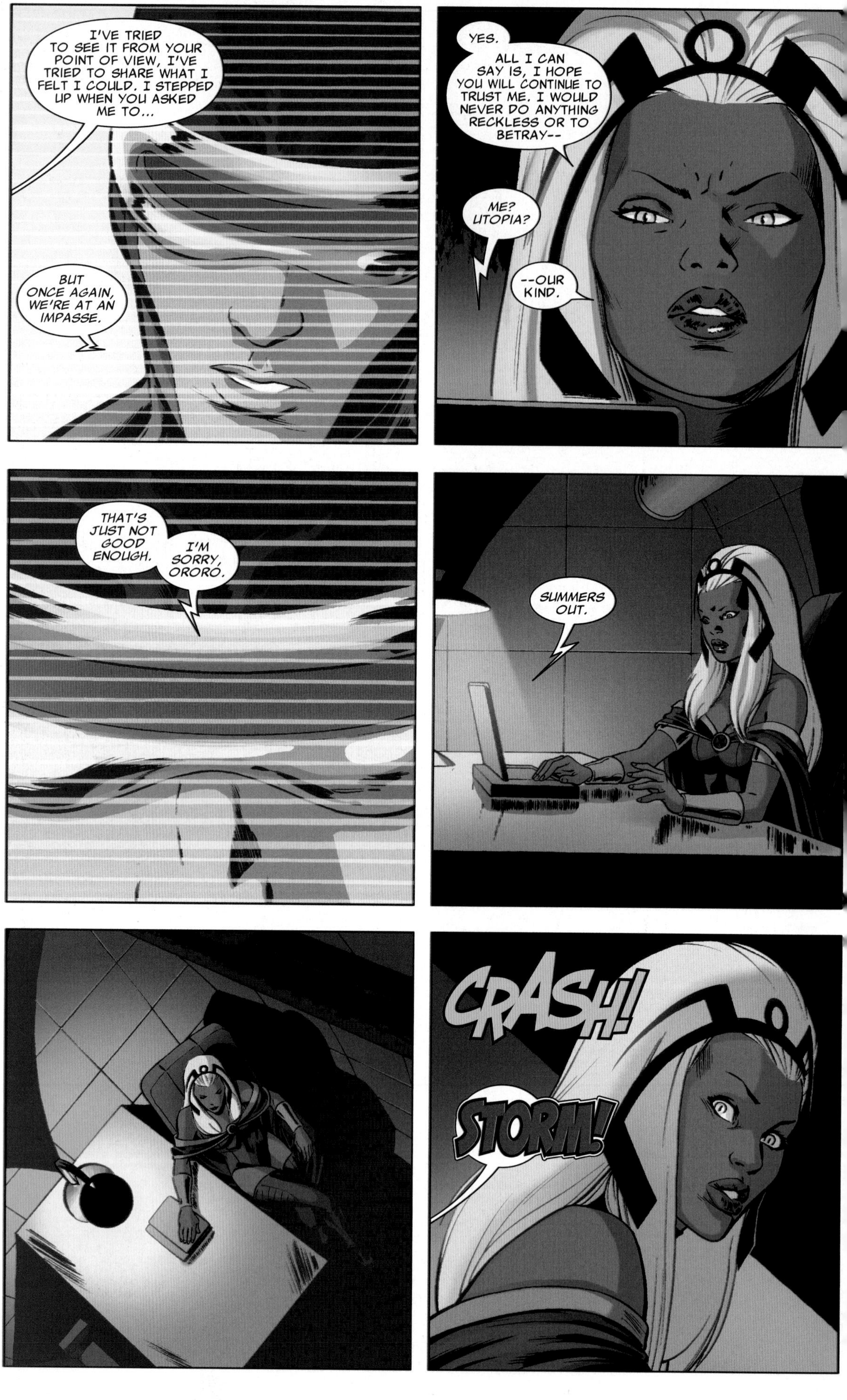
I'VE TRIED TO SEE IT FROM YOUR POINT OF VIEW, I'VE TRIED TO SHARE WHAT I FELT I COULD. I STEPPED UP WHEN YOU ASKED ME TO...
BUT ONCE AGAIN, WE'RE AT AN IMPASSE.
YES.
ALL I CAN SAY IS, I HOPE YOU WILL CONTINUE TO TRUST ME. I WOULD NEVER DO ANYTHING RECKLESS OR TO BETRAY--
ME? UTOPIA?
--OUR KIND.
THAT'S JUST NOT GOOD ENOUGH.
I'M SORRY, ORORO.
SUMMERS OUT.
CRASH!
STORM!

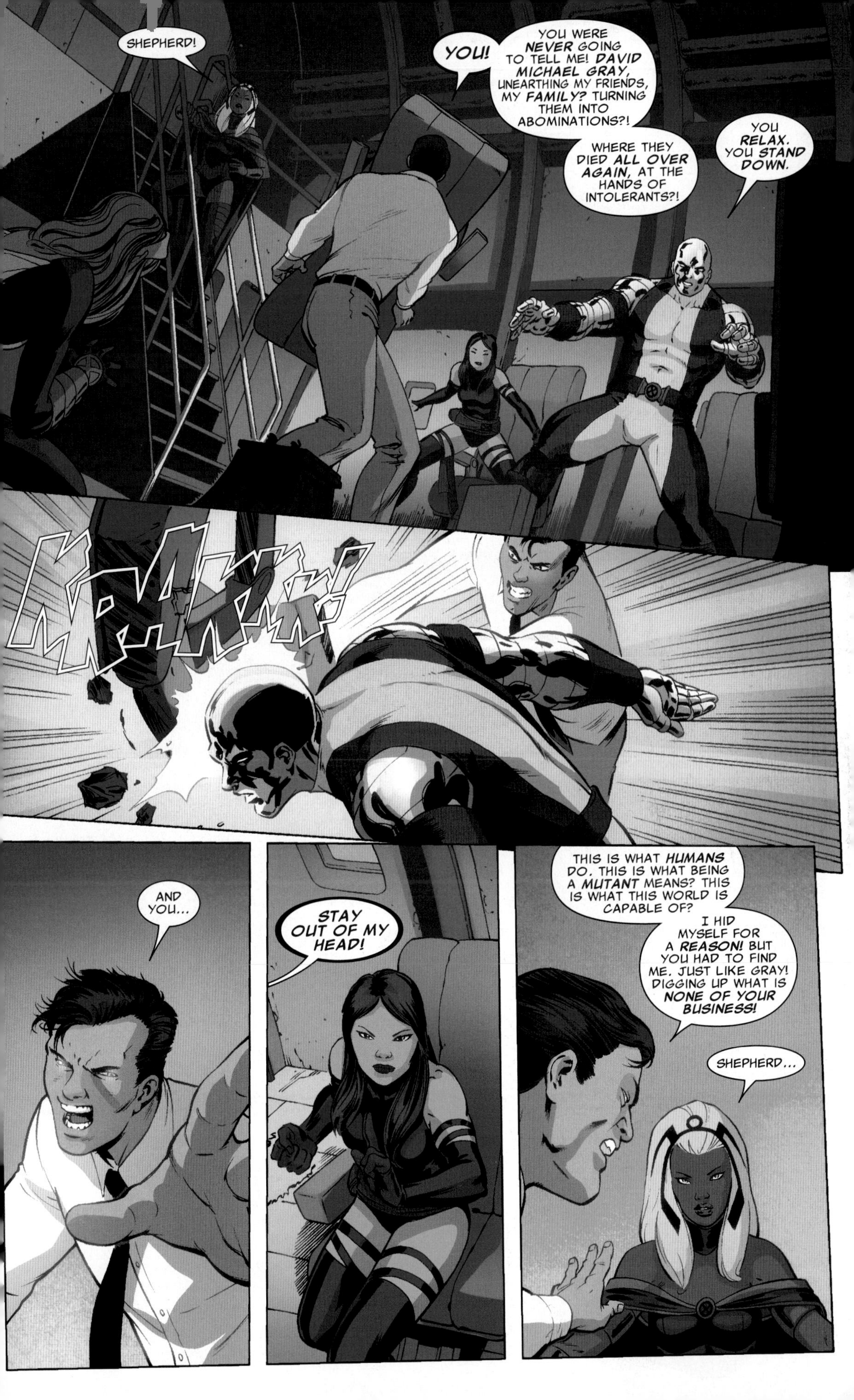
SHEPHERD!
YOU!
YOU WERE NEVER GOING TO TELL ME! DAVID MICHAEL GRAY, UNEARTHING MY FRIENDS, MY FAMILY? TURNING THEM INTO ABOMINATIONS?!
WHERE THEY DIED ALL OVER AGAIN, AT THE HANDS OF INTOLERANTS?!
YOU RELAX. YOU STAND DOWN.
K-AKKK!
AND YOU...
STAY OUT OF MY HEAD!
THIS IS WHAT HUMANS DO. THIS IS WHAT BEING A MUTANT MEANS? THIS IS WHAT THIS WORLD IS CAPABLE OF?
I HID MYSELF FOR A REASON! BUT YOU HAD TO FIND ME. JUST LIKE GRAY! DIGGING UP WHAT IS NONE OF YOUR BUSINESS!
SHEPHERD...

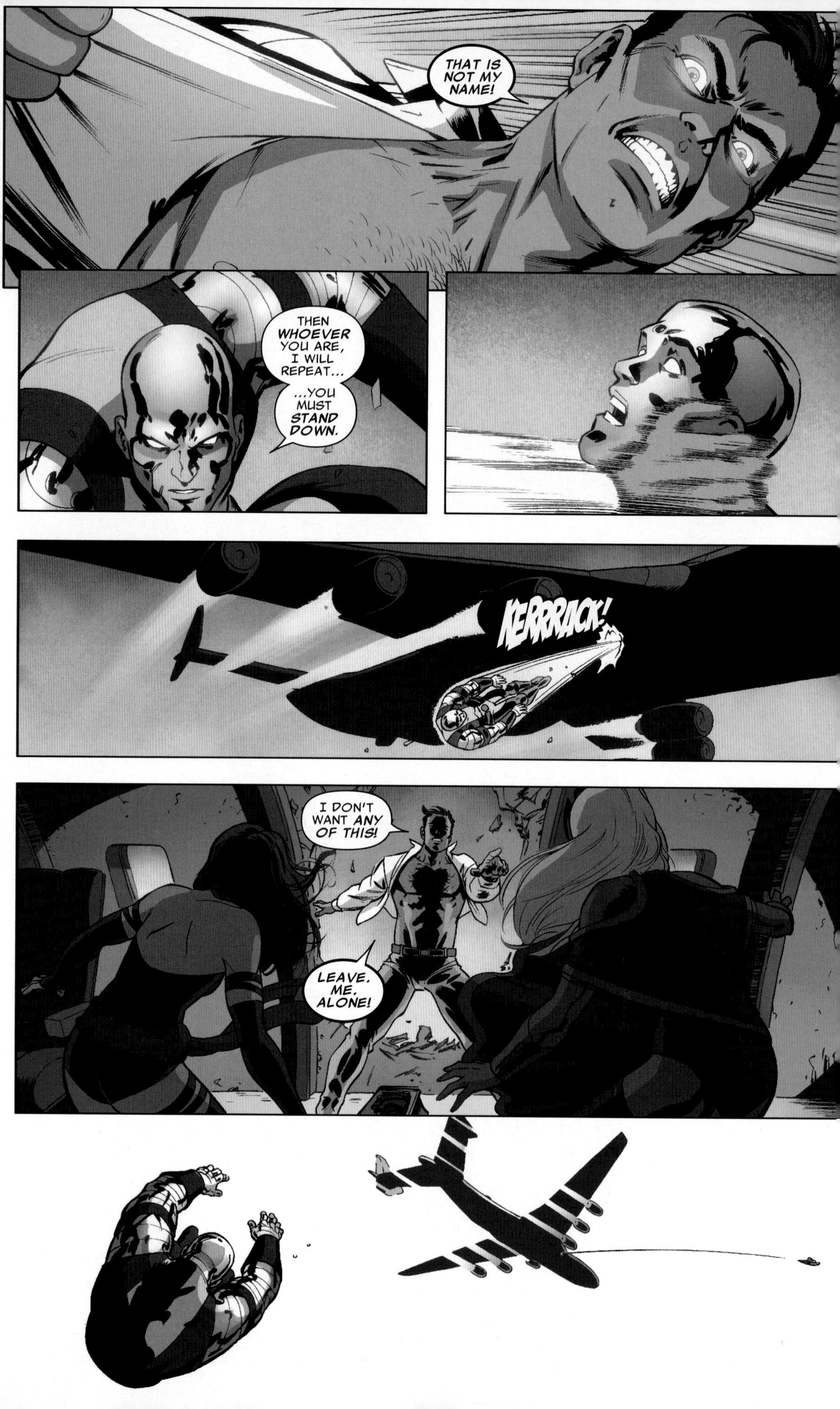
THAT IS NOT MY NAME!
THEN WHOEVER YOU ARE, I WILL REPEAT...
...YOU MUST STAND DOWN.
KERRRACK!
I DON'T WANT ANY OF THIS!
LEAVE. ME. ALONE!

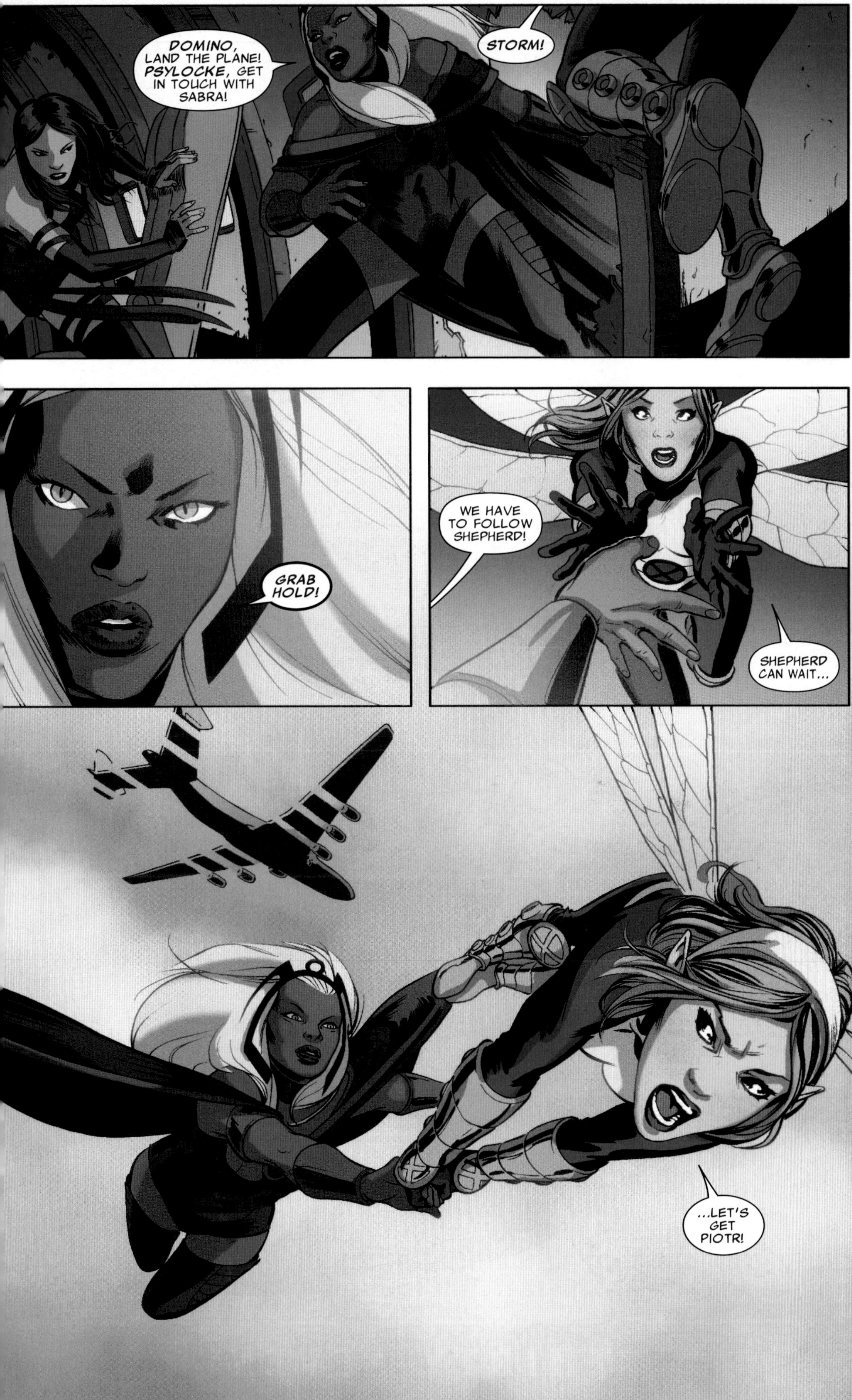
DOMINO, LAND THE PLANE! PSYLOCKE, GET IN TOUCH WITH SABRA!
STORM!
GRAB HOLD!
WE HAVE TO FOLLOW SHEPHERD!
SHEPHERD CAN WAIT...
...LET'S GET PIOTR!

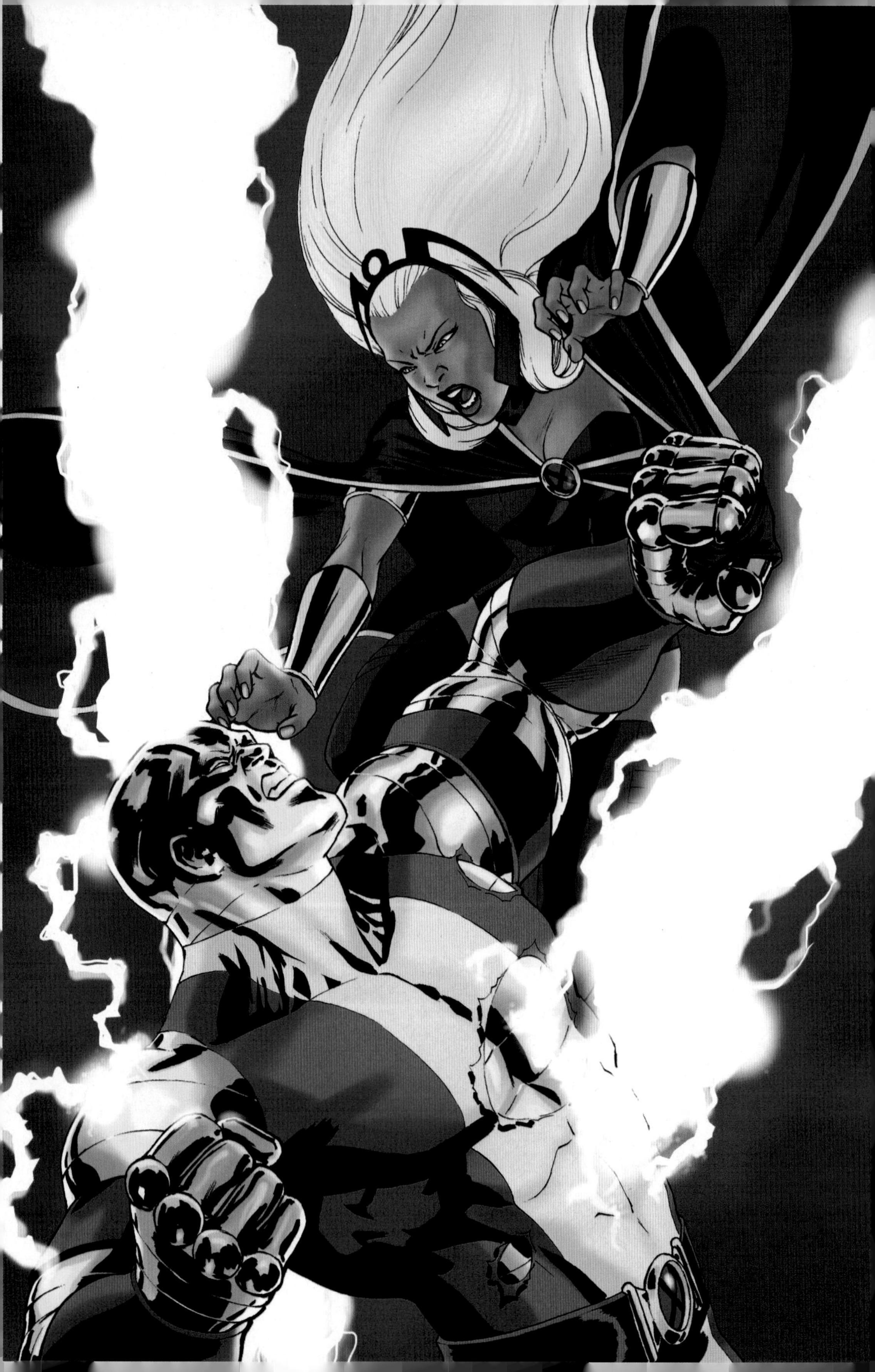

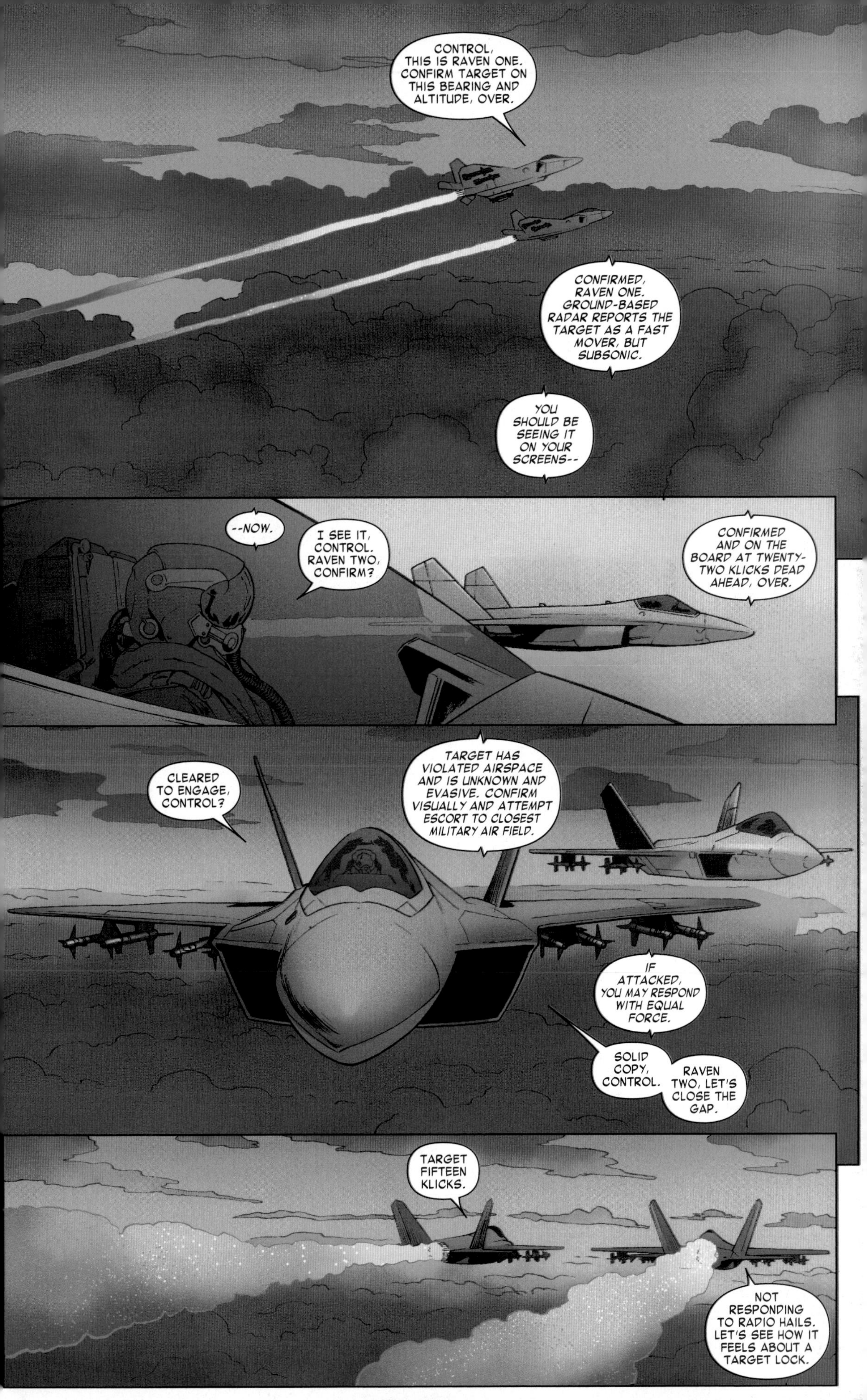
CONTROL, THIS IS RAVEN ONE. CONFIRM TARGET ON THIS BEARING AND ALTITUDE, OVER.
CONFIRMED, RAVEN ONE. GROUND-BASED RADAR REPORTS THE TARGET AS A FAST MOVER, BUT SUBSONIC.
YOU SHOULD BE SEEING IT ON YOUR SCREENS--
--NOW.
I SEE IT, CONTROL. RAVEN TWO, CONFIRM?
CONFIRMED AND ON THE BOARD AT TWENTY-TWO KLICKS DEAD AHEAD, OVER.
CLEARED TO ENGAGE, CONTROL?
TARGET HAS VIOLATED AIRSPACE AND IS UNKNOWN AND EVASIVE. CONFIRM VISUALLY AND ATTEMPT ESCORT TO CLOSEST MILITARY AIR FIELD.
IF ATTACKED, YOU MAY RESPOND WITH EQUAL FORCE.
SOLID COPY, CONTROL.
RAVEN TWO, LET'S CLOSE THE GAP.
TARGET FIFTEEN KLICKS.
NOT RESPONDING TO RADIO HAILS. LET'S SEE HOW IT FEELS ABOUT A TARGET LOCK.

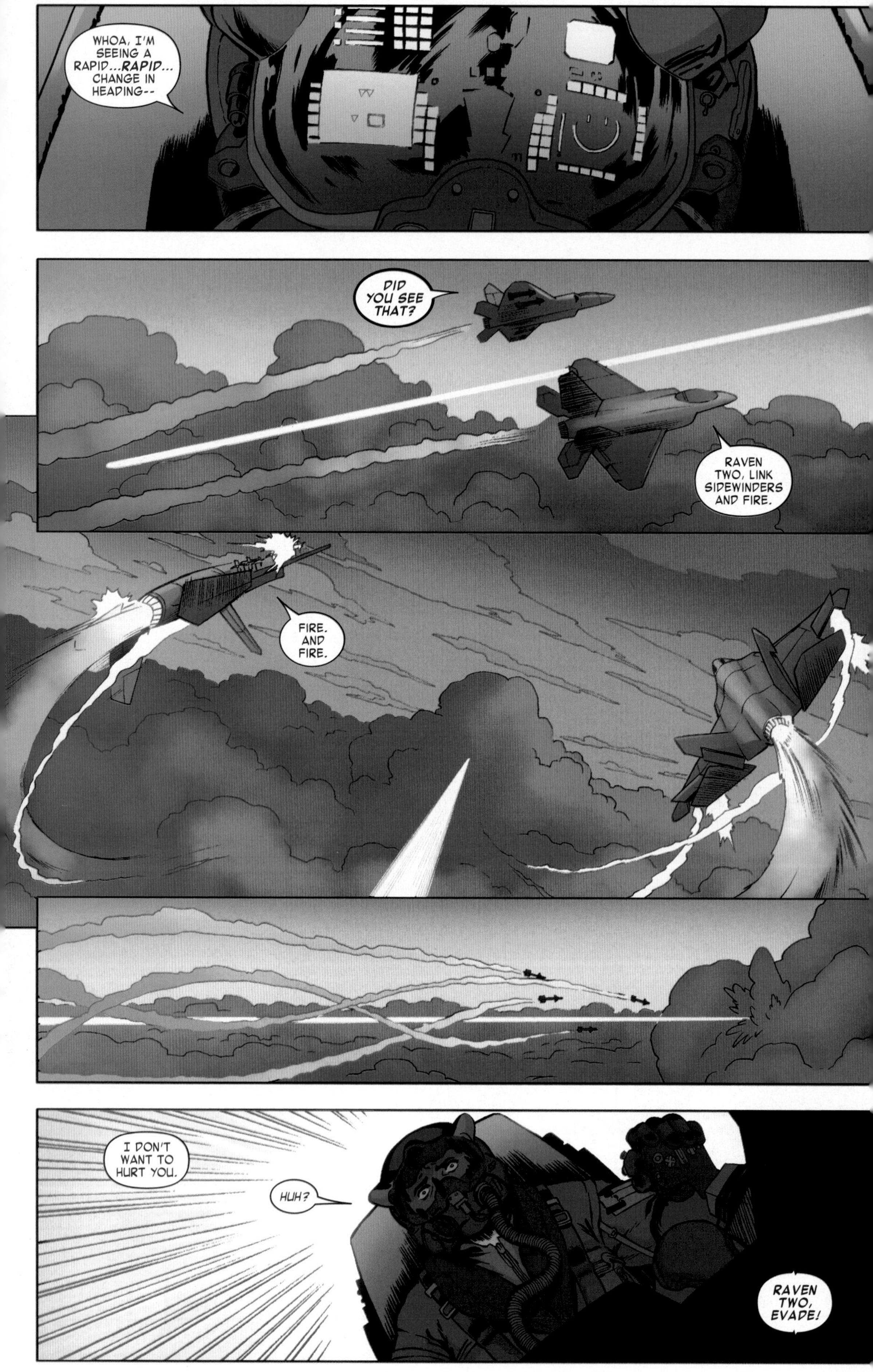
WHOA, I'M SEEING A RAPID...RAPID... CHANGE IN HEADING--
DID YOU SEE THAT?
RAVEN TWO, LINK SIDEWINDERS AND FIRE.
FIRE. AND FIRE.
I DON'T WANT TO HURT YOU.
HUH?
RAVEN TWO, EVADE!

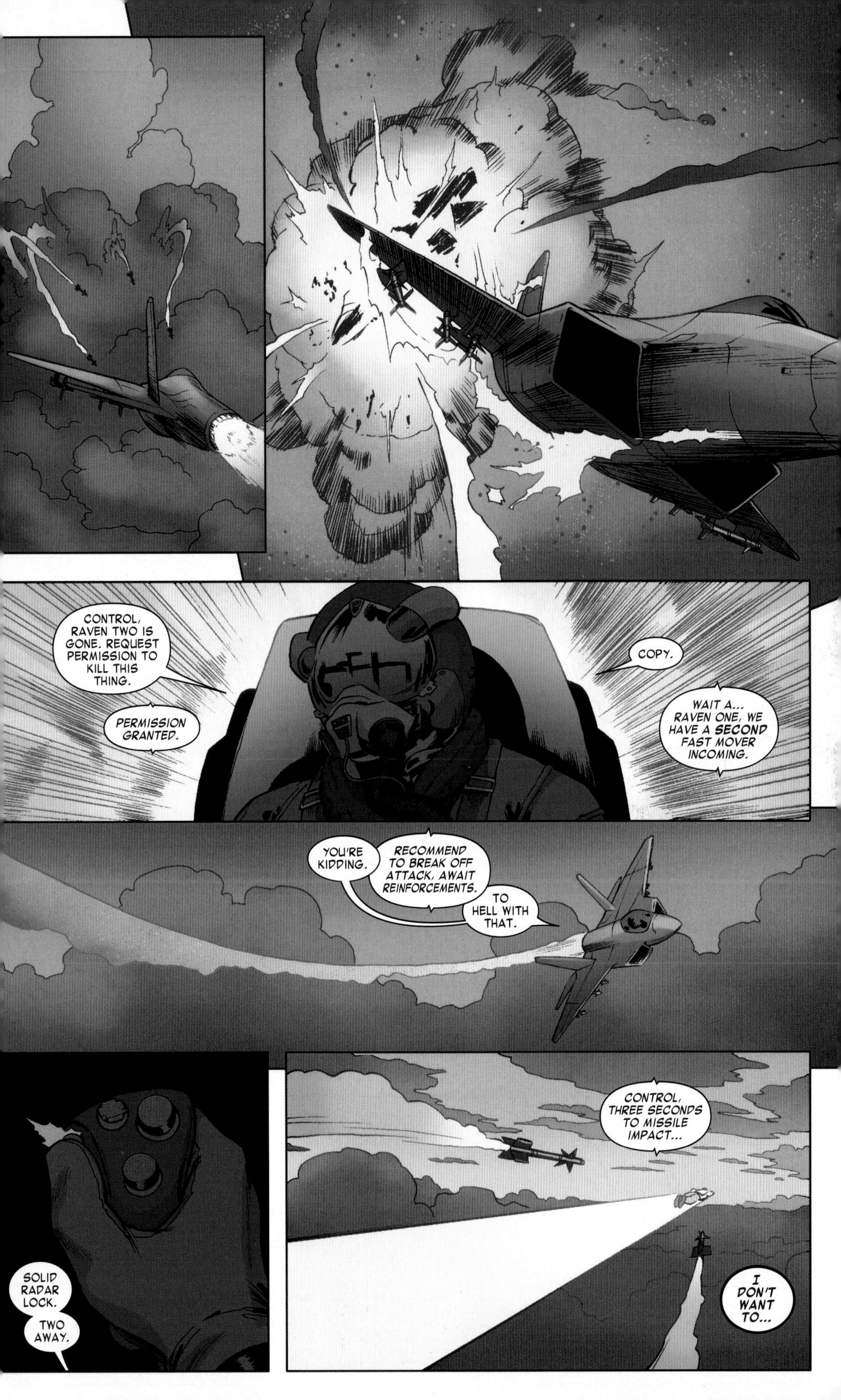
CONTROL, RAVEN TWO IS GONE. REQUEST PERMISSION TO KILL THIS THING.
PERMISSION GRANTED.
COPY.
WAIT A... RAVEN ONE, WE HAVE A SECOND FAST MOVER INCOMING.
YOU'RE KIDDING.
RECOMMEND TO BREAK OFF ATTACK, AWAIT REINFORCEMENTS.
TO HELL WITH THAT.
SOLID RADAR LOCK.
TWO AWAY.
CONTROL, THREE SECONDS TO MISSILE IMPACT...
I DON'T WANT TO...

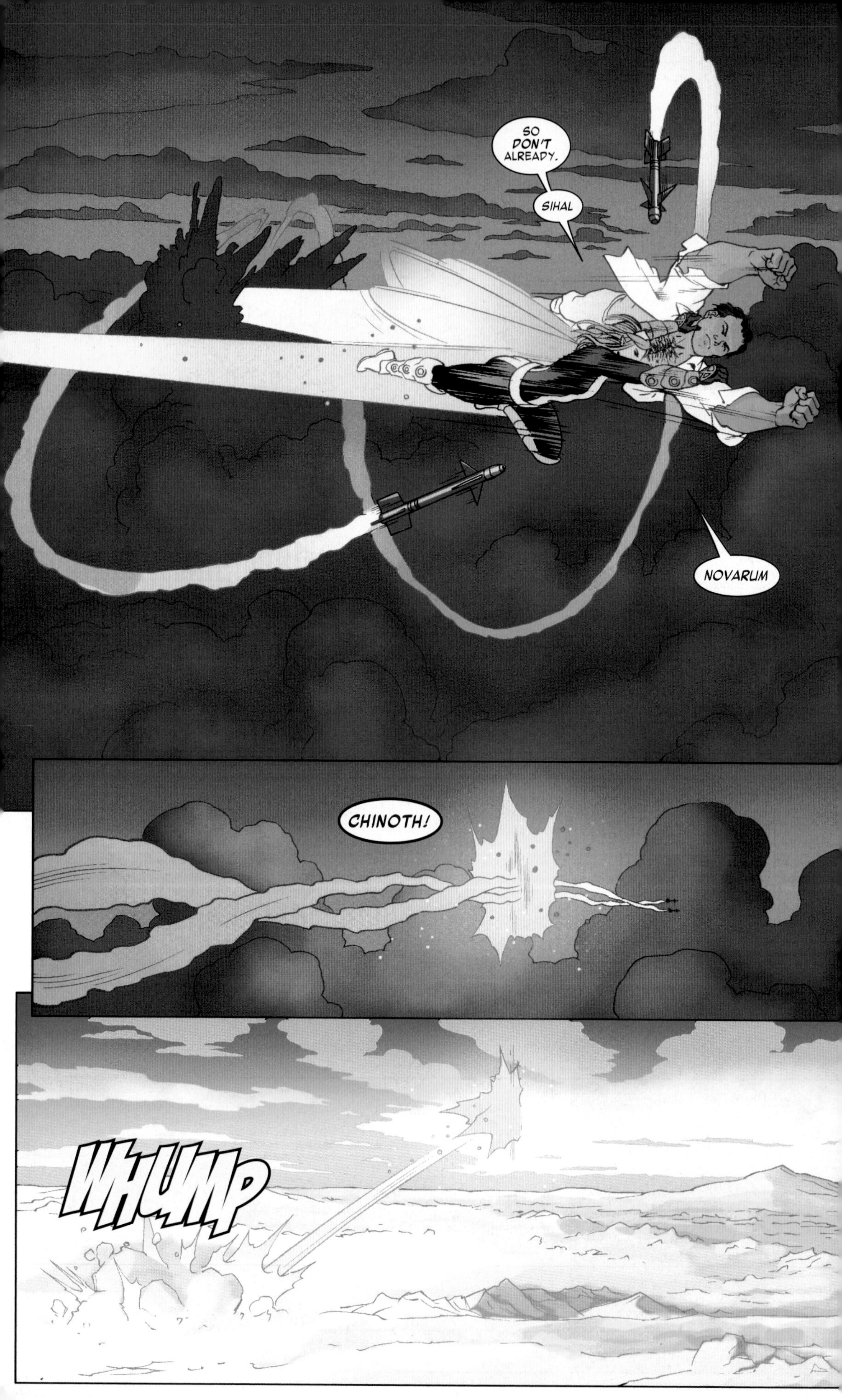
SO DON'T ALREADY.
SIHAL
NOVARUM
CHINOTH!
WHUMP

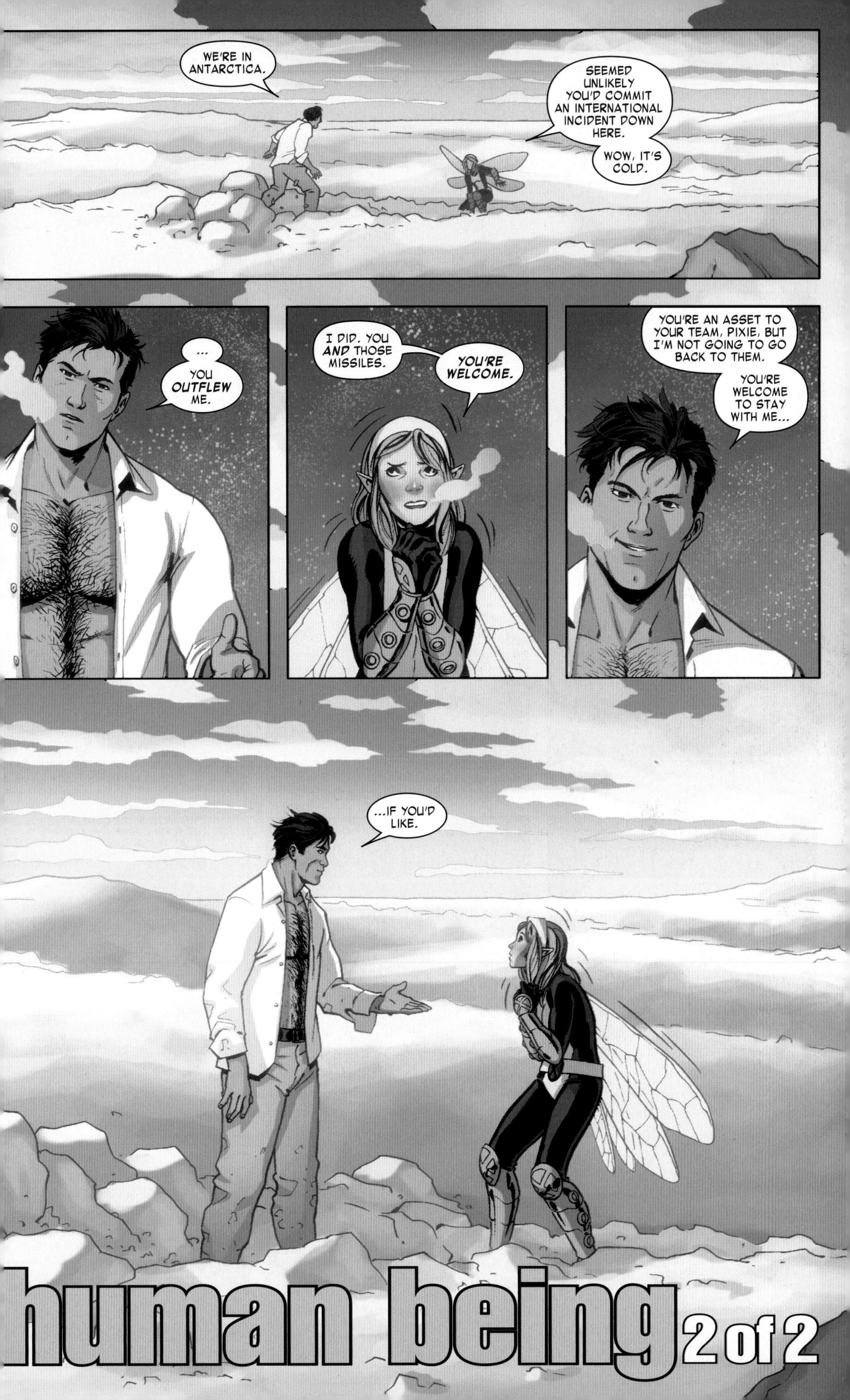
WE'RE IN ANTARCTICA.
SEEMED UNLIKELY YOU'D COMMIT AN INTERNATIONAL INCIDENT DOWN HERE.
WOW, IT'S COLD.
... YOU OUTFLEW ME.
I DID. YOU AND THOSE MISSILES.
YOU'RE WELCOME.
YOU'RE AN ASSET TO YOUR TEAM, PIXIE, BUT I'M NOT GOING TO GO BACK TO THEM.
YOU'RE WELCOME TO STAY WITH ME...
...IF YOU'D LIKE.
human being 2 of 2

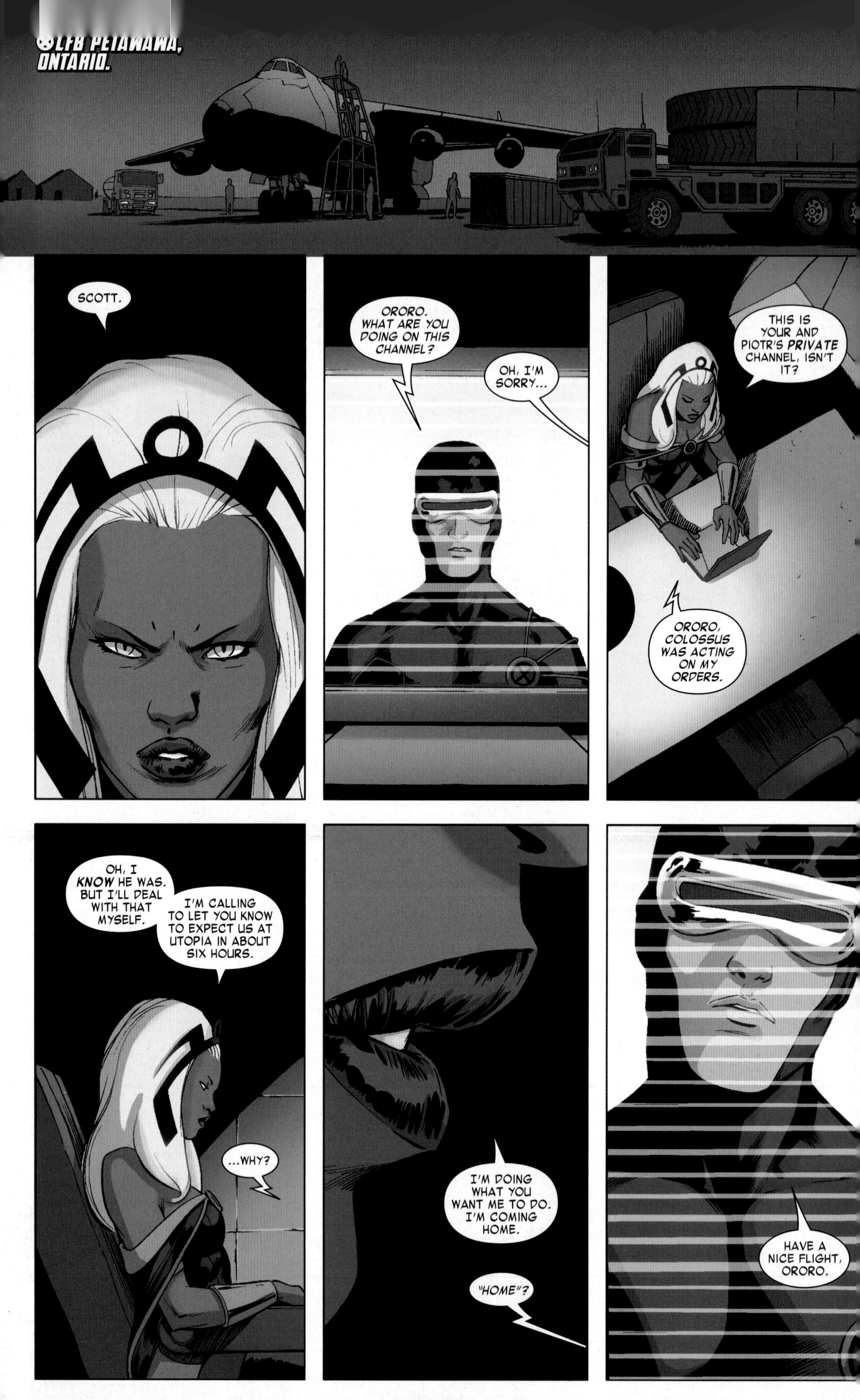
CFB PETAWAWA, ONTARIO.
SCOTT.
ORORO. WHAT ARE YOU DOING ON THIS CHANNEL?
OH, I'M SORRY...
THIS IS YOUR AND PIOTR'S PRIVATE CHANNEL, ISN'T IT?
ORORO, COLOSSUS WAS ACTING ON MY ORDERS.
OH, I KNOW HE WAS. BUT I'LL DEAL WITH THAT MYSELF.
I'M CALLING TO LET YOU KNOW TO EXPECT US AT UTOPIA IN ABOUT SIX HOURS.
...WHY?
I'M DOING WHAT YOU WANT ME TO DO. I'M COMING HOME.
"HOME"?
HAVE A NICE FLIGHT, ORORO.

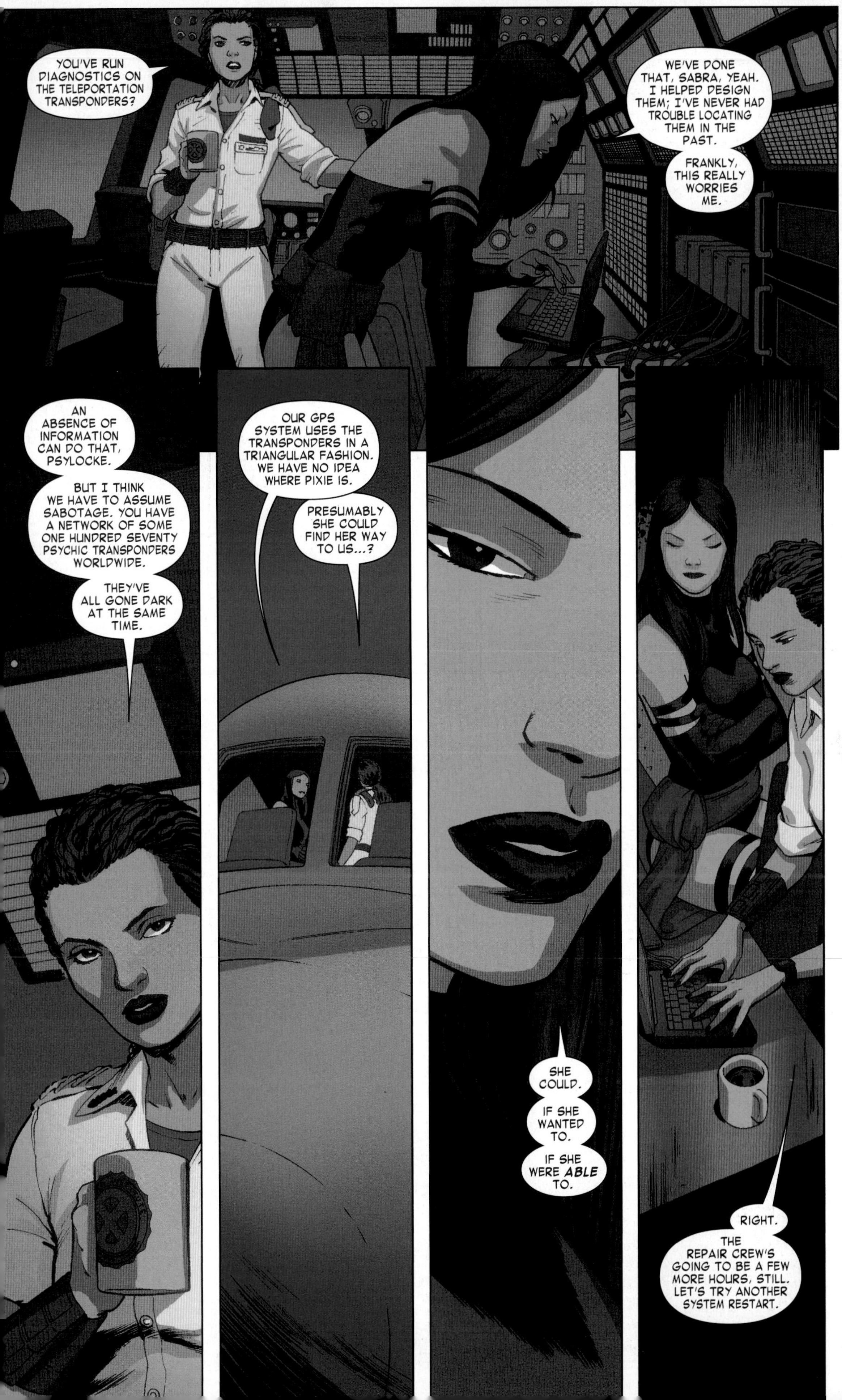
YOU'VE RUN DIAGNOSTICS ON THE TELEPORTATION TRANSPONDERS?
WE'VE DONE THAT, SABRA, YEAH. I HELPED DESIGN THEM; I'VE NEVER HAD TROUBLE LOCATING THEM IN THE PAST.
FRANKLY, THIS REALLY WORRIES ME.
AN ABSENCE OF INFORMATION CAN DO THAT, PSYLOCKE.
BUT I THINK WE HAVE TO ASSUME SABOTAGE. YOU HAVE A NETWORK OF SOME ONE HUNDRED SEVENTY PSYCHIC TRANSPONDERS WORLDWIDE.
THEY'VE ALL GONE DARK AT THE SAME TIME.
OUR GPS SYSTEM USES THE TRANSPONDERS IN A TRIANGULAR FASHION. WE HAVE NO IDEA WHERE PIXIE IS.
PRESUMABLY SHE COULD FIND HER WAY TO US...?
SHE COULD.
IF SHE WANTED TO.
IF SHE WERE *ABLE* TO.
RIGHT.
THE REPAIR CREW'S GOING TO BE A FEW MORE HOURS, STILL. LET'S TRY ANOTHER SYSTEM RESTART.

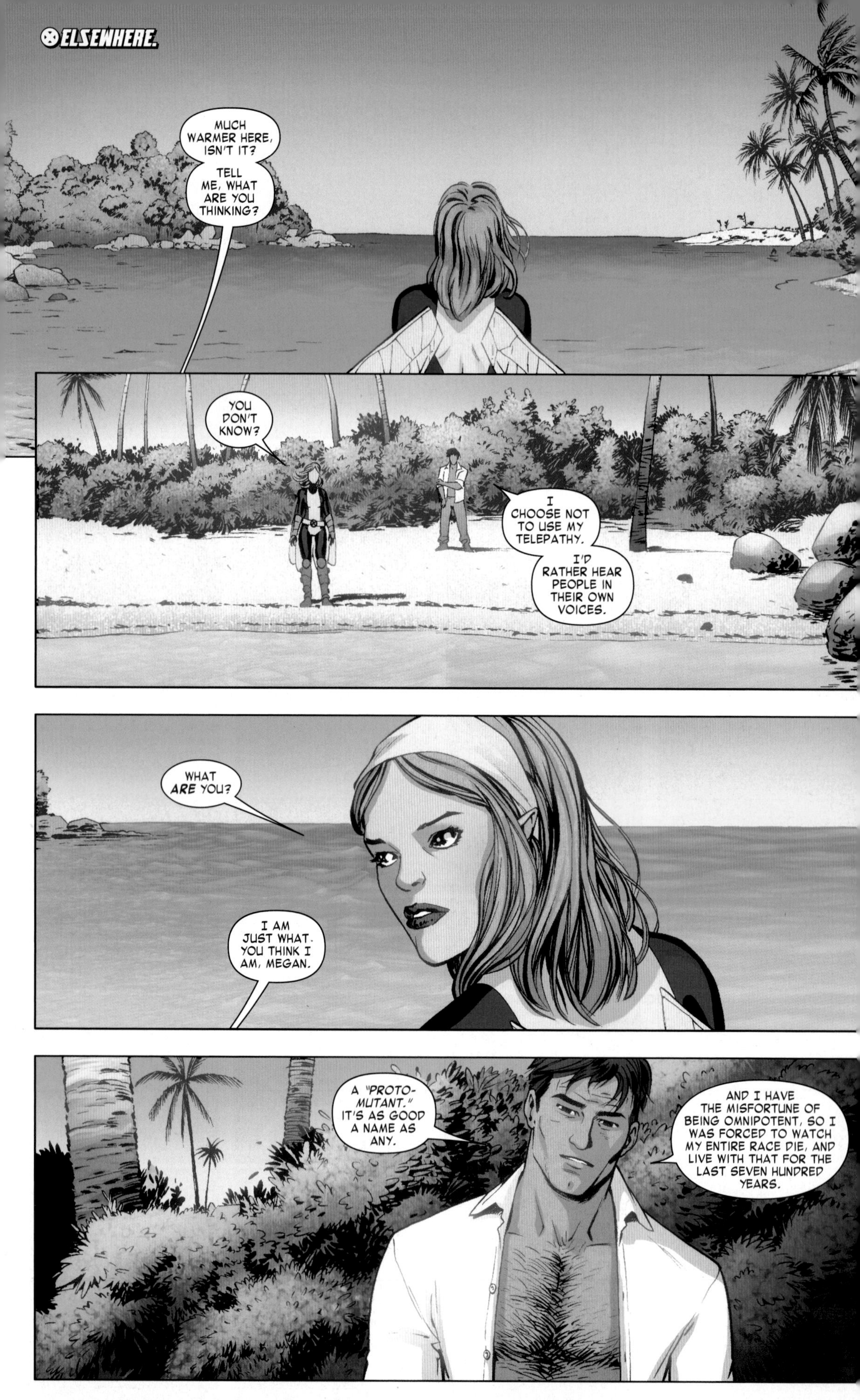
ELSEWHERE.
MUCH WARMER HERE, ISN'T IT?
TELL ME, WHAT ARE YOU THINKING?
YOU DON'T KNOW?
I CHOOSE NOT TO USE MY TELEPATHY.
I'D RATHER HEAR PEOPLE IN THEIR OWN VOICES.
WHAT ARE YOU?
I AM JUST WHAT YOU THINK I AM, MEGAN.
A "PROTO-MUTANT." IT'S AS GOOD A NAME AS ANY.
AND I HAVE THE MISFORTUNE OF BEING OMNIPOTENT, SO I WAS FORCED TO WATCH MY ENTIRE RACE DIE, AND LIVE WITH THAT FOR THE LAST SEVEN HUNDRED YEARS.

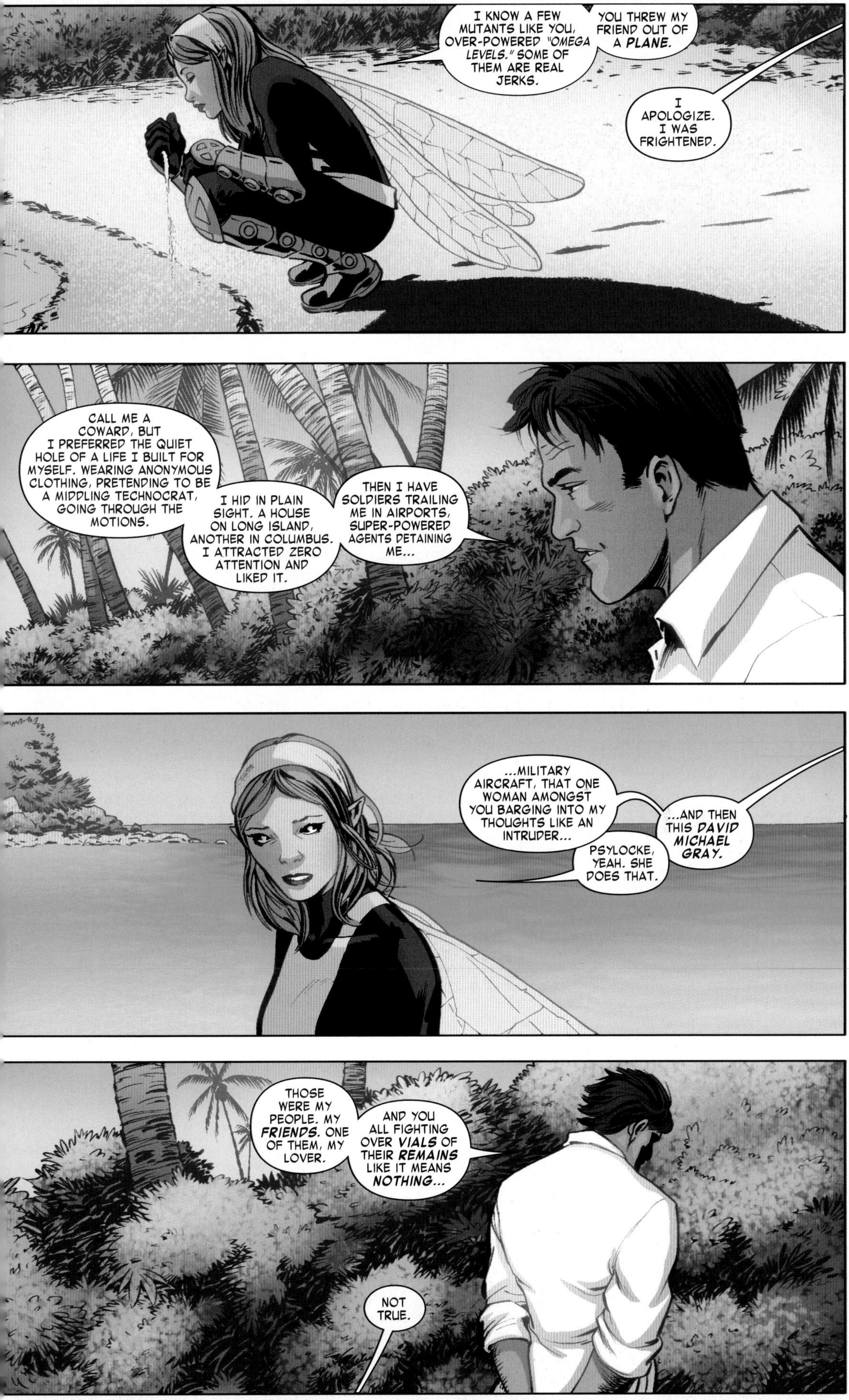

I KNOW A FEW MUTANTS LIKE YOU, OVER-POWERED "OMEGA LEVELS." SOME OF THEM ARE REAL JERKS.
YOU THREW MY FRIEND OUT OF A *PLANE*.
I APOLOGIZE. I WAS FRIGHTENED.
CALL ME A COWARD, BUT I PREFERRED THE QUIET HOLE OF A LIFE I BUILT FOR MYSELF. WEARING ANONYMOUS CLOTHING, PRETENDING TO BE A MIDDLING TECHNOCRAT, GOING THROUGH THE MOTIONS.
I HID IN PLAIN SIGHT. A HOUSE ON LONG ISLAND, ANOTHER IN COLUMBUS. I ATTRACTED ZERO ATTENTION AND LIKED IT.
THEN I HAVE SOLDIERS TRAILING ME IN AIRPORTS, SUPER-POWERED AGENTS DETAINING ME...
...MILITARY AIRCRAFT, THAT ONE WOMAN AMONGST YOU BARGING INTO MY THOUGHTS LIKE AN INTRUDER...
...AND THEN THIS *DAVID MICHAEL GRAY*.
PSYLOCKE, YEAH. SHE DOES THAT.
THOSE WERE MY PEOPLE. MY *FRIENDS*. ONE OF THEM, MY LOVER.
AND YOU ALL FIGHTING OVER *VIALS* OF THEIR *REMAINS* LIKE IT MEANS *NOTHING*...
NOT TRUE.

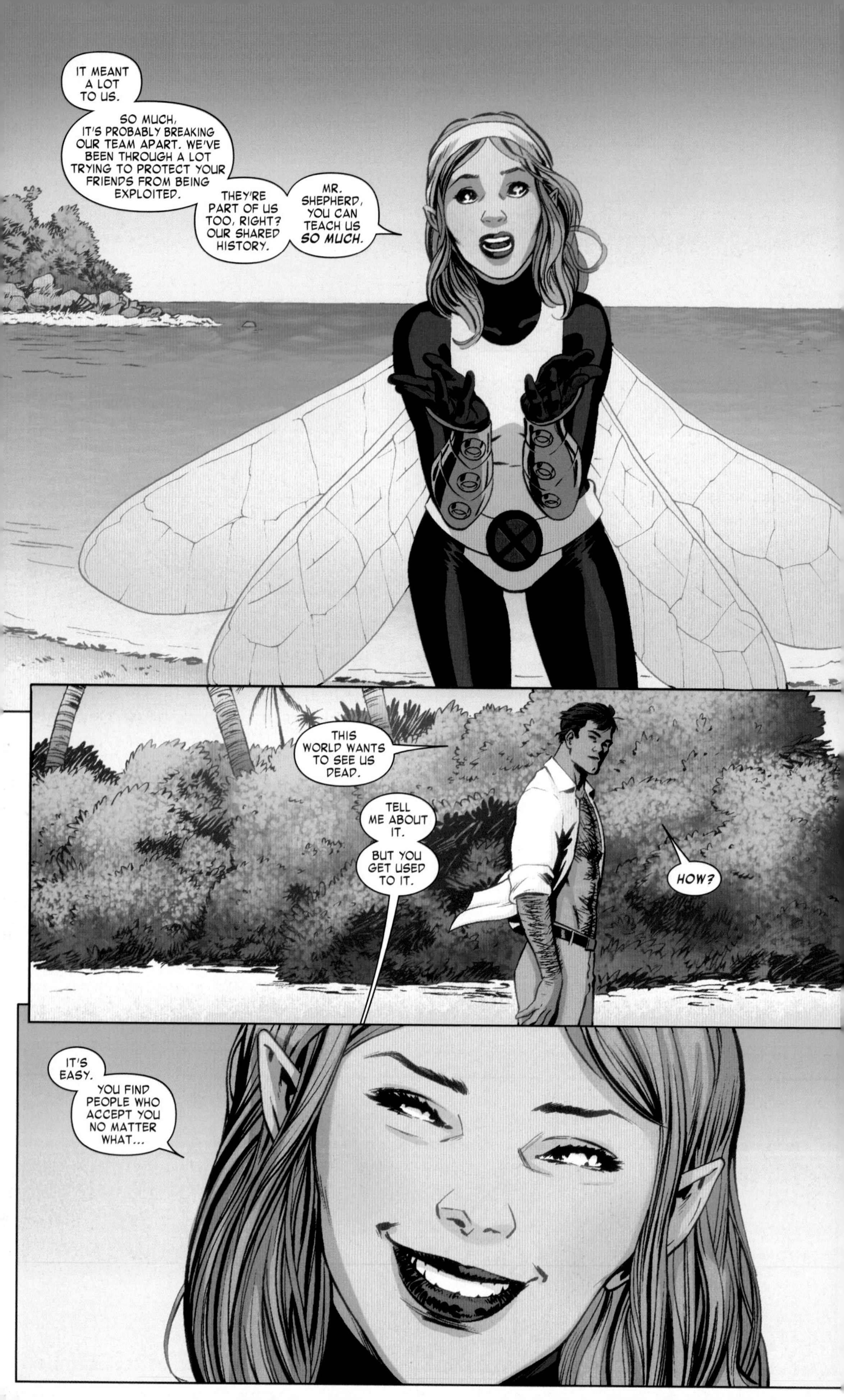
IT MEANT A LOT TO US.
SO MUCH, IT'S PROBABLY BREAKING OUR TEAM APART. WE'VE BEEN THROUGH A LOT TRYING TO PROTECT YOUR FRIENDS FROM BEING EXPLOITED.
THEY'RE PART OF US TOO, RIGHT? OUR SHARED HISTORY.
MR. SHEPHERD, YOU CAN TEACH US SO MUCH.
THIS WORLD WANTS TO SEE US DEAD.
TELL ME ABOUT IT.
BUT YOU GET USED TO IT.
HOW?
IT'S EASY.
YOU FIND PEOPLE WHO ACCEPT YOU NO MATTER WHAT...

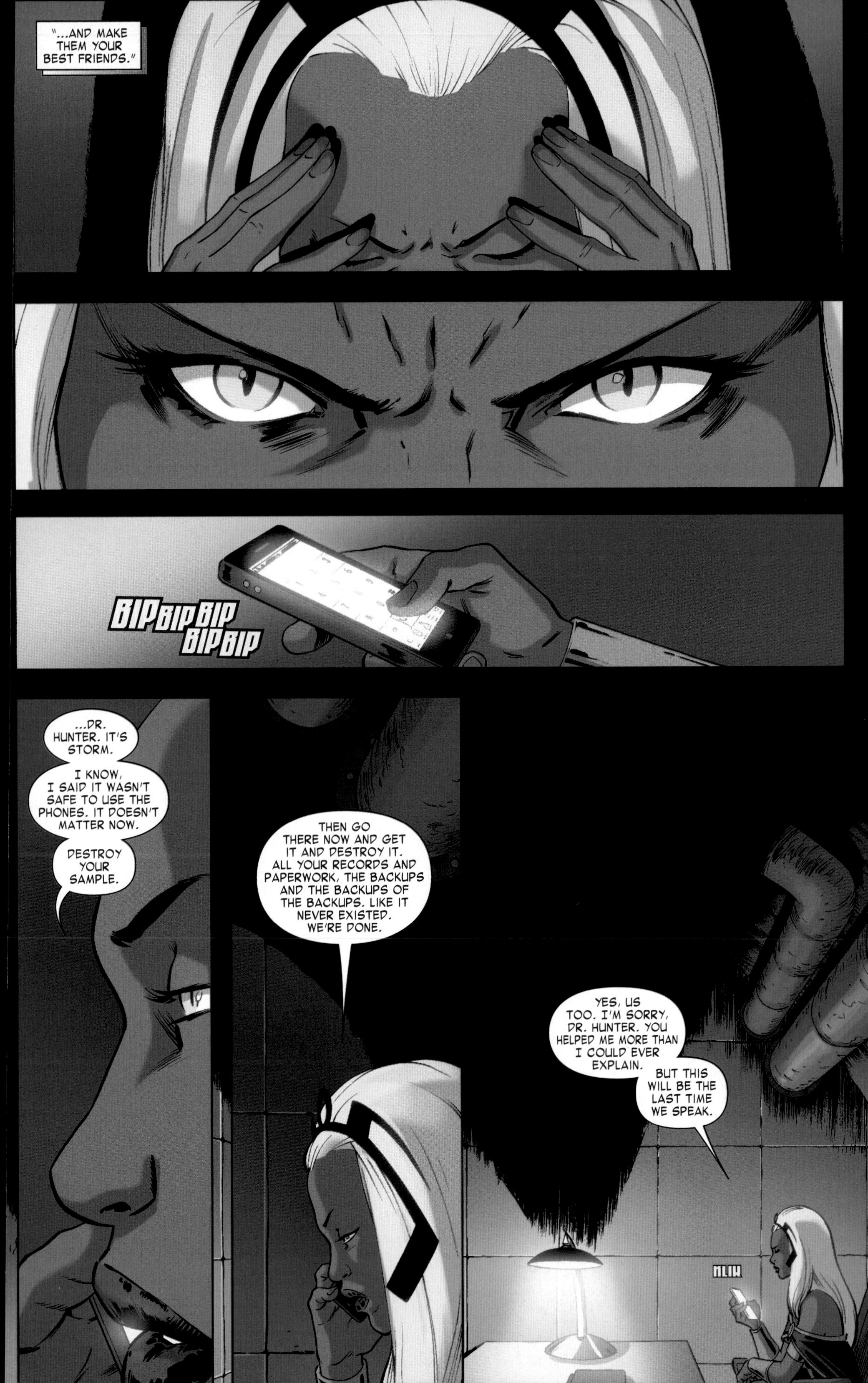
"...AND MAKE THEM YOUR BEST FRIENDS."
BIPBIPBIP BIPBIP
...DR. HUNTER. IT'S STORM.
I KNOW, I SAID IT WASN'T SAFE TO USE THE PHONES. IT DOESN'T MATTER NOW.
DESTROY YOUR SAMPLE.
THEN GO THERE NOW AND GET IT AND DESTROY IT. ALL YOUR RECORDS AND PAPERWORK, THE BACKUPS AND THE BACKUPS OF THE BACKUPS. LIKE IT NEVER EXISTED. WE'RE DONE.
YES, US TOO. I'M SORRY, DR. HUNTER. YOU HELPED ME MORE THAN I COULD EVER EXPLAIN.
BUT THIS WILL BE THE LAST TIME WE SPEAK.

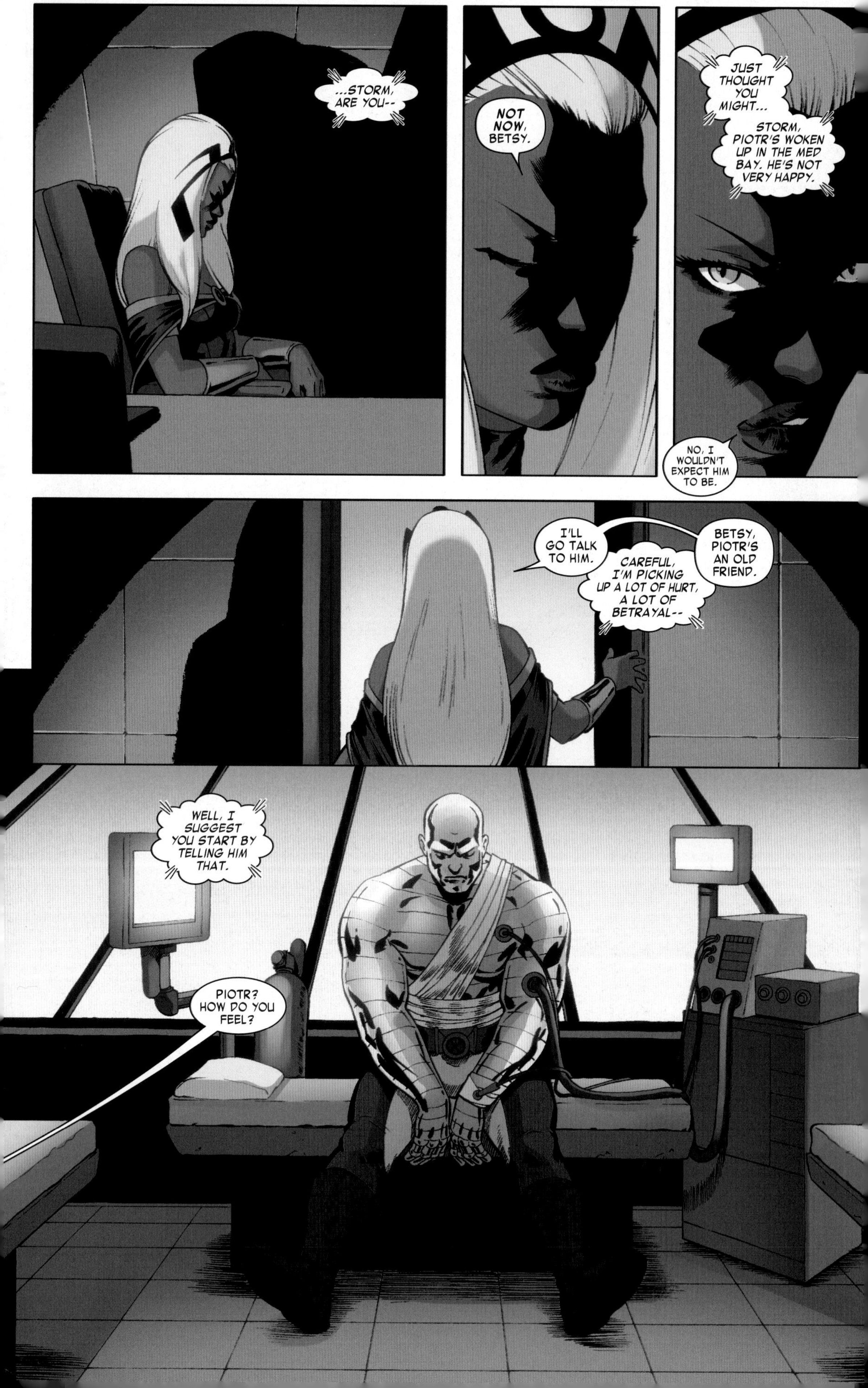
...STORM, ARE YOU--
NOT NOW, BETSY.
JUST THOUGHT YOU MIGHT...
STORM, PIOTR'S WOKEN UP IN THE MED BAY. HE'S NOT VERY HAPPY.
NO, I WOULDN'T EXPECT HIM TO BE.
I'LL GO TALK TO HIM.
CAREFUL, I'M PICKING UP A LOT OF HURT, A LOT OF BETRAYAL--
BETSY, PIOTR'S AN OLD FRIEND.
WELL, I SUGGEST YOU START BY TELLING HIM THAT.
PIOTR? HOW DO YOU FEEL?

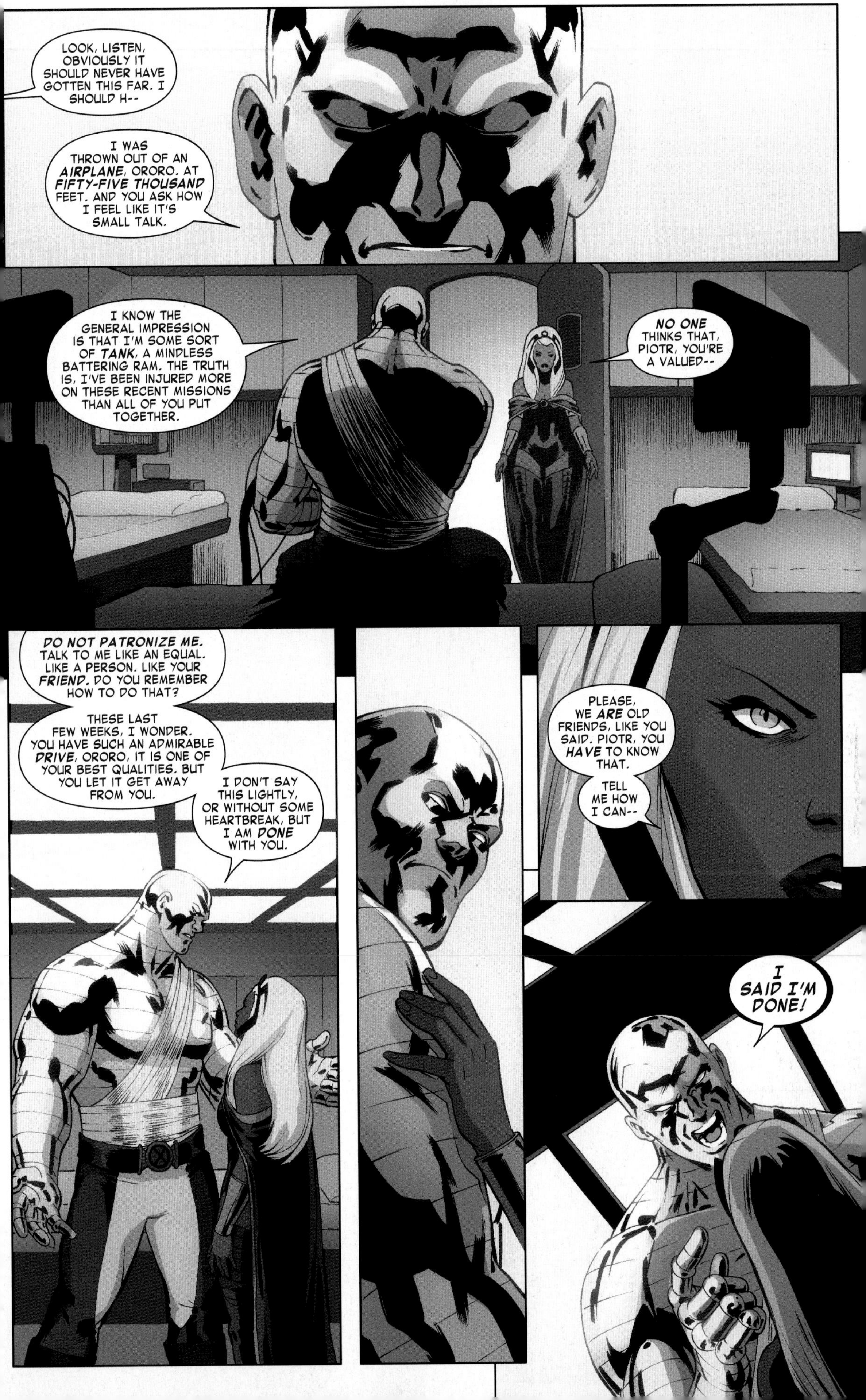
LOOK, LISTEN, OBVIOUSLY IT SHOULD NEVER HAVE GOTTEN THIS FAR. I SHOULD H--
I WAS THROWN OUT OF AN AIRPLANE, ORORO. AT FIFTY-FIVE THOUSAND FEET. AND YOU ASK HOW I FEEL LIKE IT'S SMALL TALK.
I KNOW THE GENERAL IMPRESSION IS THAT I'M SOME SORT OF TANK, A MINDLESS BATTERING RAM. THE TRUTH IS, I'VE BEEN INJURED MORE ON THESE RECENT MISSIONS THAN ALL OF YOU PUT TOGETHER.
NO ONE THINKS THAT, PIOTR, YOU'RE A VALUED--
DO NOT PATRONIZE ME. TALK TO ME LIKE AN EQUAL. LIKE A PERSON. LIKE YOUR FRIEND. DO YOU REMEMBER HOW TO DO THAT?
THESE LAST FEW WEEKS, I WONDER. YOU HAVE SUCH AN ADMIRABLE DRIVE, ORORO, IT IS ONE OF YOUR BEST QUALITIES. BUT YOU LET IT GET AWAY FROM YOU.
I DON'T SAY THIS LIGHTLY, OR WITHOUT SOME HEARTBREAK, BUT I AM DONE WITH YOU.
PLEASE, WE ARE OLD FRIENDS, LIKE YOU SAID. PIOTR, YOU HAVE TO KNOW THAT.
TELL ME HOW I CAN--
I SAID I'M DONE!

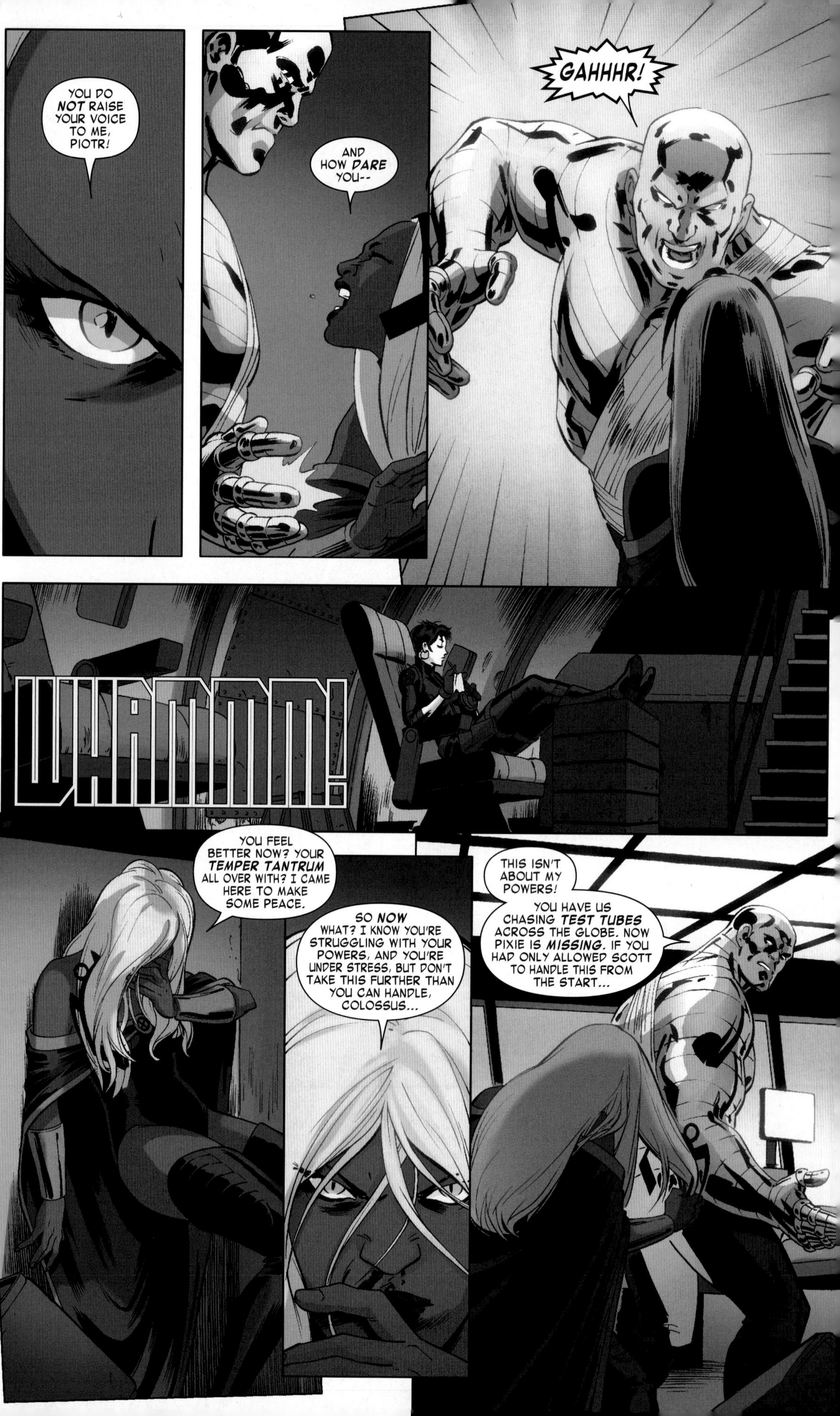
YOU DO NOT RAISE YOUR VOICE TO ME, PIOTR!
AND HOW DARE YOU--
GAHHHR!
WHAMMM!
YOU FEEL BETTER NOW? YOUR TEMPER TANTRUM ALL OVER WITH? I CAME HERE TO MAKE SOME PEACE.
SO NOW WHAT? I KNOW YOU'RE STRUGGLING WITH YOUR POWERS, AND YOU'RE UNDER STRESS, BUT DON'T TAKE THIS FURTHER THAN YOU CAN HANDLE, COLOSSUS...
THIS ISN'T ABOUT MY POWERS!
YOU HAVE US CHASING TEST TUBES ACROSS THE GLOBE. NOW PIXIE IS MISSING. IF YOU HAD ONLY ALLOWED SCOTT TO HANDLE THIS FROM THE START...

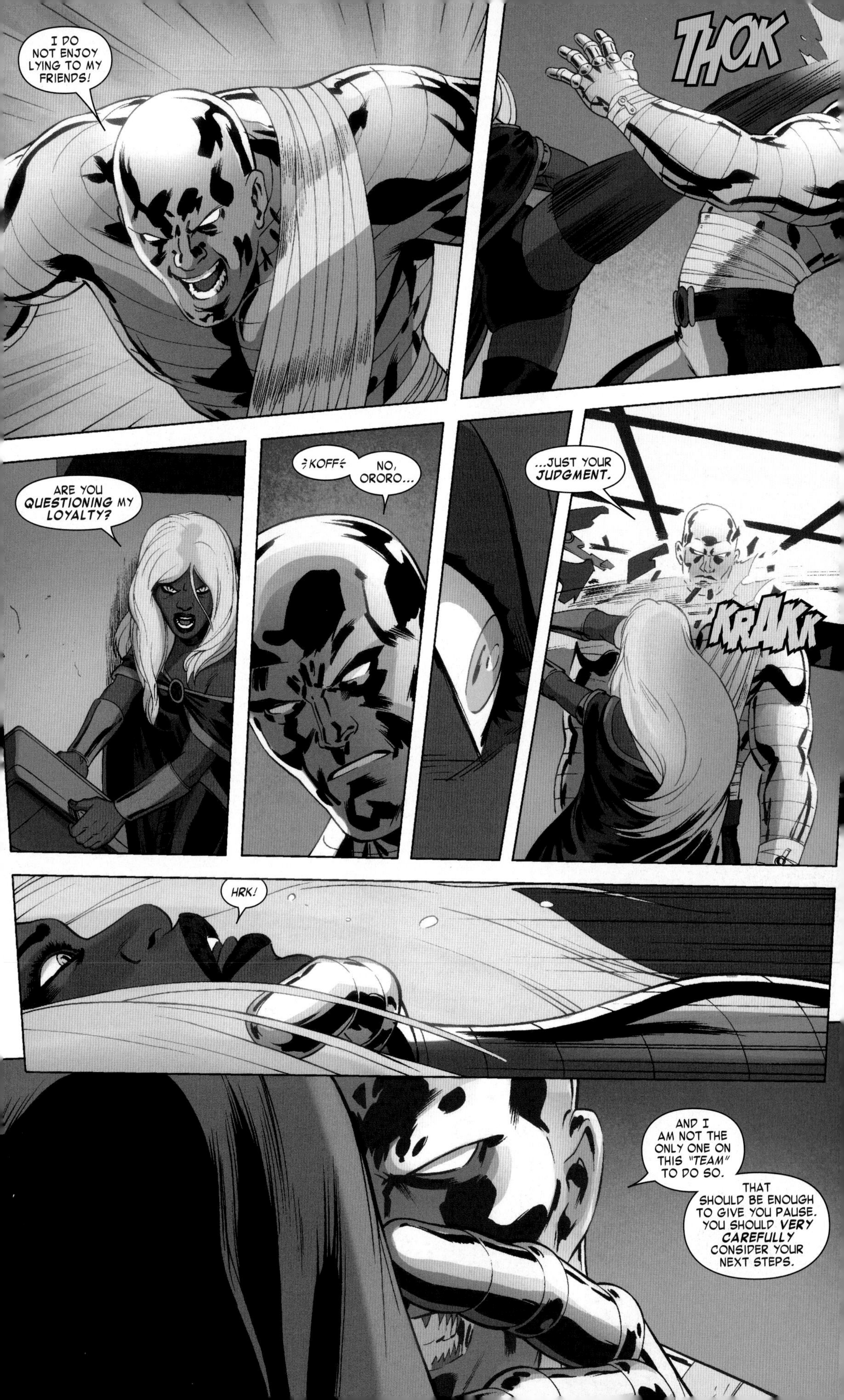
I DO NOT ENJOY LYING TO MY FRIENDS!
THOK
ARE YOU QUESTIONING MY LOYALTY?
KOFF NO, ORORO...
...JUST YOUR JUDGMENT.
KRAKK
HRK!
AND I AM NOT THE ONLY ONE ON THIS "TEAM" TO DO SO.
THAT SHOULD BE ENOUGH TO GIVE YOU PAUSE. YOU SHOULD VERY CAREFULLY CONSIDER YOUR NEXT STEPS.

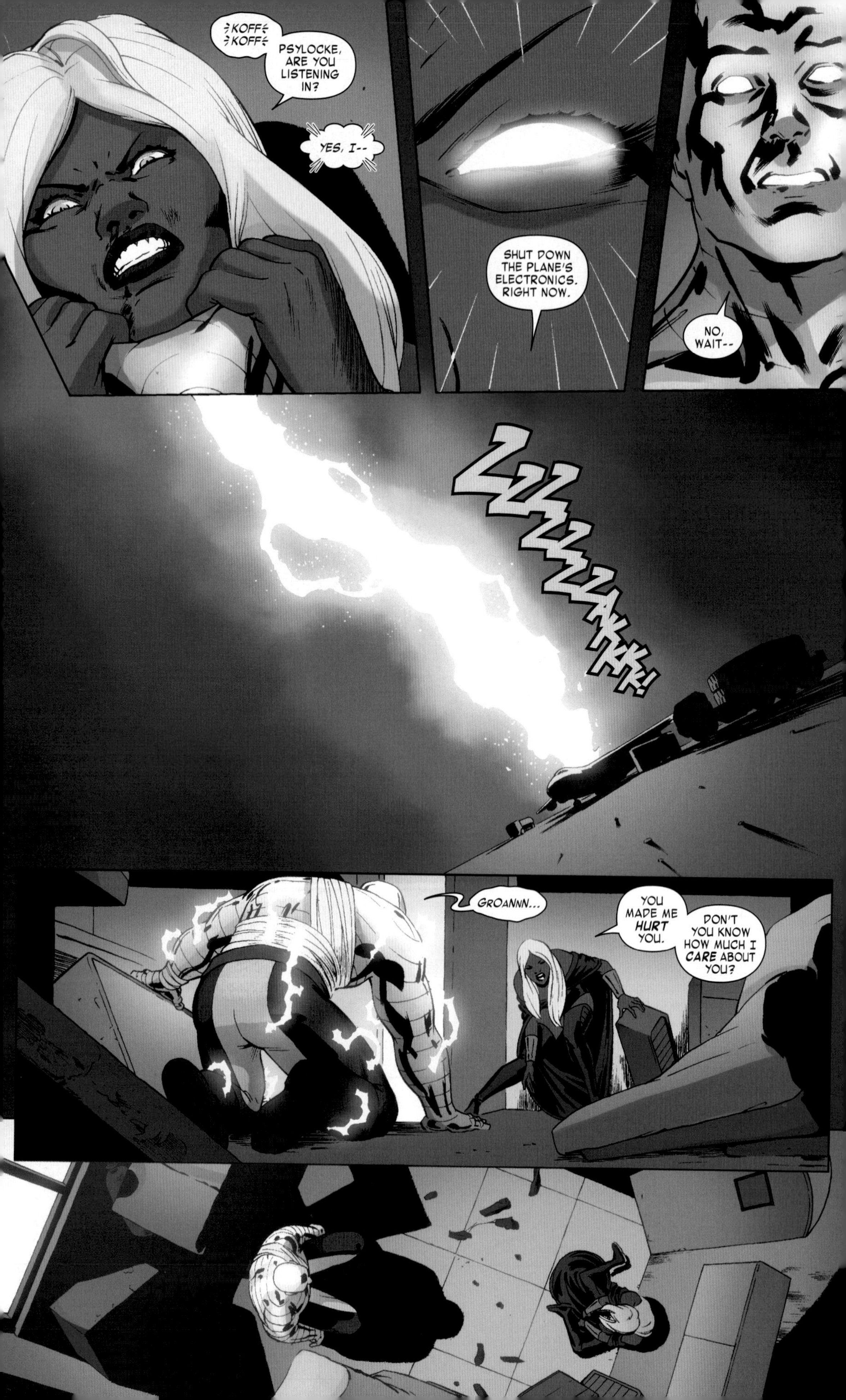

≷KOFF≶ ≷KOFF≶
PSYLOCKE, ARE YOU LISTENING IN?
YES, I--
SHUT DOWN THE PLANE'S ELECTRONICS. RIGHT NOW.
NO, WAIT--
ZZZZZZAKKK!
GROANNN...
YOU MADE ME HURT YOU.
DON'T YOU KNOW HOW MUCH I CARE ABOUT YOU?

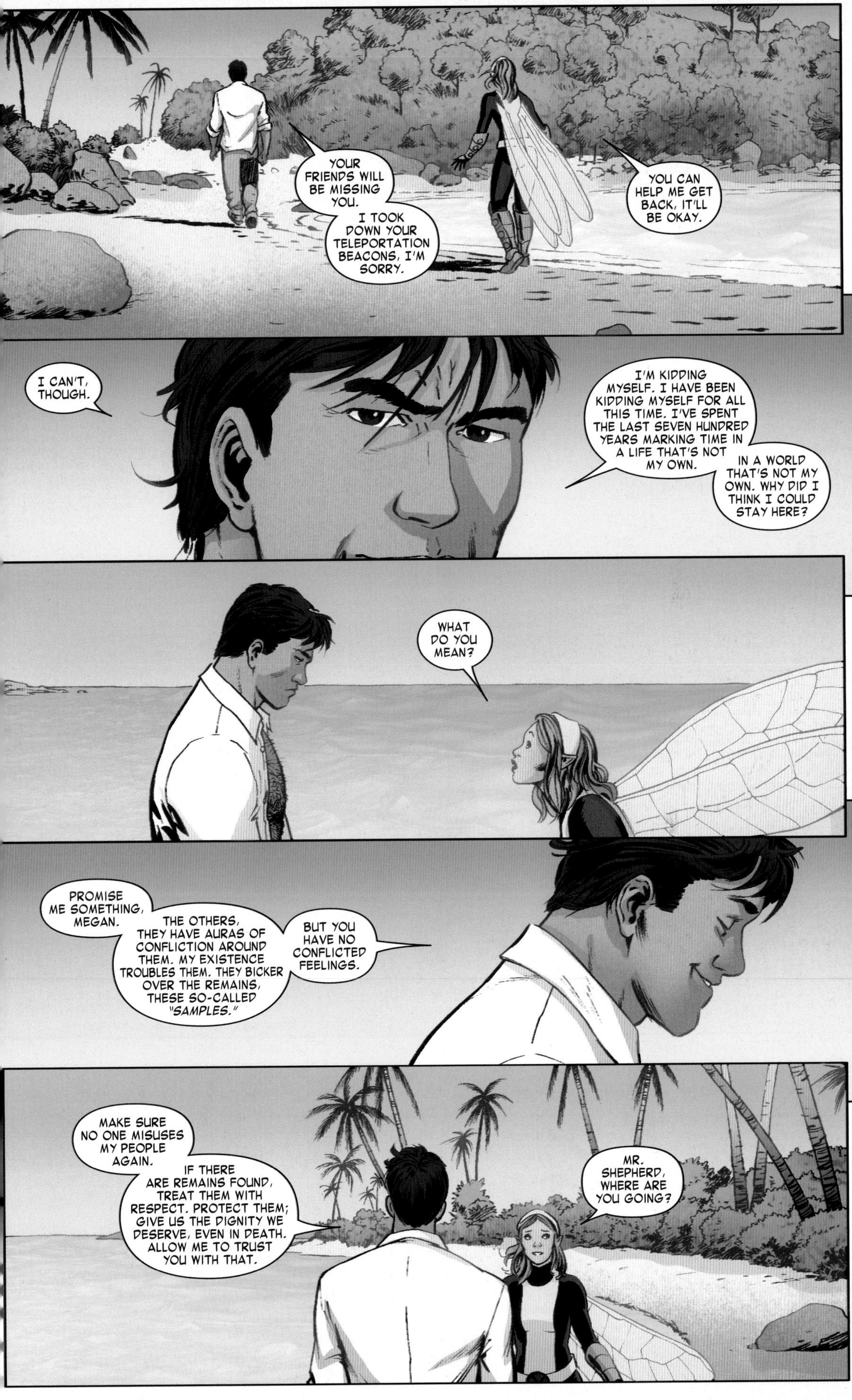
YOUR FRIENDS WILL BE MISSING YOU.
I TOOK DOWN YOUR TELEPORTATION BEACONS, I'M SORRY.
YOU CAN HELP ME GET BACK, IT'LL BE OKAY.
I CAN'T, THOUGH.
I'M KIDDING MYSELF. I HAVE BEEN KIDDING MYSELF FOR ALL THIS TIME. I'VE SPENT THE LAST SEVEN HUNDRED YEARS MARKING TIME IN A LIFE THAT'S NOT MY OWN.
IN A WORLD THAT'S NOT MY OWN. WHY DID I THINK I COULD STAY HERE?
WHAT DO YOU MEAN?
PROMISE ME SOMETHING, MEGAN.
THE OTHERS, THEY HAVE AURAS OF CONFLICTION AROUND THEM. MY EXISTENCE TROUBLES THEM. THEY BICKER OVER THE REMAINS, THESE SO-CALLED "SAMPLES."
BUT YOU HAVE NO CONFLICTED FEELINGS.
MAKE SURE NO ONE MISUSES MY PEOPLE AGAIN.
IF THERE ARE REMAINS FOUND, TREAT THEM WITH RESPECT. PROTECT THEM; GIVE US THE DIGNITY WE DESERVE, EVEN IN DEATH. ALLOW ME TO TRUST YOU WITH THAT.
MR. SHEPHERD, WHERE ARE YOU GOING?

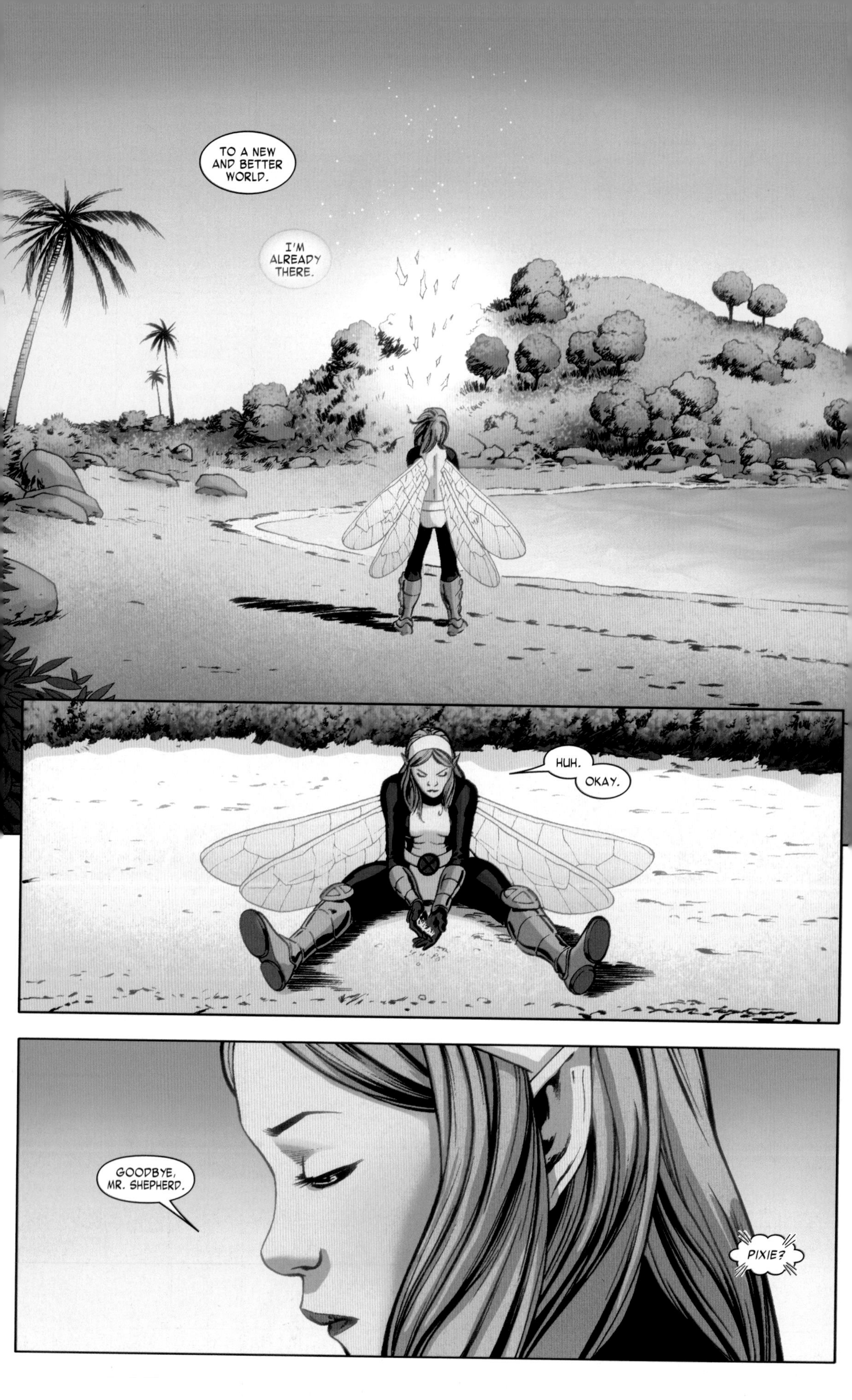
TO A NEW AND BETTER WORLD.
I'M ALREADY THERE.
HUH.
OKAY.
GOODBYE, MR. SHEPHERD.
PIXIE?

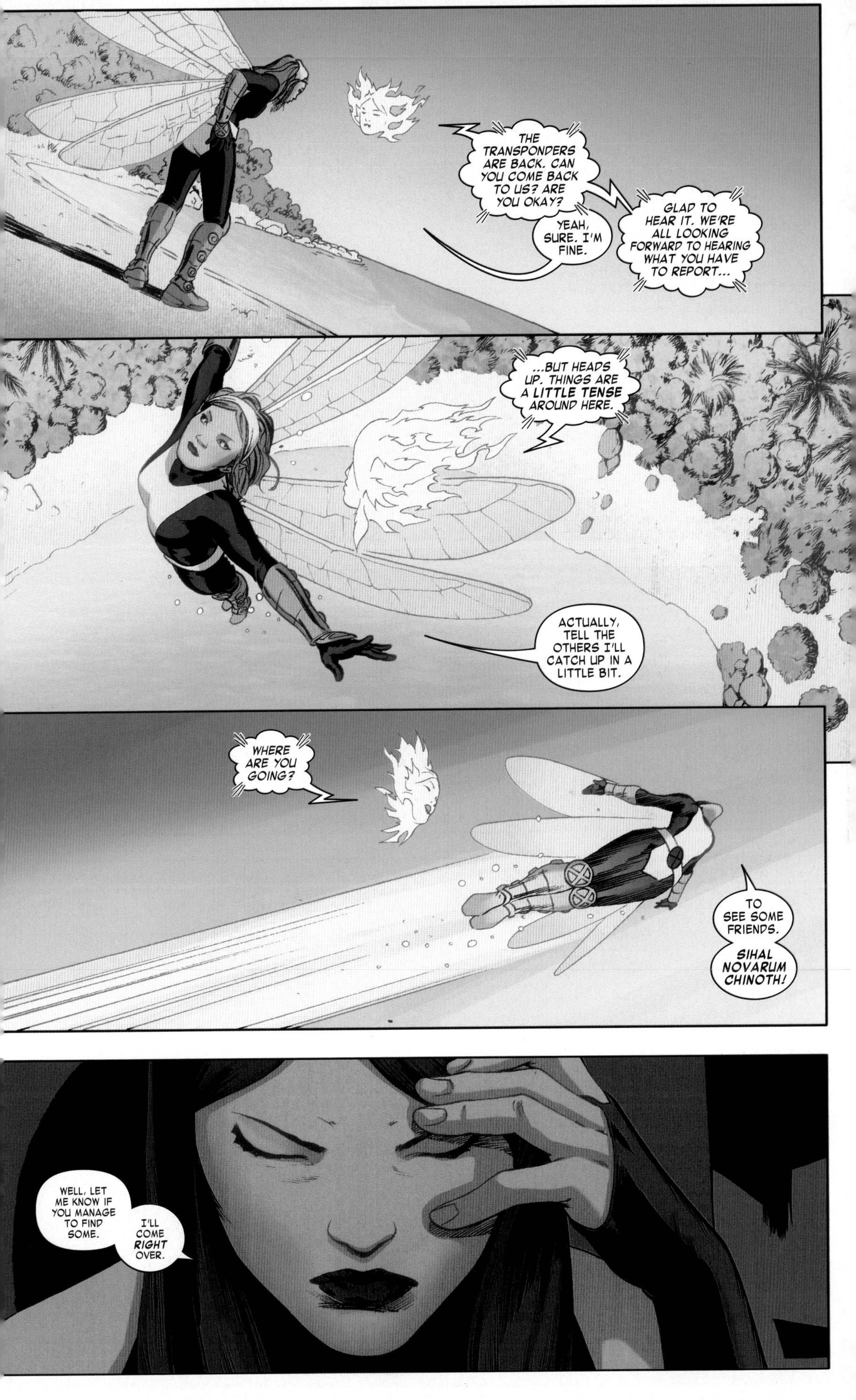
THE TRANSPONDERS ARE BACK. CAN YOU COME BACK TO US? ARE YOU OKAY?
YEAH, SURE. I'M FINE.
GLAD TO HEAR IT. WE'RE ALL LOOKING FORWARD TO HEARING WHAT YOU HAVE TO REPORT...
...BUT HEADS UP. THINGS ARE A LITTLE TENSE AROUND HERE.
ACTUALLY, TELL THE OTHERS I'LL CATCH UP IN A LITTLE BIT.
WHERE ARE YOU GOING?
TO SEE SOME FRIENDS.
SIHAL NOVARUM CHINOTH!
WELL, LET ME KNOW IF YOU MANAGE TO FIND SOME.
I'LL COME RIGHT OVER.

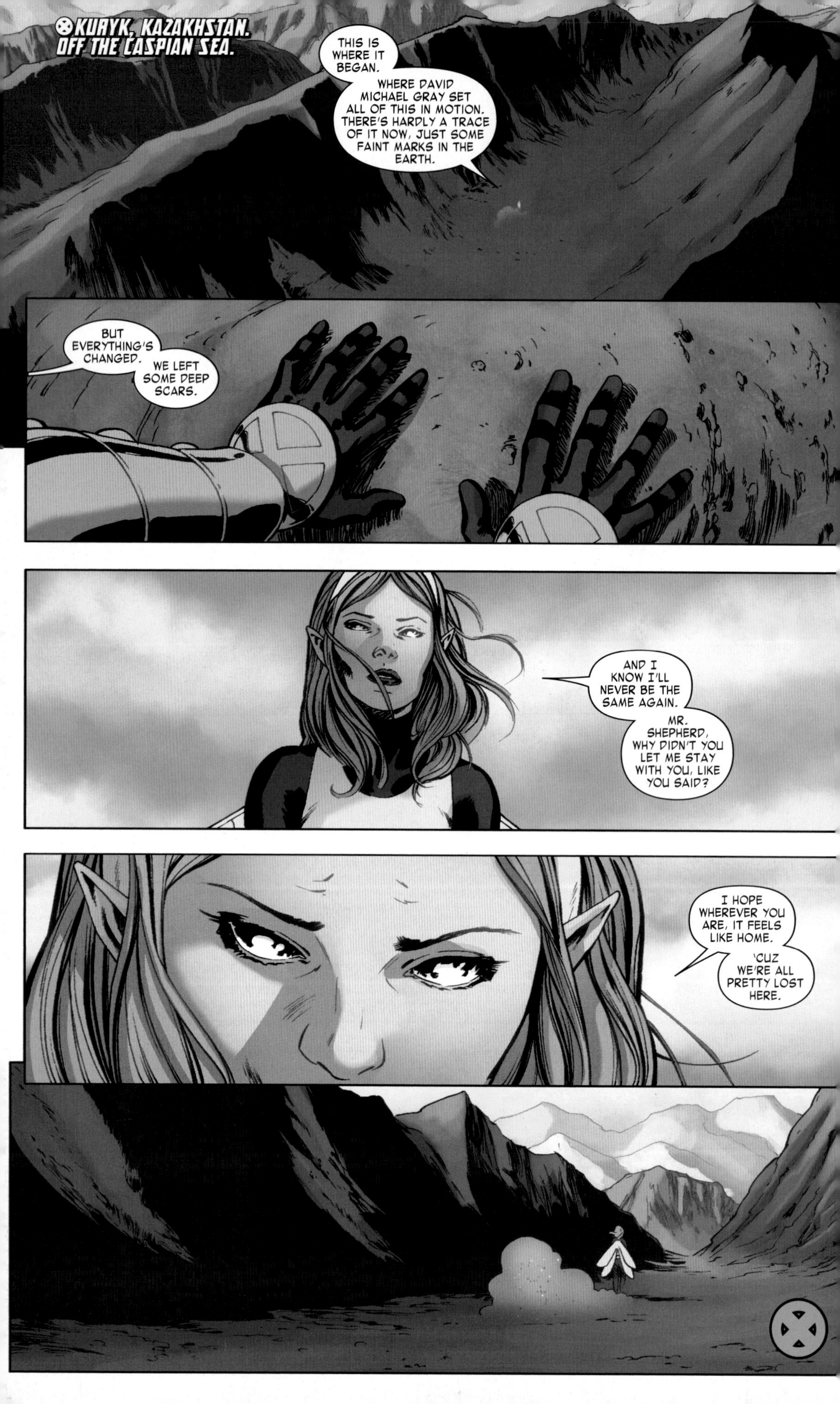

KURYK, KAZAKHSTAN. OFF THE CASPIAN SEA.
THIS IS WHERE IT BEGAN.
WHERE DAVID MICHAEL GRAY SET ALL OF THIS IN MOTION. THERE'S HARDLY A TRACE OF IT NOW, JUST SOME FAINT MARKS IN THE EARTH.
BUT EVERYTHING'S CHANGED.
WE LEFT SOME DEEP SCARS.
AND I KNOW I'LL NEVER BE THE SAME AGAIN.
MR. SHEPHERD, WHY DIDN'T YOU LET ME STAY WITH YOU, LIKE YOU SAID?
I HOPE WHEREVER YOU ARE, IT FEELS LIKE HOME.
'CUZ WE'RE ALL PRETTY LOST HERE.

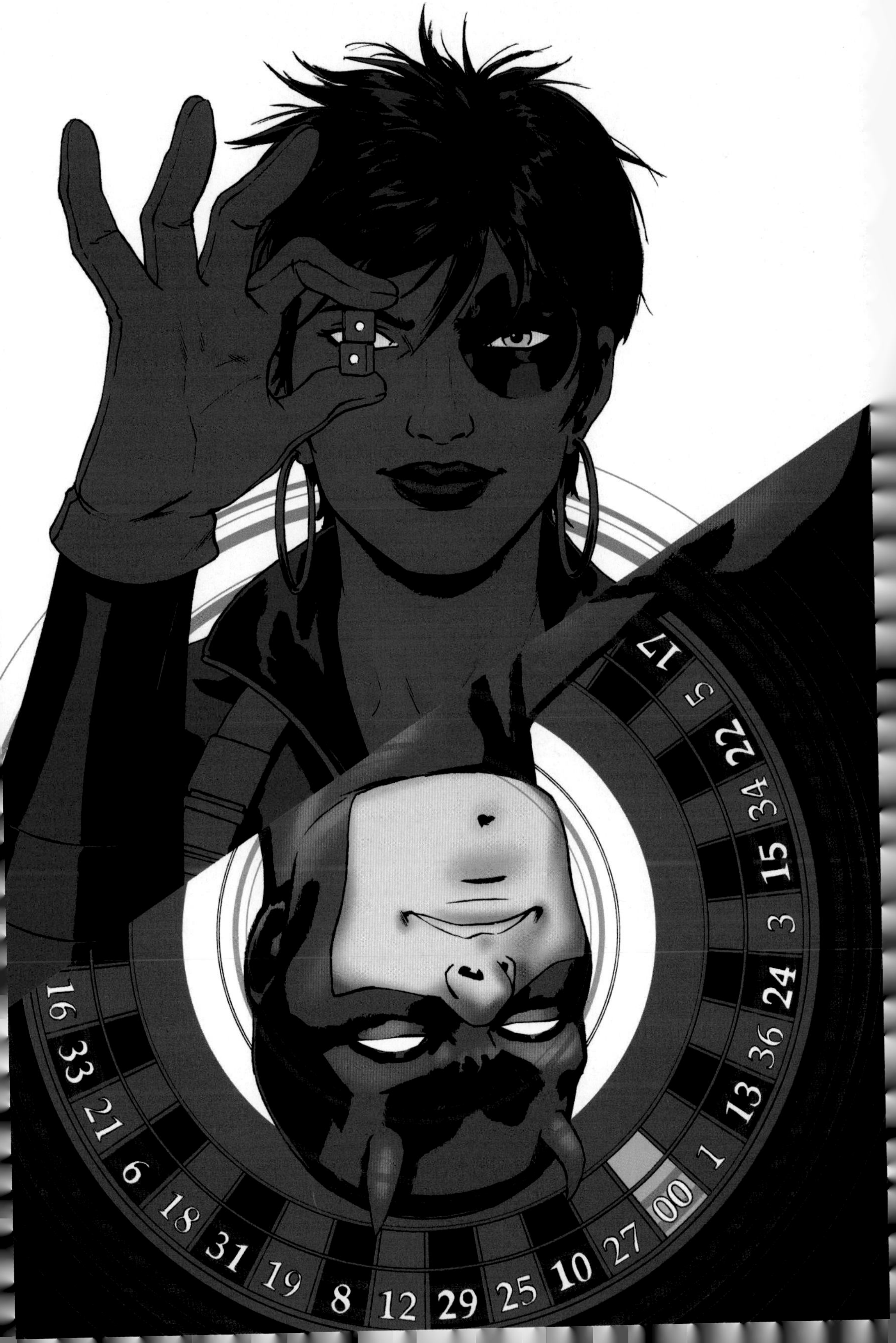

17 5 22 34 15 3 24 36 13 1 00 27 10 25 29 12 8 19 31 18 6 21 33 16

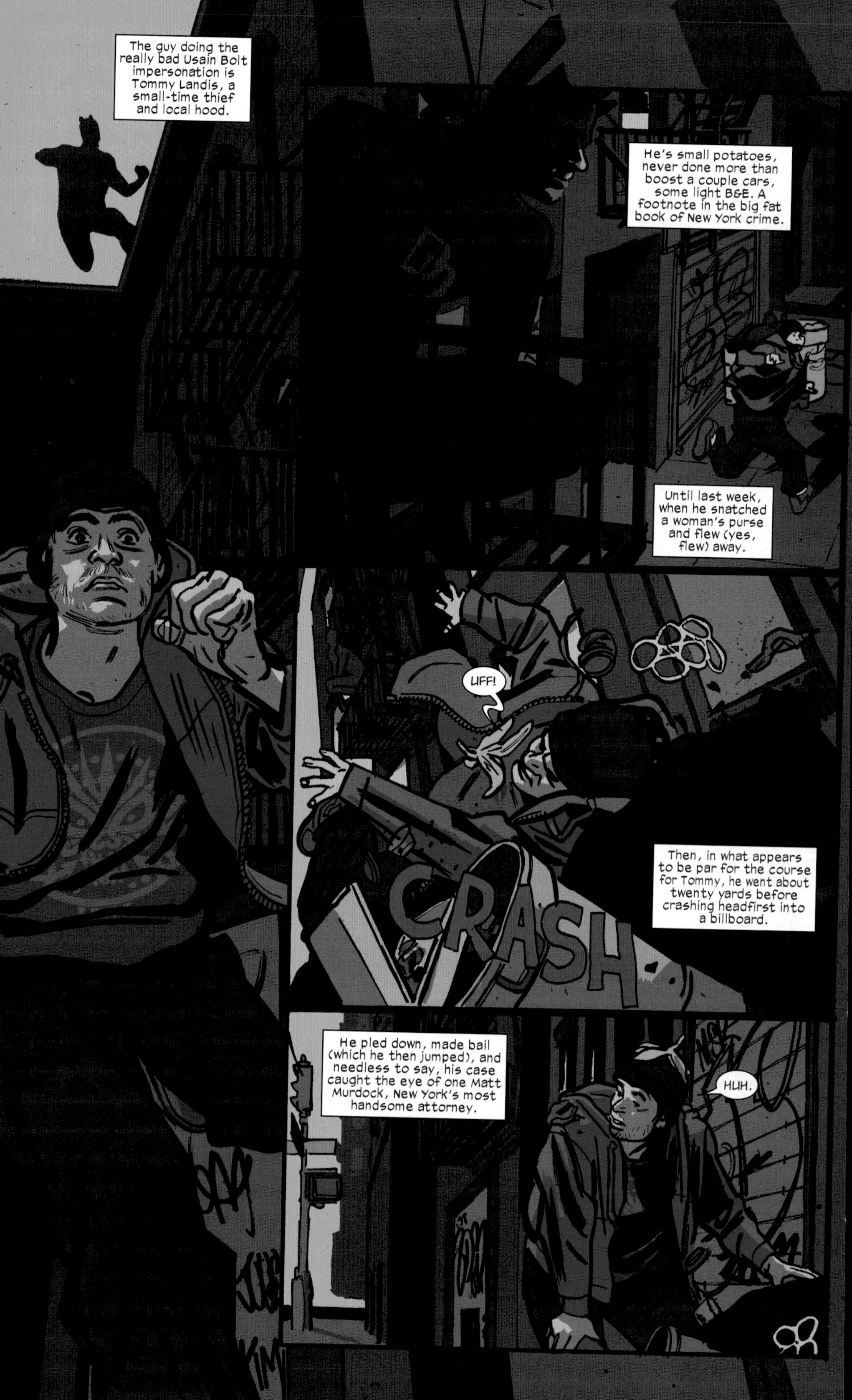
The guy doing the really bad Usain Bolt impersonation is Tommy Landis, a small-time thief and local hood.
He's small potatoes, never done more than boost a couple cars, some light B&E. A footnote in the big fat book of New York crime.
Until last week, when he snatched a woman's purse and flew (yes, flew) away.
UFF!
CRASH
Then, in what appears to be par for the course for Tommy, he went about twenty yards before crashing headfirst into a billboard.
He pled down, made bail (which he then jumped), and needless to say, his case caught the eye of one Matt Murdock, New York's most handsome attorney.
HUH.

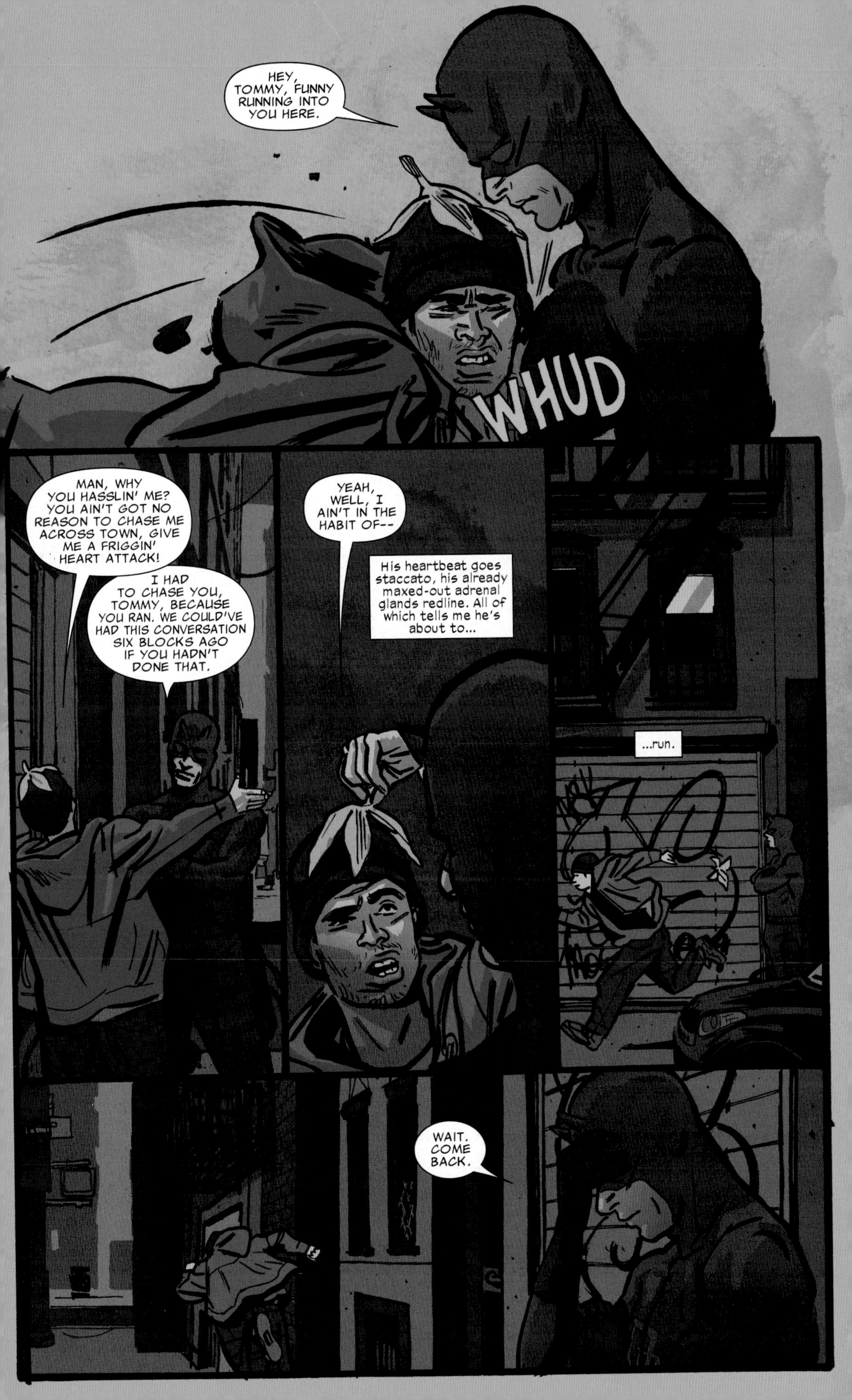
HEY, TOMMY, FUNNY RUNNING INTO YOU HERE.
WHUD
MAN, WHY YOU HASSLIN' ME? YOU AIN'T GOT NO REASON TO CHASE ME ACROSS TOWN, GIVE ME A FRIGGIN' HEART ATTACK!
I HAD TO CHASE YOU, TOMMY, BECAUSE YOU RAN. WE COULD'VE HAD THIS CONVERSATION SIX BLOCKS AGO IF YOU HADN'T DONE THAT.
YEAH, WELL, I AIN'T IN THE HABIT OF--
His heartbeat goes staccato, his already maxed-out adrenal glands redline. All of which tells me he's about to...
...run.
WAIT. COME BACK.

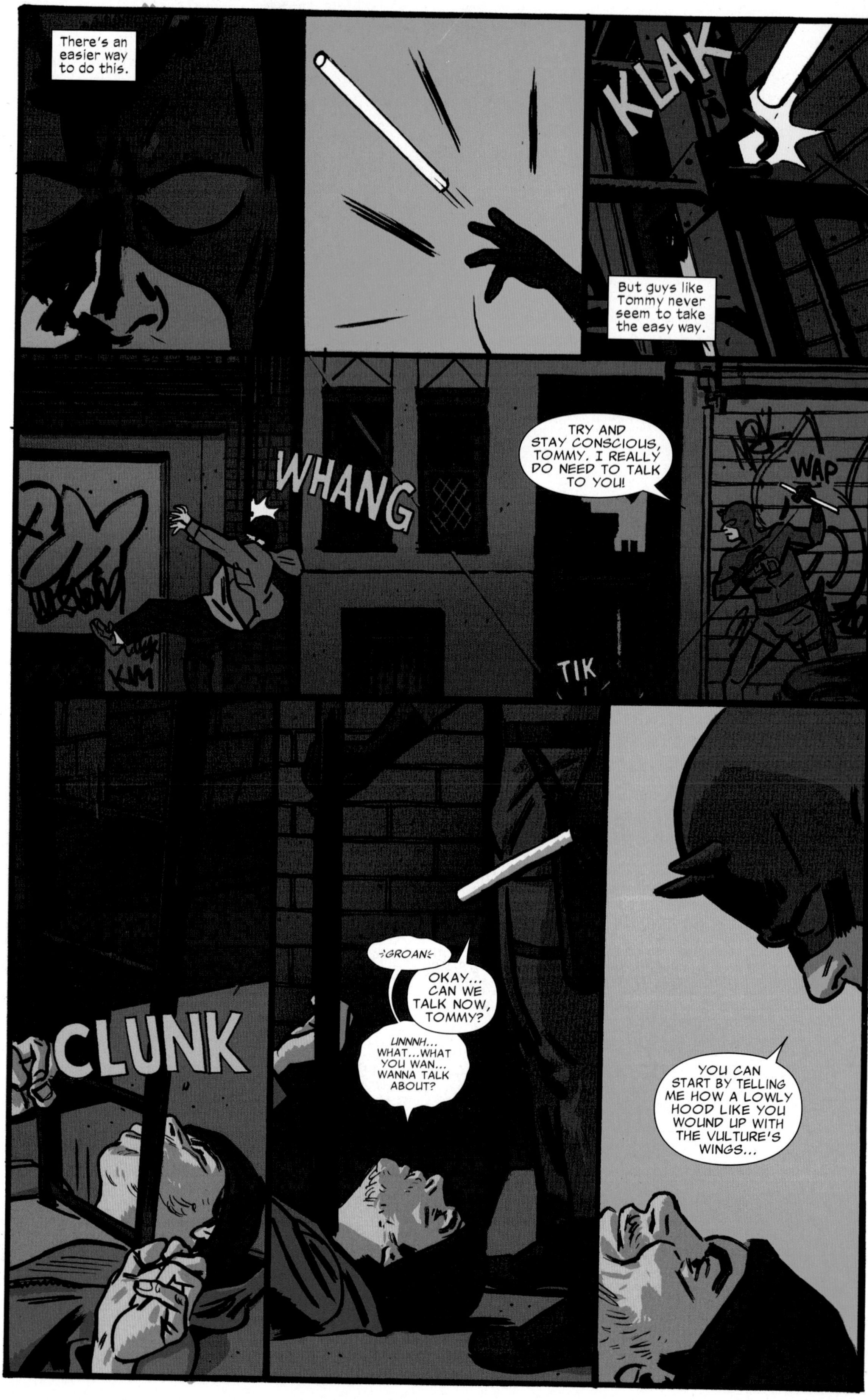
There's an easier way to do this.
KLAK
But guys like Tommy never seem to take the easy way.
WHANG
TRY AND STAY CONSCIOUS, TOMMY. I REALLY DO NEED TO TALK TO YOU!
WAP
TIK
CLUNK
GROAN
OKAY... CAN WE TALK NOW, TOMMY?
UNNNH... WHAT...WHAT YOU WAN... WANNA TALK ABOUT?
YOU CAN START BY TELLING ME HOW A LOWLY HOOD LIKE YOU WOUND UP WITH THE VULTURE'S WINGS...

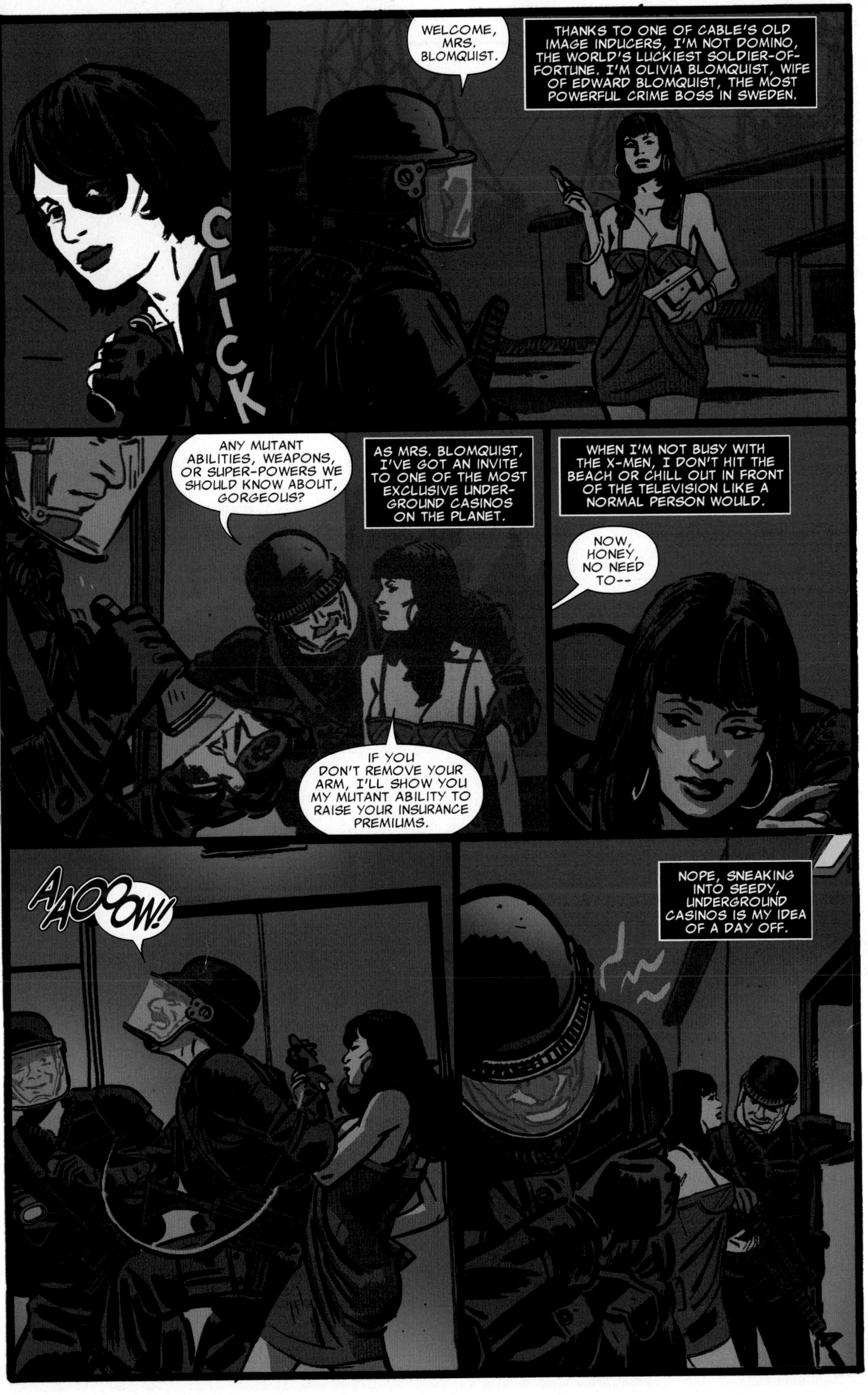

CLICK
WELCOME, MRS. BLOMQUIST.
THANKS TO ONE OF CABLE'S OLD IMAGE INDUCERS, I'M NOT DOMINO, THE WORLD'S LUCKIEST SOLDIER-OF-FORTUNE. I'M OLIVIA BLOMQUIST, WIFE OF EDWARD BLOMQUIST, THE MOST POWERFUL CRIME BOSS IN SWEDEN.
ANY MUTANT ABILITIES, WEAPONS, OR SUPER-POWERS WE SHOULD KNOW ABOUT, GORGEOUS?
AS MRS. BLOMQUIST, I'VE GOT AN INVITE TO ONE OF THE MOST EXCLUSIVE UNDER-GROUND CASINOS ON THE PLANET.
IF YOU DON'T REMOVE YOUR ARM, I'LL SHOW YOU MY MUTANT ABILITY TO RAISE YOUR INSURANCE PREMIUMS.
WHEN I'M NOT BUSY WITH THE X-MEN, I DON'T HIT THE BEACH OR CHILL OUT IN FRONT OF THE TELEVISION LIKE A NORMAL PERSON WOULD.
NOW, HONEY, NO NEED TO--
AAOOOW!
NOPE, SNEAKING INTO SEEDY, UNDERGROUND CASINOS IS MY IDEA OF A DAY OFF.

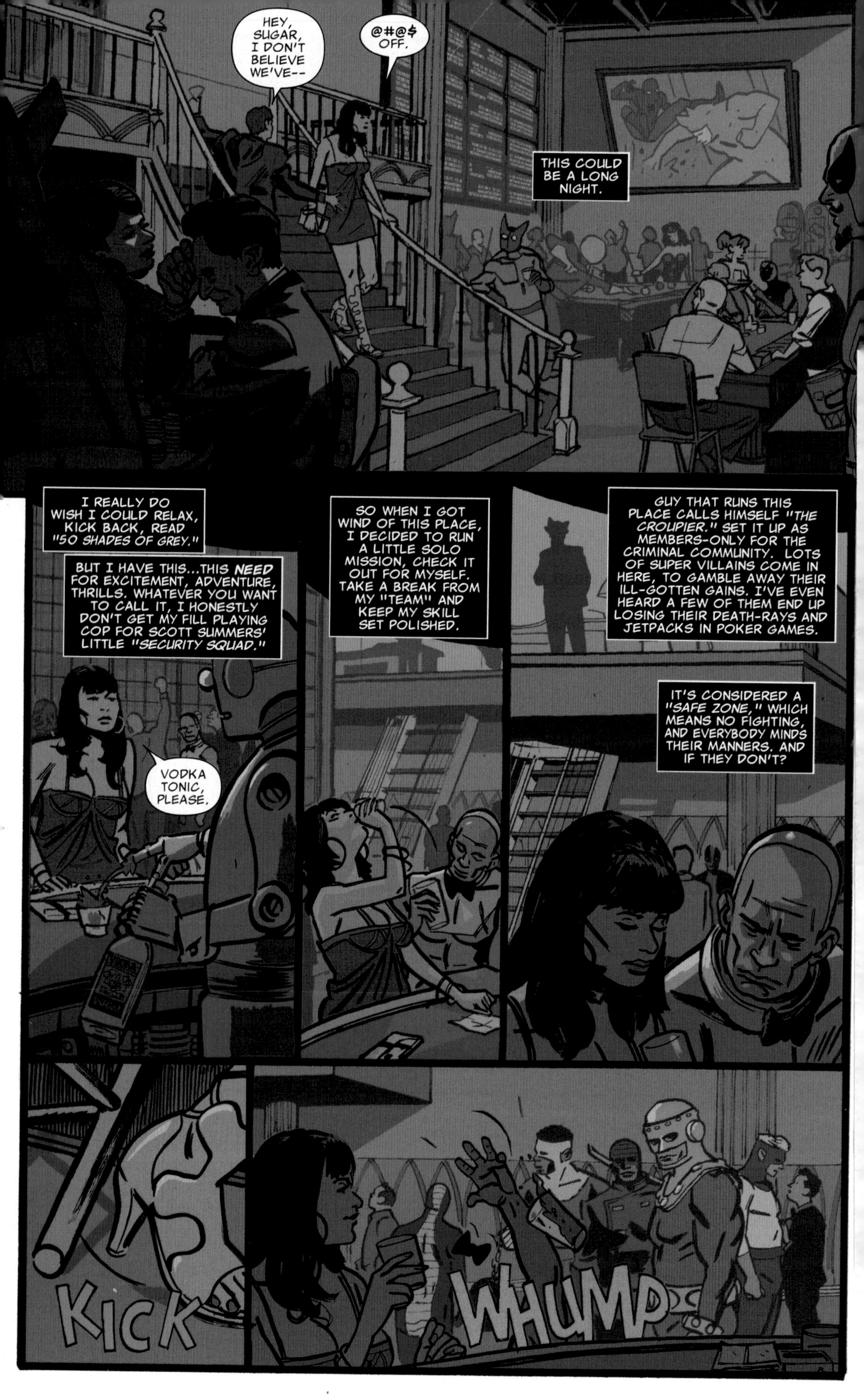
HEY, SUGAR, I DON'T BELIEVE WE'VE--
@#@$ OFF.
THIS COULD BE A LONG NIGHT.
I REALLY DO WISH I COULD RELAX, KICK BACK, READ "50 SHADES OF GREY."
BUT I HAVE THIS...THIS NEED FOR EXCITEMENT, ADVENTURE, THRILLS. WHATEVER YOU WANT TO CALL IT, I HONESTLY DON'T GET MY FILL PLAYING COP FOR SCOTT SUMMERS' LITTLE "SECURITY SQUAD."
VODKA TONIC, PLEASE.
SO WHEN I GOT WIND OF THIS PLACE, I DECIDED TO RUN A LITTLE SOLO MISSION, CHECK IT OUT FOR MYSELF. TAKE A BREAK FROM MY "TEAM" AND KEEP MY SKILL SET POLISHED.
GUY THAT RUNS THIS PLACE CALLS HIMSELF "THE CROUPIER." SET IT UP AS MEMBERS-ONLY FOR THE CRIMINAL COMMUNITY. LOTS OF SUPER VILLAINS COME IN HERE, TO GAMBLE AWAY THEIR ILL-GOTTEN GAINS. I'VE EVEN HEARD A FEW OF THEM END UP LOSING THEIR DEATH-RAYS AND JETPACKS IN POKER GAMES.
IT'S CONSIDERED A "SAFE ZONE," WHICH MEANS NO FIGHTING, AND EVERYBODY MINDS THEIR MANNERS. AND IF THEY DON'T?
KICK
WHUMP

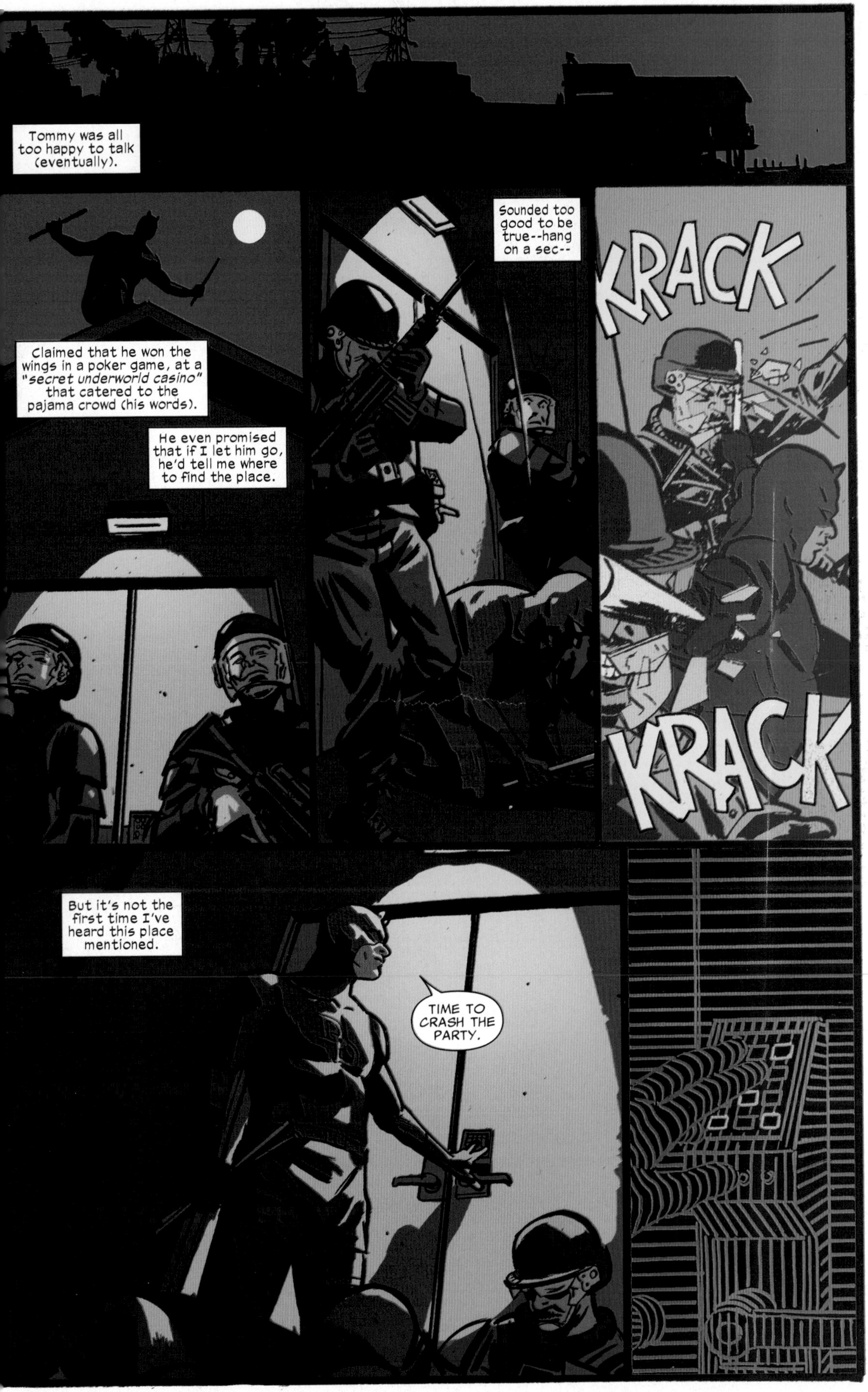
Tommy was all too happy to talk (eventually).
Claimed that he won the wings in a poker game, at a "secret underworld casino" that catered to the pajama crowd (his words).
He even promised that if I let him go, he'd tell me where to find the place.
Sounded too good to be true--hang on a sec--
KRACK
KRACK
But it's not the first time I've heard this place mentioned.
TIME TO CRASH THE PARTY.

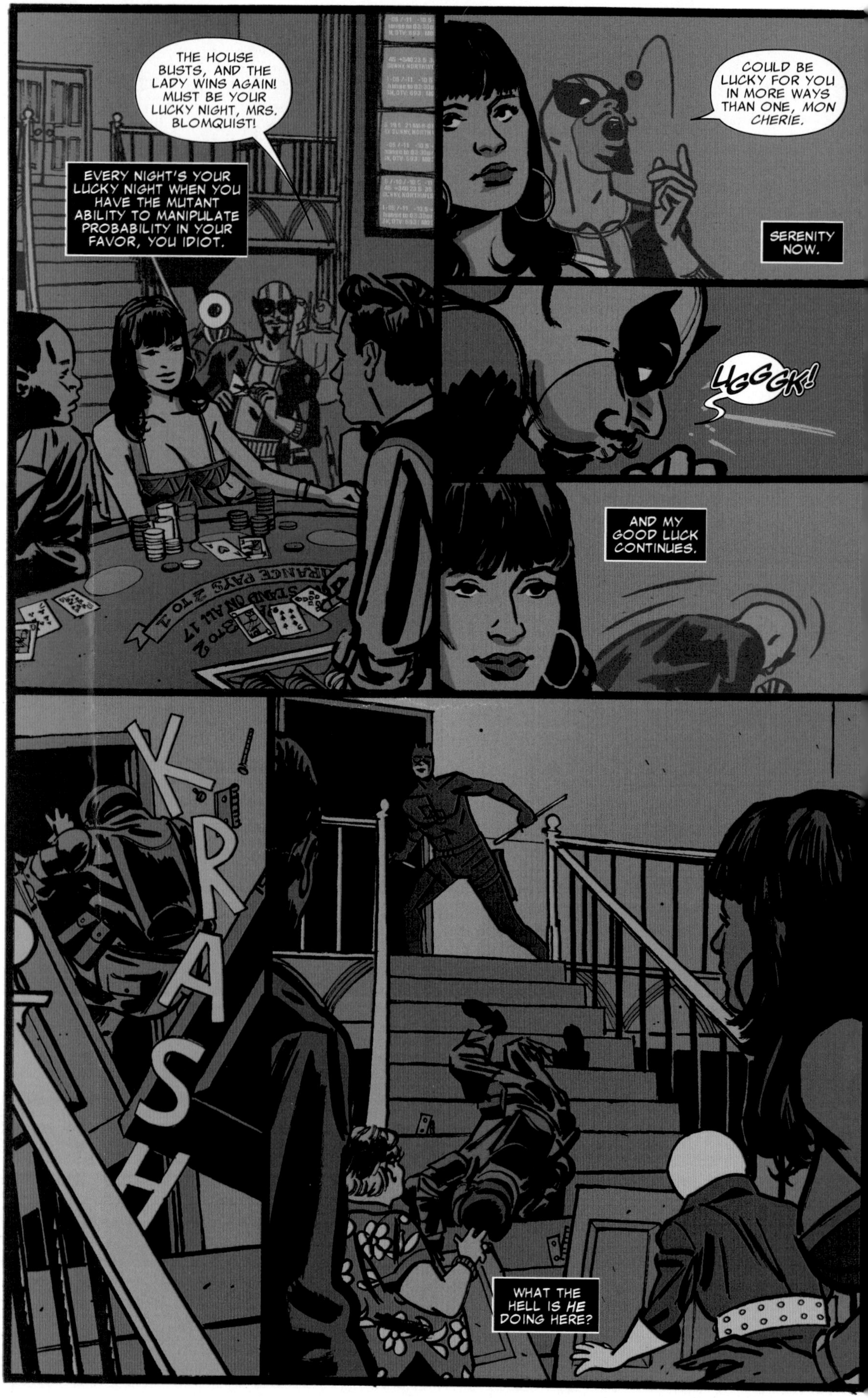
THE HOUSE BUSTS, AND THE LADY WINS AGAIN! MUST BE YOUR LUCKY NIGHT, MRS. BLOMQUIST!
EVERY NIGHT'S YOUR LUCKY NIGHT WHEN YOU HAVE THE MUTANT ABILITY TO MANIPULATE PROBABILITY IN YOUR FAVOR, YOU IDIOT.
COULD BE LUCKY FOR YOU IN MORE WAYS THAN ONE, MON CHERIE.
SERENITY NOW.
UGGGK!
AND MY GOOD LUCK CONTINUES.
K R A S H
WHAT THE HELL IS *HE* DOING HERE?

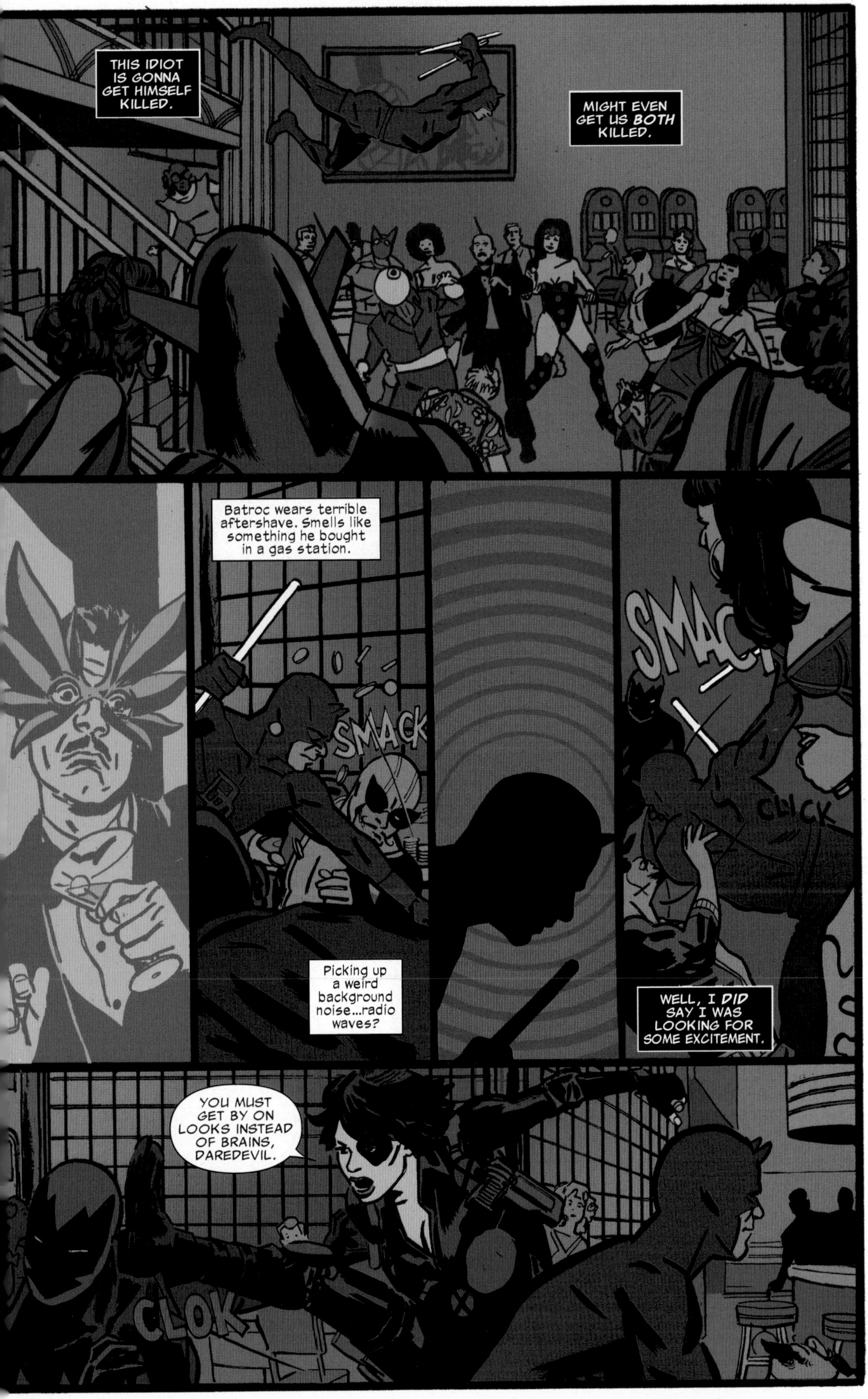
THIS IDIOT IS GONNA GET HIMSELF KILLED.
MIGHT EVEN GET US BOTH KILLED.
Batroc wears terrible aftershave. Smells like something he bought in a gas station.
SMACK
Picking up a weird background noise...radio waves?
SMACK
CLICK
WELL, I DID SAY I WAS LOOKING FOR SOME EXCITEMENT.
YOU MUST GET BY ON LOOKS INSTEAD OF BRAINS, DAREDEVIL.
CLOK

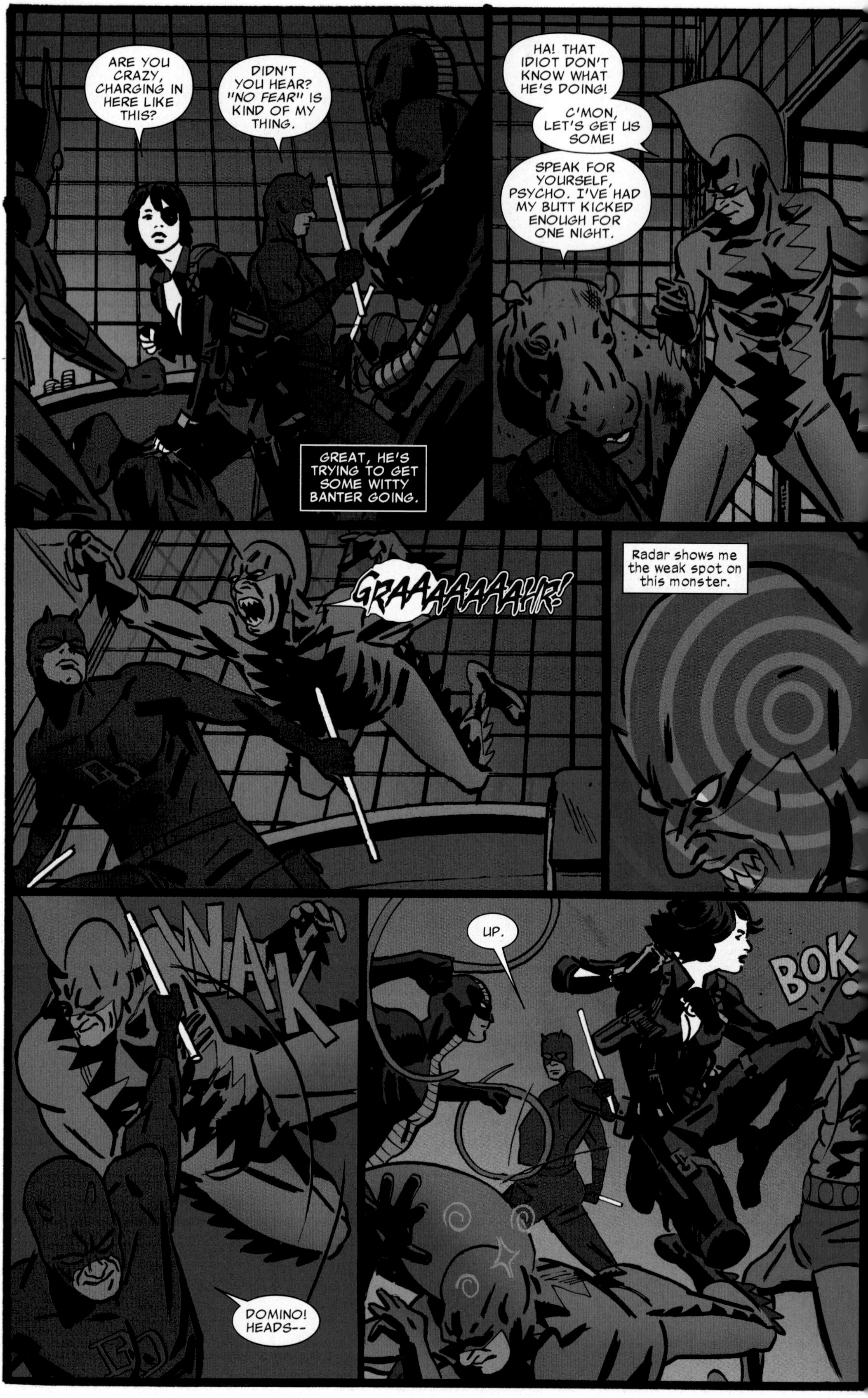
ARE YOU CRAZY, CHARGING IN HERE LIKE THIS?
DIDN'T YOU HEAR? "NO FEAR" IS KIND OF MY THING.
GREAT, HE'S TRYING TO GET SOME WITTY BANTER GOING.
HA! THAT IDIOT DON'T KNOW WHAT HE'S DOING!
C'MON, LET'S GET US SOME!
SPEAK FOR YOURSELF, PSYCHO. I'VE HAD MY BUTT KICKED ENOUGH FOR ONE NIGHT.
GRAAAAAAAHR!
Radar shows me the weak spot on this monster.
WAK
DOMINO! HEADS--
UP.
BOK

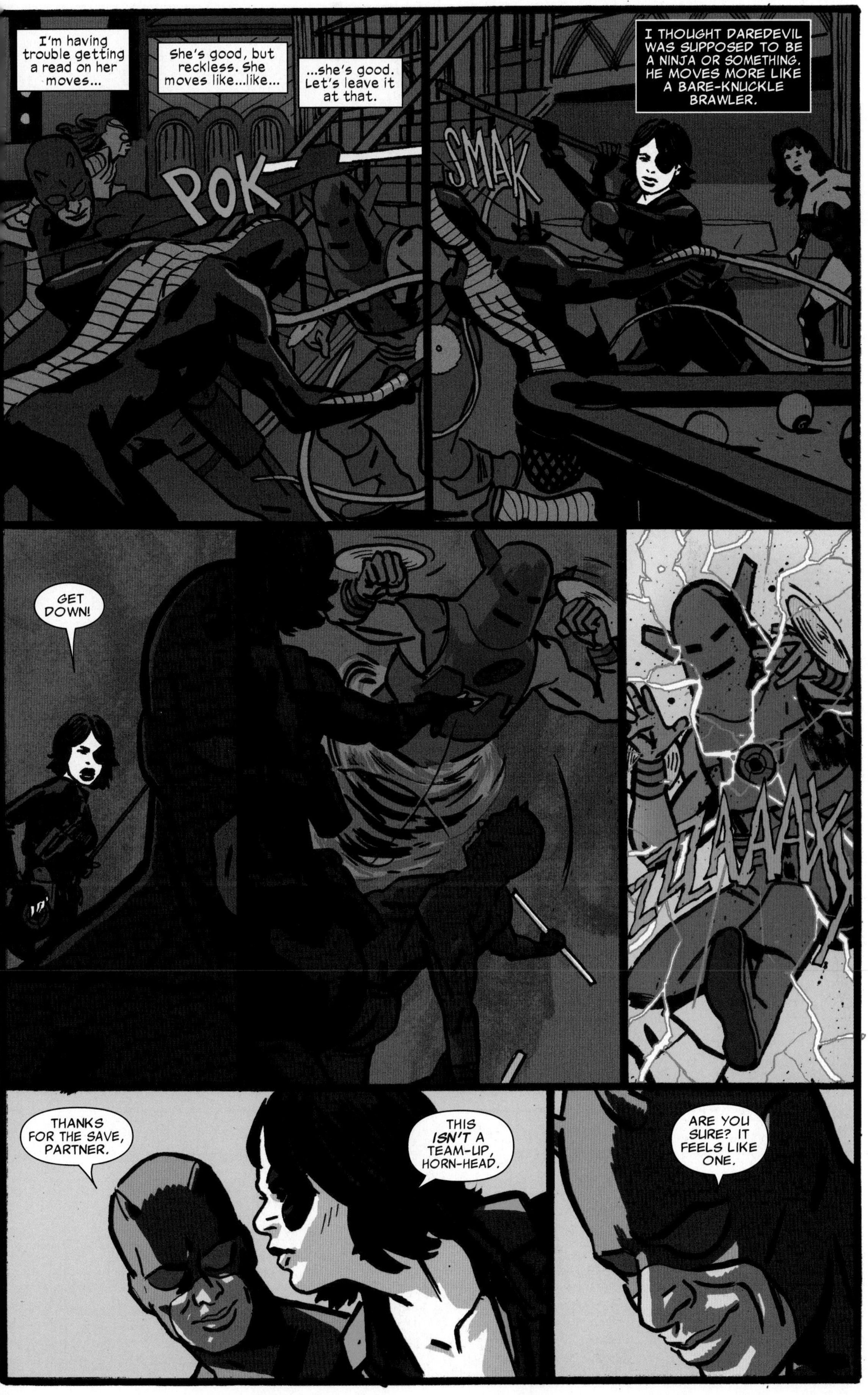

I'm having trouble getting a read on her moves...
She's good, but reckless. She moves like...like...
...she's good. Let's leave it at that.
POK
SMAK
I THOUGHT DAREDEVIL WAS SUPPOSED TO BE A NINJA OR SOMETHING. HE MOVES MORE LIKE A BARE-KNUCKLE BRAWLER.
GET DOWN!
ZZZAAAAK
THANKS FOR THE SAVE, PARTNER.
THIS *ISN'T* A TEAM-UP, HORN-HEAD.
ARE YOU SURE? IT FEELS LIKE ONE.

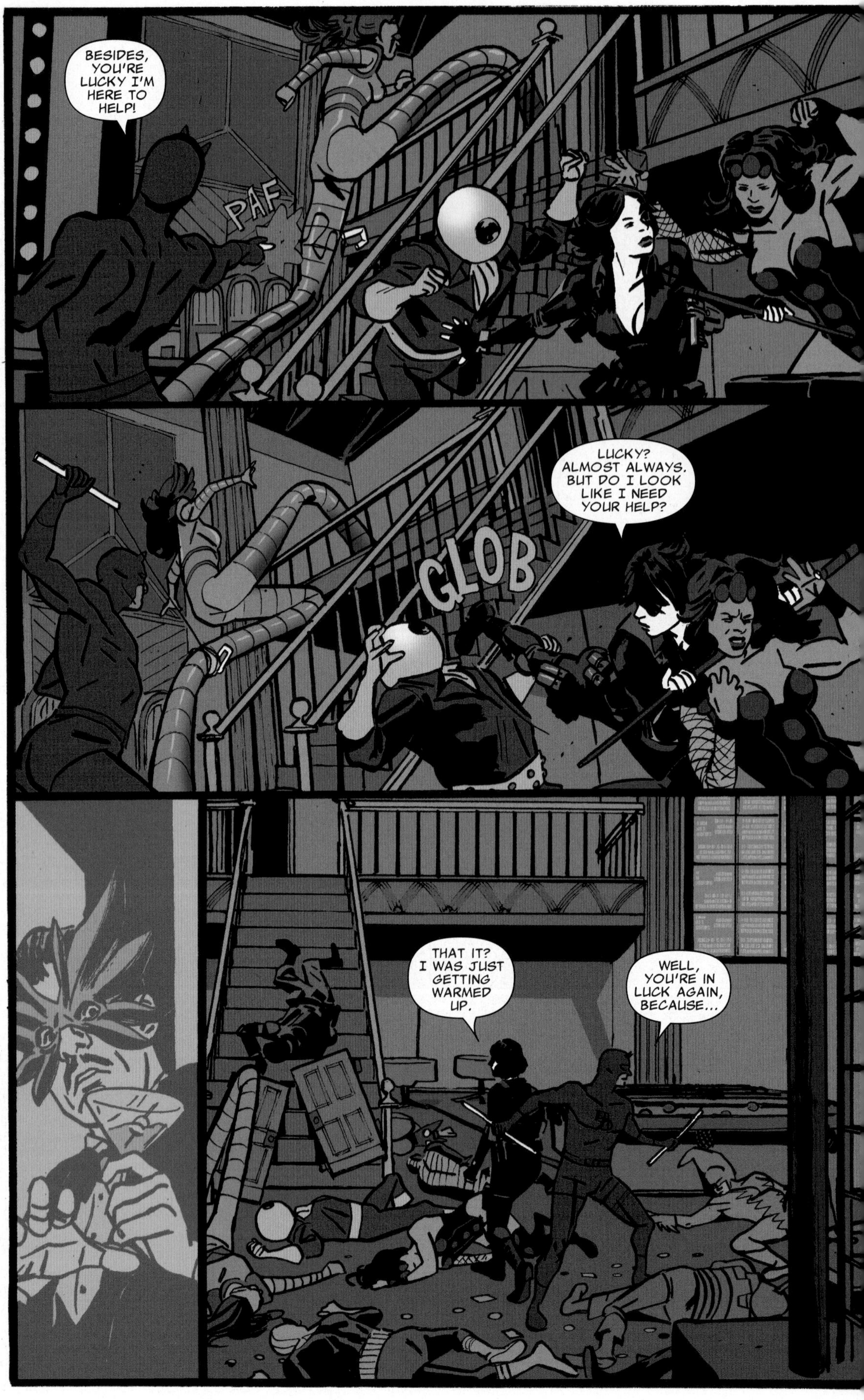
BESIDES, YOU'RE LUCKY I'M HERE TO HELP!
PAF
LUCKY? ALMOST ALWAYS. BUT DO I LOOK LIKE I NEED YOUR HELP?
GLOB
THAT IT? I WAS JUST GETTING WARMED UP.
WELL, YOU'RE IN LUCK AGAIN, BECAUSE...

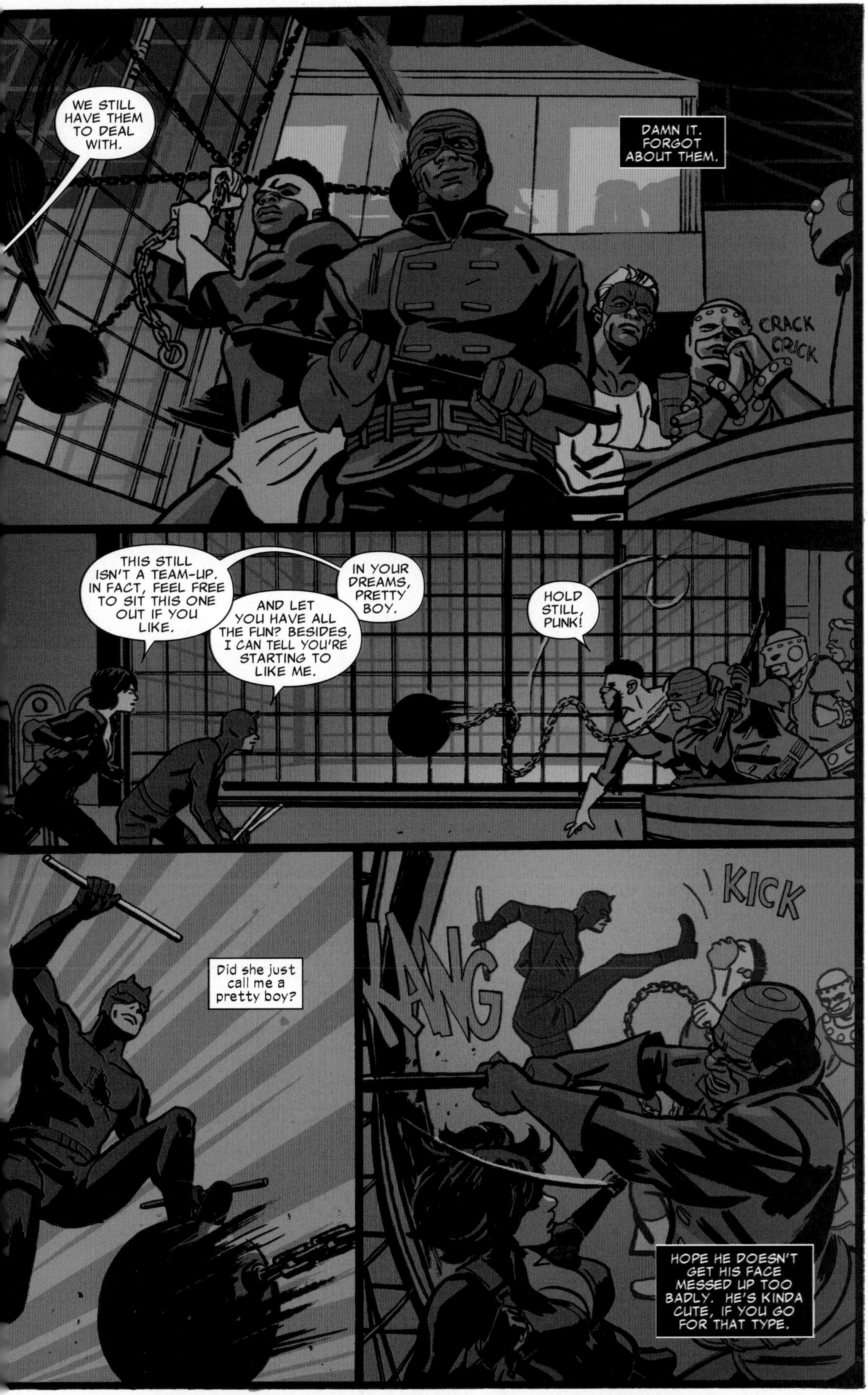
WE STILL HAVE THEM TO DEAL WITH.
DAMN IT. FORGOT ABOUT THEM.
CRACK
CRICK
THIS STILL ISN'T A TEAM-UP. IN FACT, FEEL FREE TO SIT THIS ONE OUT IF YOU LIKE.
AND LET YOU HAVE ALL THE FUN? BESIDES, I CAN TELL YOU'RE STARTING TO LIKE ME.
IN YOUR DREAMS, PRETTY BOY.
HOLD STILL, PUNK!
Did she just call me a pretty boy?
KICK
KANG
HOPE HE DOESN'T GET HIS FACE MESSED UP TOO BADLY. HE'S KINDA CUTE, IF YOU GO FOR THAT TYPE.

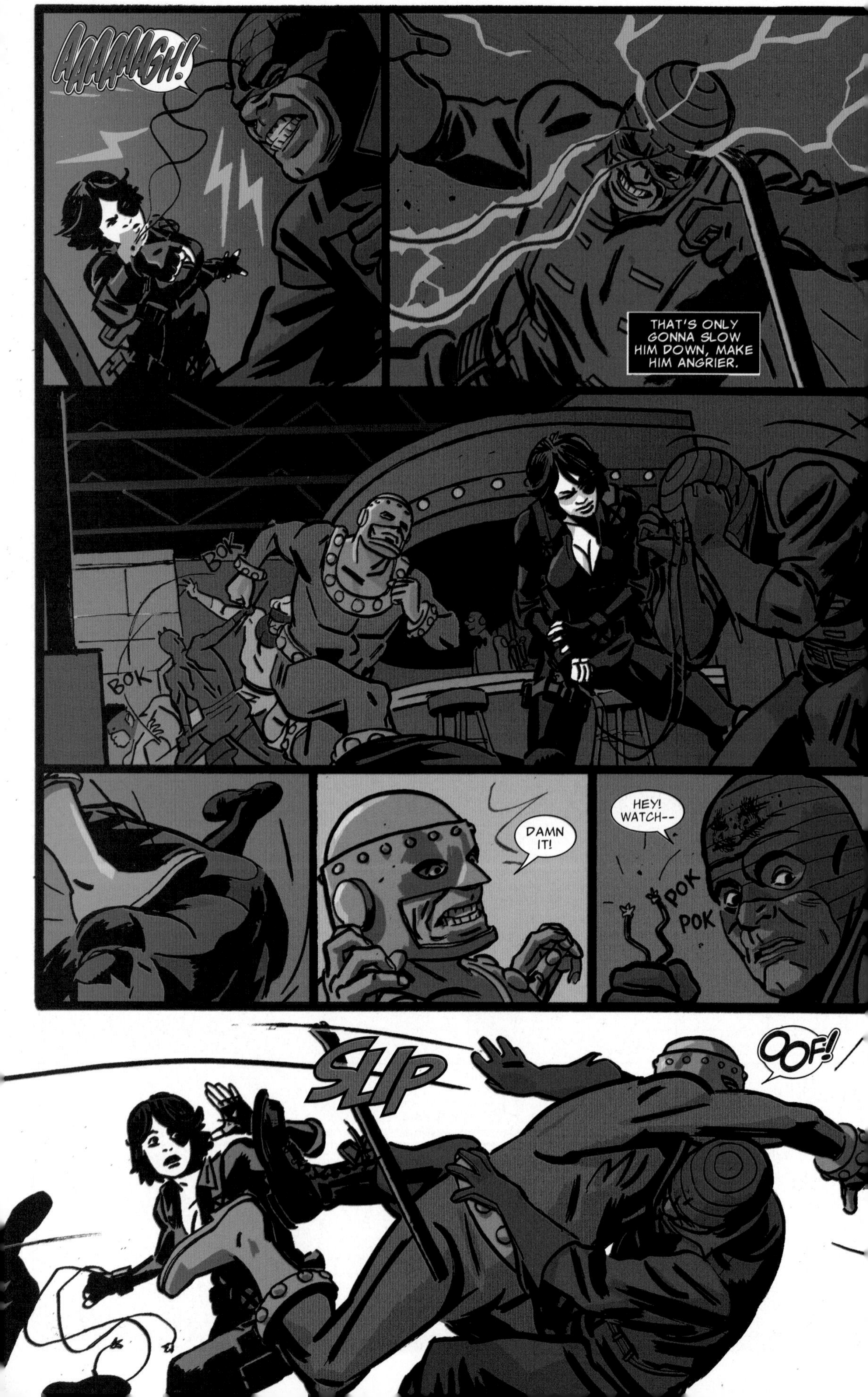
AAAAAAGH!
THAT'S ONLY GONNA SLOW HIM DOWN, MAKE HIM ANGRIER.
BOK
BOK
DAMN IT!
HEY! WATCH--
POK
POK
SLIP
OOF!

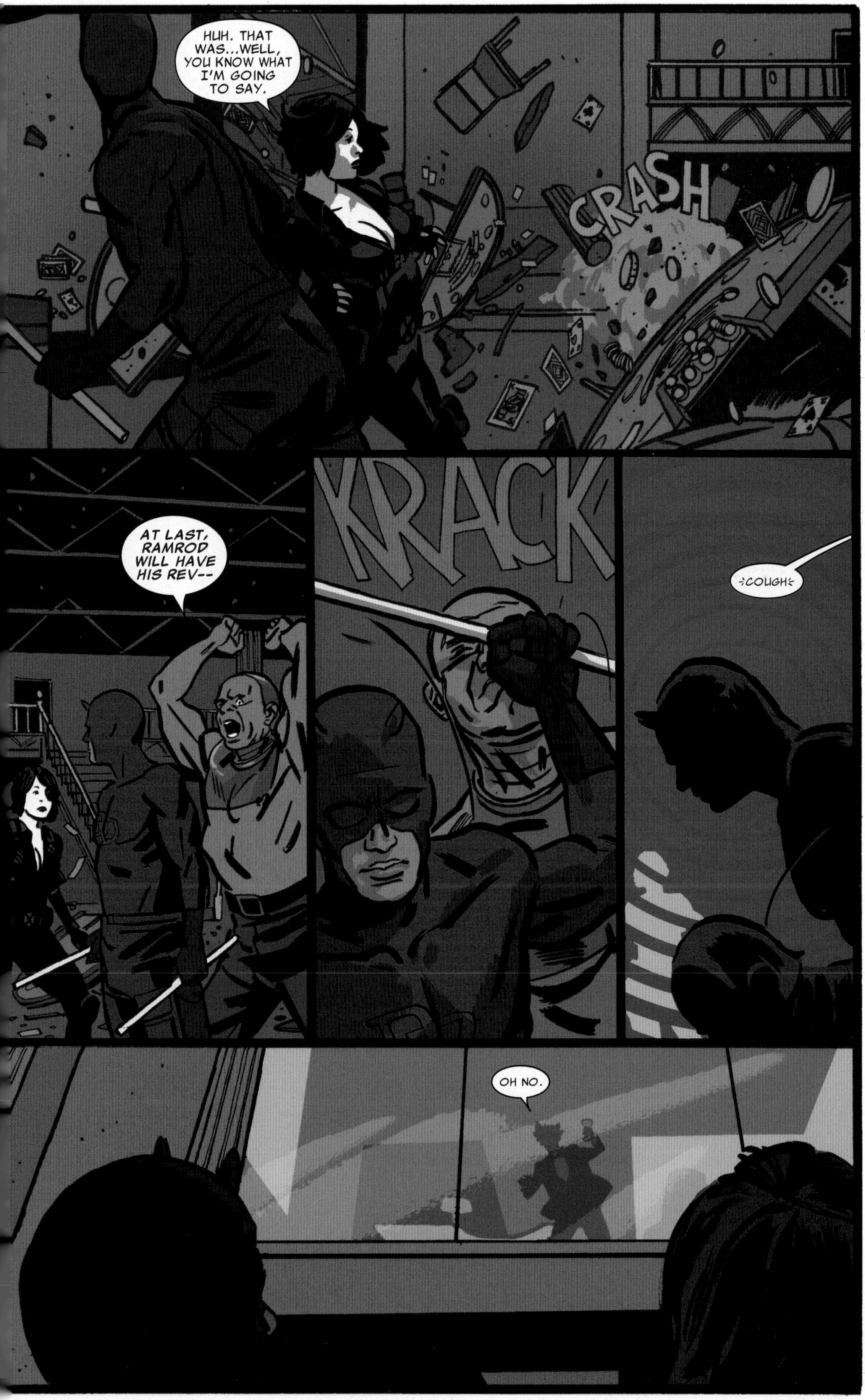
HUH. THAT WAS...WELL, YOU KNOW WHAT I'M GOING TO SAY.
CRASH
AT LAST, RAMROD WILL HAVE HIS REV--
KRACK
COUGH
OH NO.

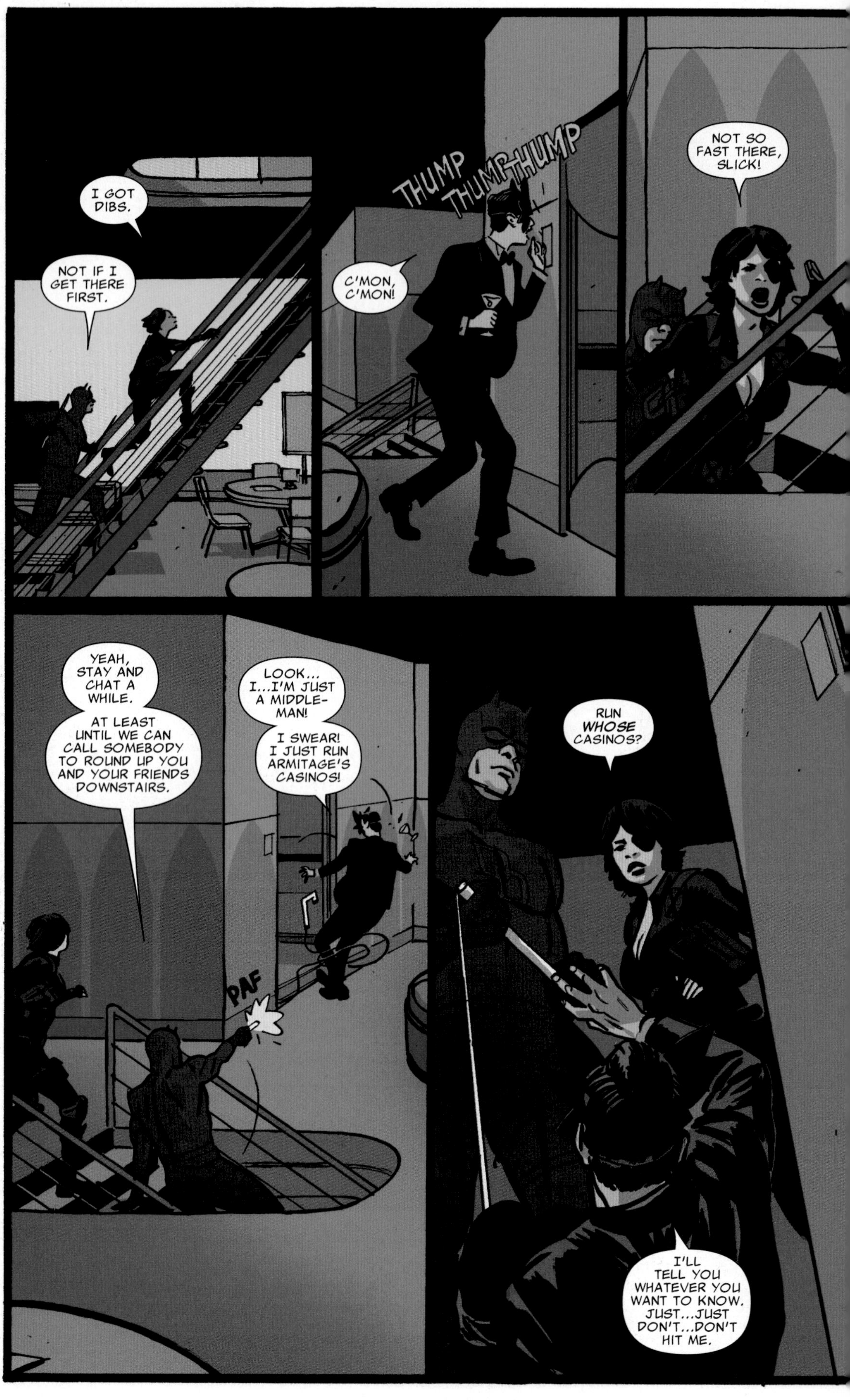
I GOT DIBS.
NOT IF I GET THERE FIRST.
THUMP THUMP THUMP
C'MON, C'MON!
NOT SO FAST THERE, SLICK!
YEAH, STAY AND CHAT A WHILE.
AT LEAST UNTIL WE CAN CALL SOMEBODY TO ROUND UP YOU AND YOUR FRIENDS DOWNSTAIRS.
LOOK... I...I'M JUST A MIDDLE-MAN!
I SWEAR! I JUST RUN ARMITAGE'S CASINOS!
PAF
RUN WHOSE CASINOS?
I'LL TELL YOU WHATEVER YOU WANT TO KNOW. JUST...JUST DON'T...DON'T HIT ME.

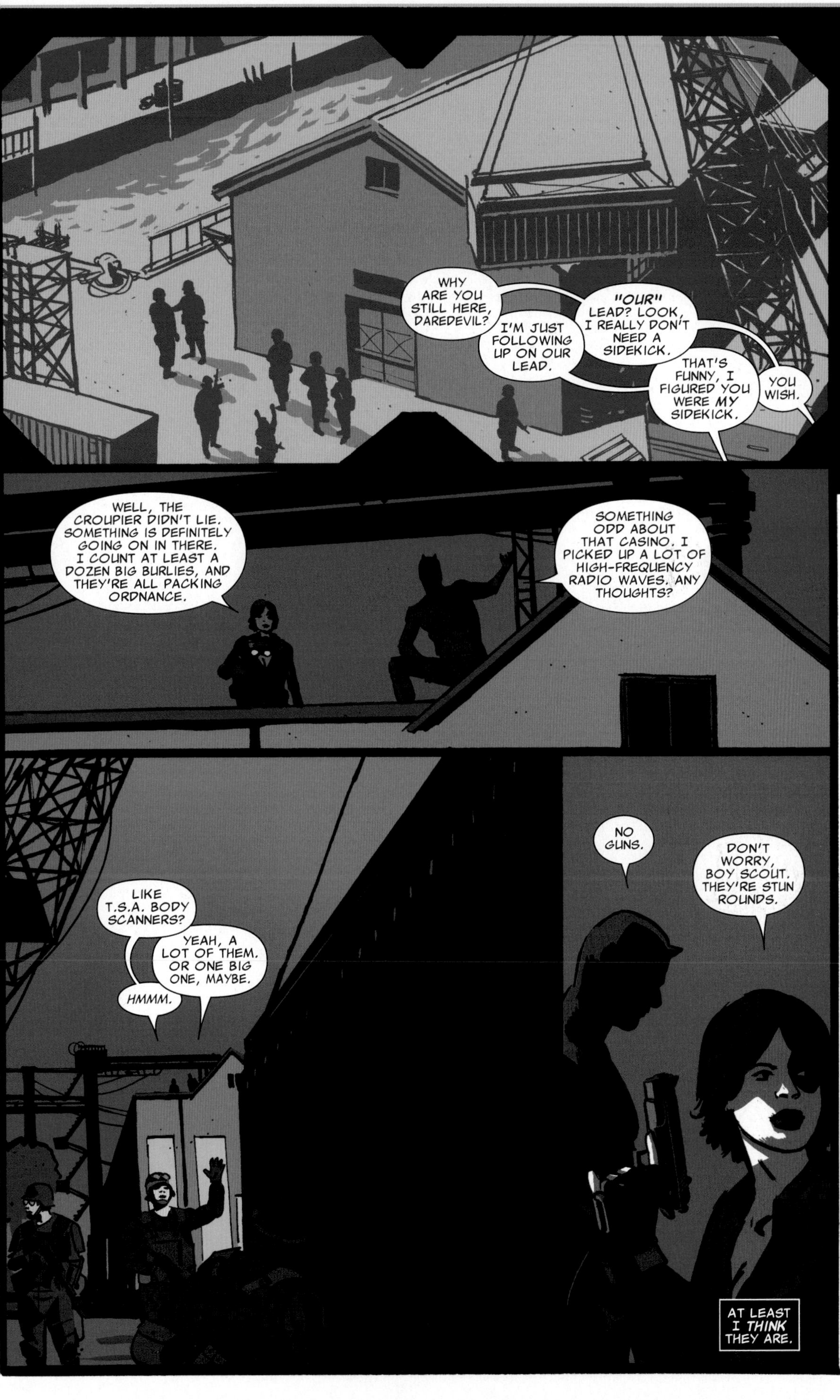
WHY ARE YOU STILL HERE, DAREDEVIL?
I'M JUST FOLLOWING UP ON OUR LEAD.
"OUR" LEAD? LOOK, I REALLY DON'T NEED A SIDEKICK.
THAT'S FUNNY, I FIGURED YOU WERE MY SIDEKICK.
YOU WISH.
WELL, THE CROUPIER DIDN'T LIE. SOMETHING IS DEFINITELY GOING ON IN THERE. I COUNT AT LEAST A DOZEN BIG BURLIES, AND THEY'RE ALL PACKING ORDNANCE.
SOMETHING ODD ABOUT THAT CASINO. I PICKED UP A LOT OF HIGH-FREQUENCY RADIO WAVES. ANY THOUGHTS?
LIKE T.S.A. BODY SCANNERS?
YEAH, A LOT OF THEM. OR ONE BIG ONE, MAYBE.
HMMM.
NO GUNS.
DON'T WORRY, BOY SCOUT. THEY'RE STUN ROUNDS.
AT LEAST I THINK THEY ARE.

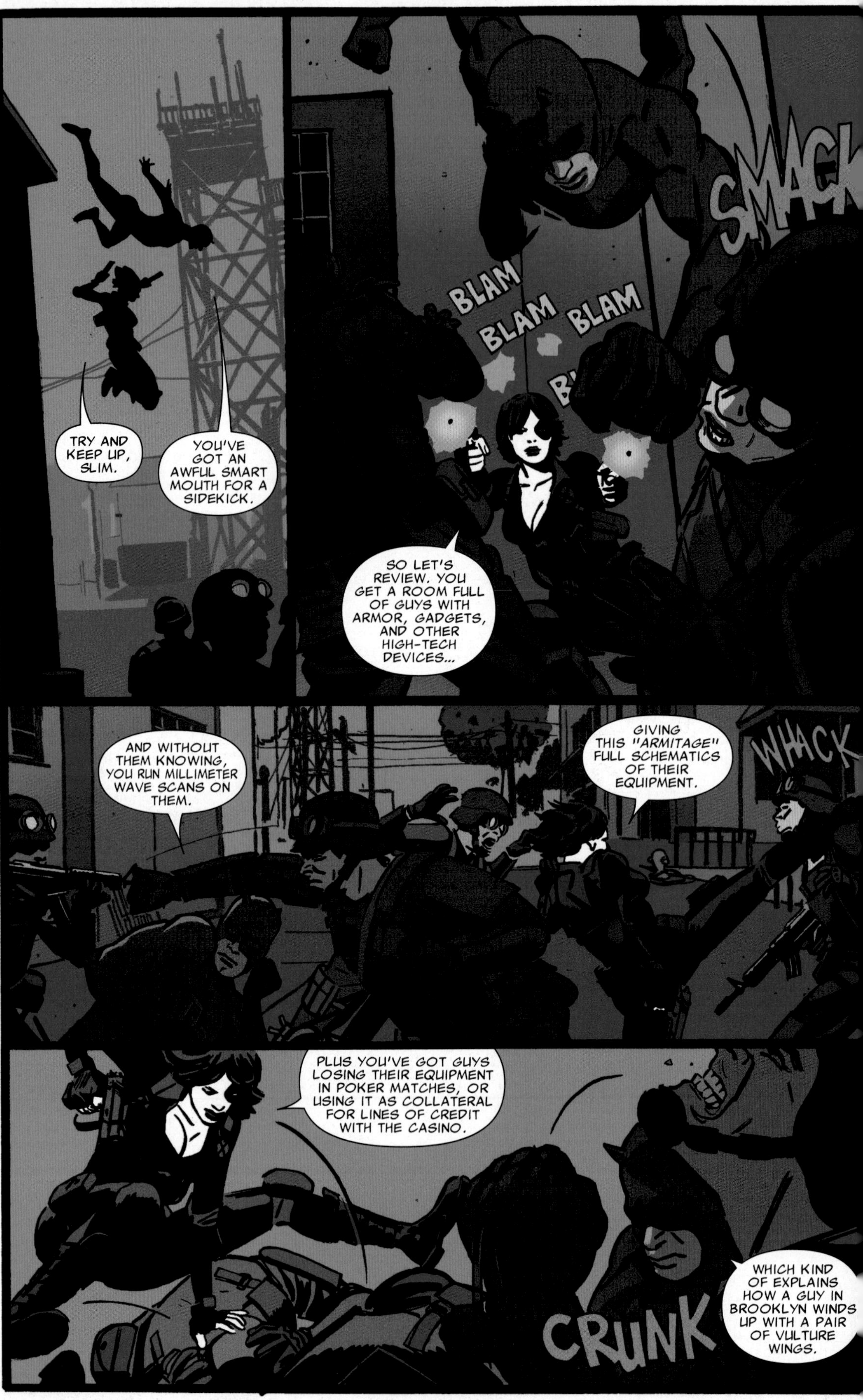

TRY AND KEEP UP, SLIM.
YOU'VE GOT AN AWFUL SMART MOUTH FOR A SIDEKICK.
SMACK
BLAM
BLAM
BLAM
SO LET'S REVIEW. YOU GET A ROOM FULL OF GUYS WITH ARMOR, GADGETS, AND OTHER HIGH-TECH DEVICES...
AND WITHOUT THEM KNOWING, YOU RUN MILLIMETER WAVE SCANS ON THEM.
GIVING THIS "ARMITAGE" FULL SCHEMATICS OF THEIR EQUIPMENT.
WHACK
PLUS YOU'VE GOT GUYS LOSING THEIR EQUIPMENT IN POKER MATCHES, OR USING IT AS COLLATERAL FOR LINES OF CREDIT WITH THE CASINO.
CRUNK
WHICH KIND OF EXPLAINS HOW A GUY IN BROOKLYN WINDS UP WITH A PAIR OF VULTURE WINGS.

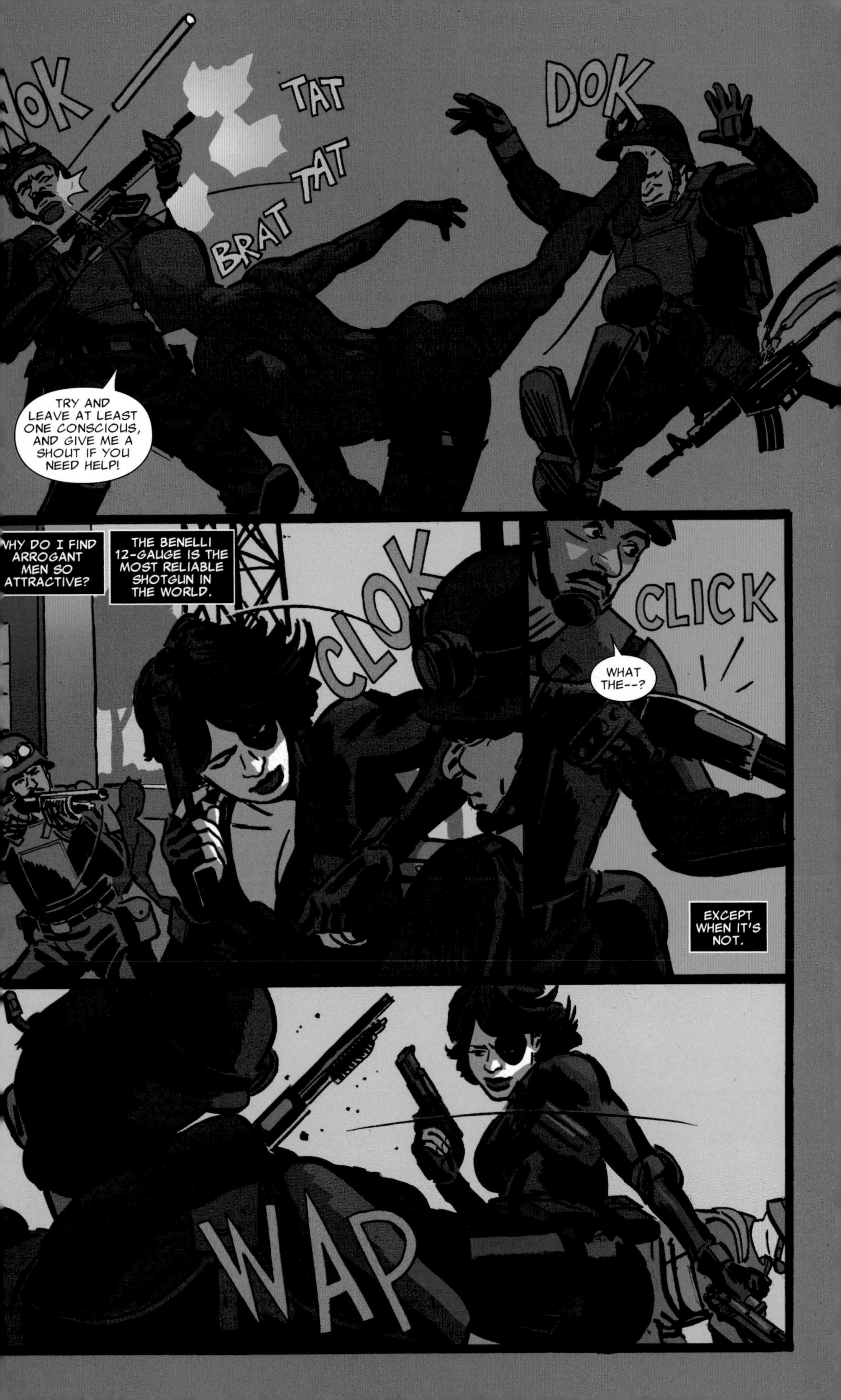

WOK
TAT
BRAT TAT
DOK
TRY AND LEAVE AT LEAST ONE CONSCIOUS, AND GIVE ME A SHOUT IF YOU NEED HELP!
WHY DO I FIND ARROGANT MEN SO ATTRACTIVE?
THE BENELLI 12-GAUGE IS THE MOST RELIABLE SHOTGUN IN THE WORLD.
CLOK
CLICK
WHAT THE--?
EXCEPT WHEN IT'S NOT.
WAP

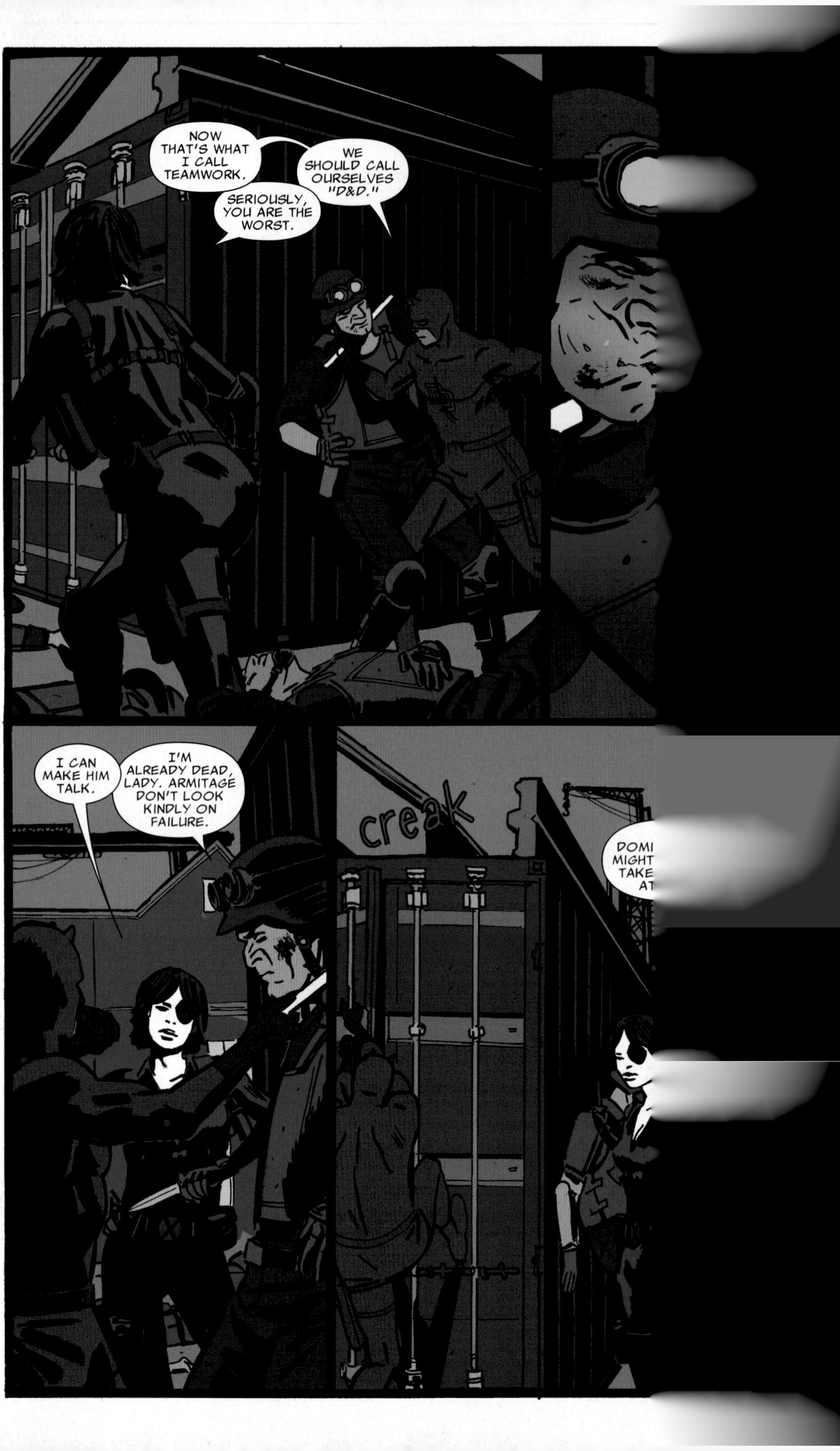
NOW THAT'S WHAT I CALL TEAMWORK.
WE SHOULD CALL OURSELVES "D&D."
SERIOUSLY, YOU ARE THE WORST.
I CAN MAKE HIM TALK.
I'M ALREADY DEAD, LADY. ARMITAGE DON'T LOOK KINDLY ON FAILURE.
creak

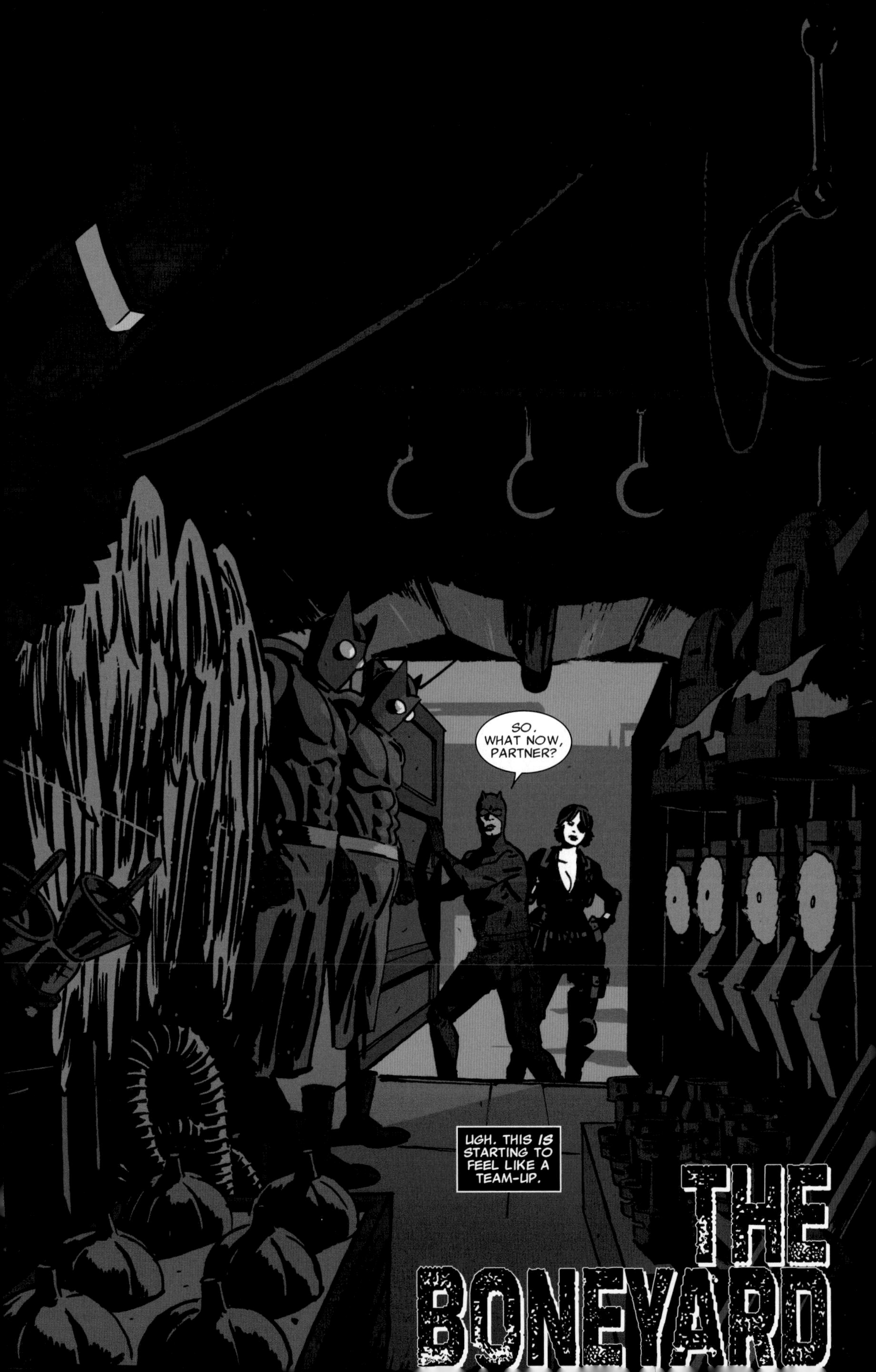
SO, WHAT NOW, PARTNER?
UGH. THIS IS STARTING TO FEEL LIKE A TEAM-UP.
THE BONEYARD

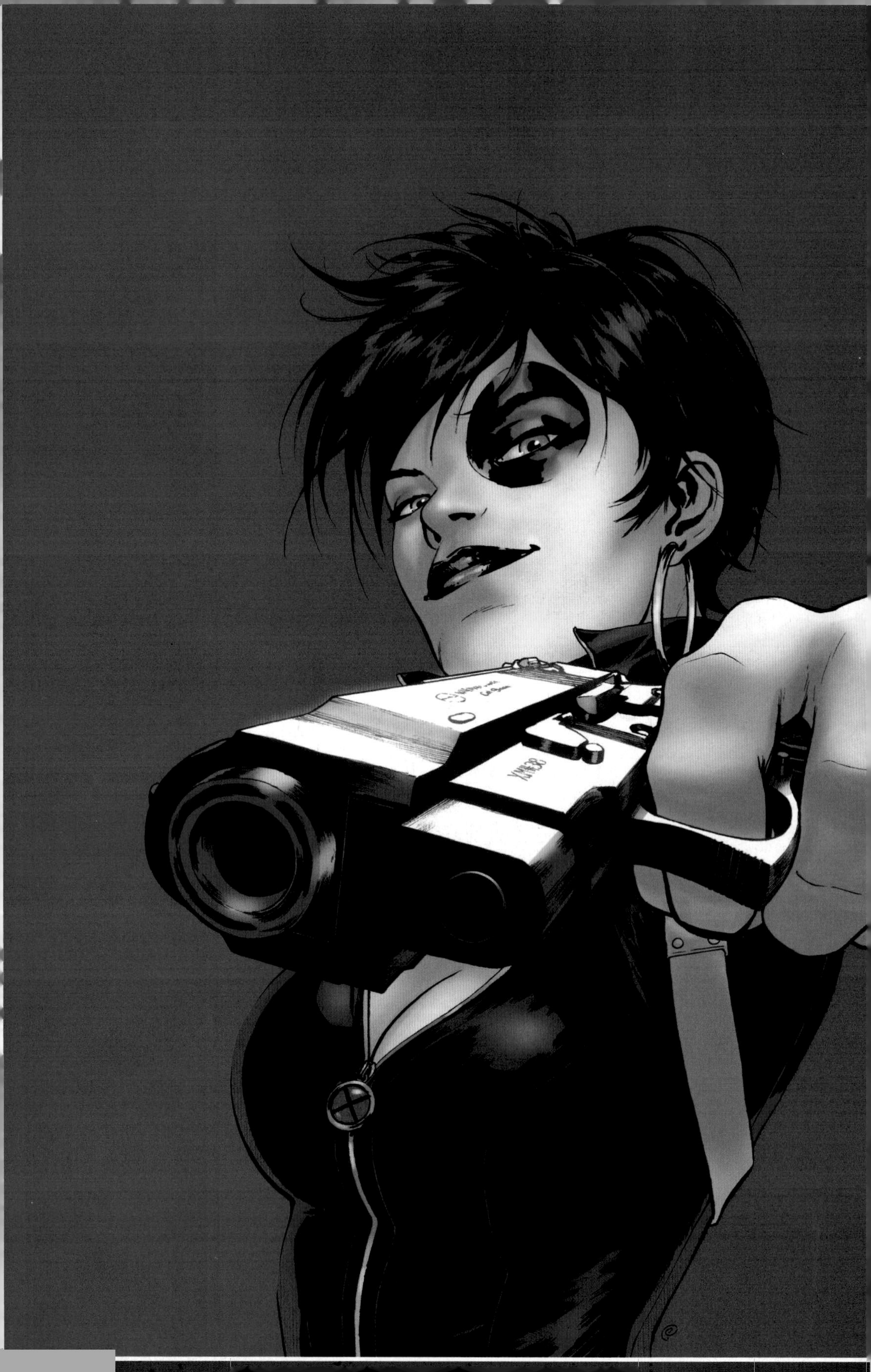

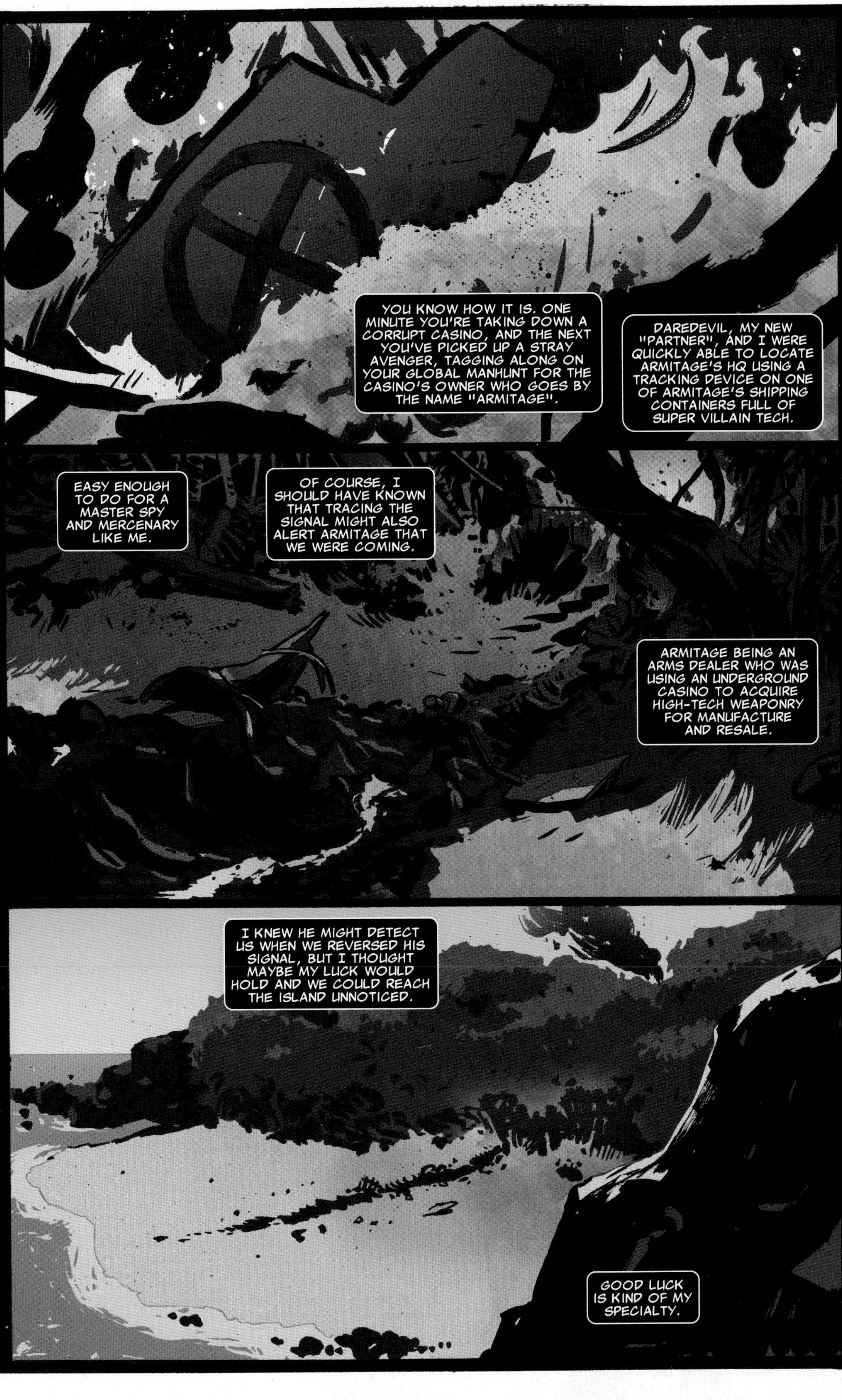
YOU KNOW HOW IT IS. ONE MINUTE YOU'RE TAKING DOWN A CORRUPT CASINO, AND THE NEXT YOU'VE PICKED UP A STRAY AVENGER, TAGGING ALONG ON YOUR GLOBAL MANHUNT FOR THE CASINO'S OWNER WHO GOES BY THE NAME "ARMITAGE".
DAREDEVIL, MY NEW "PARTNER", AND I WERE QUICKLY ABLE TO LOCATE ARMITAGE'S HQ USING A TRACKING DEVICE ON ONE OF ARMITAGE'S SHIPPING CONTAINERS FULL OF SUPER VILLAIN TECH.
EASY ENOUGH TO DO FOR A MASTER SPY AND MERCENARY LIKE ME.
OF COURSE, I SHOULD HAVE KNOWN THAT TRACING THE SIGNAL MIGHT ALSO ALERT ARMITAGE THAT WE WERE COMING.
ARMITAGE BEING AN ARMS DEALER WHO WAS USING AN UNDERGROUND CASINO TO ACQUIRE HIGH-TECH WEAPONRY FOR MANUFACTURE AND RESALE.
I KNEW HE MIGHT DETECT US WHEN WE REVERSED HIS SIGNAL, BUT I THOUGHT MAYBE MY LUCK WOULD HOLD AND WE COULD REACH THE ISLAND UNNOTICED.
GOOD LUCK IS KIND OF MY SPECIALTY.

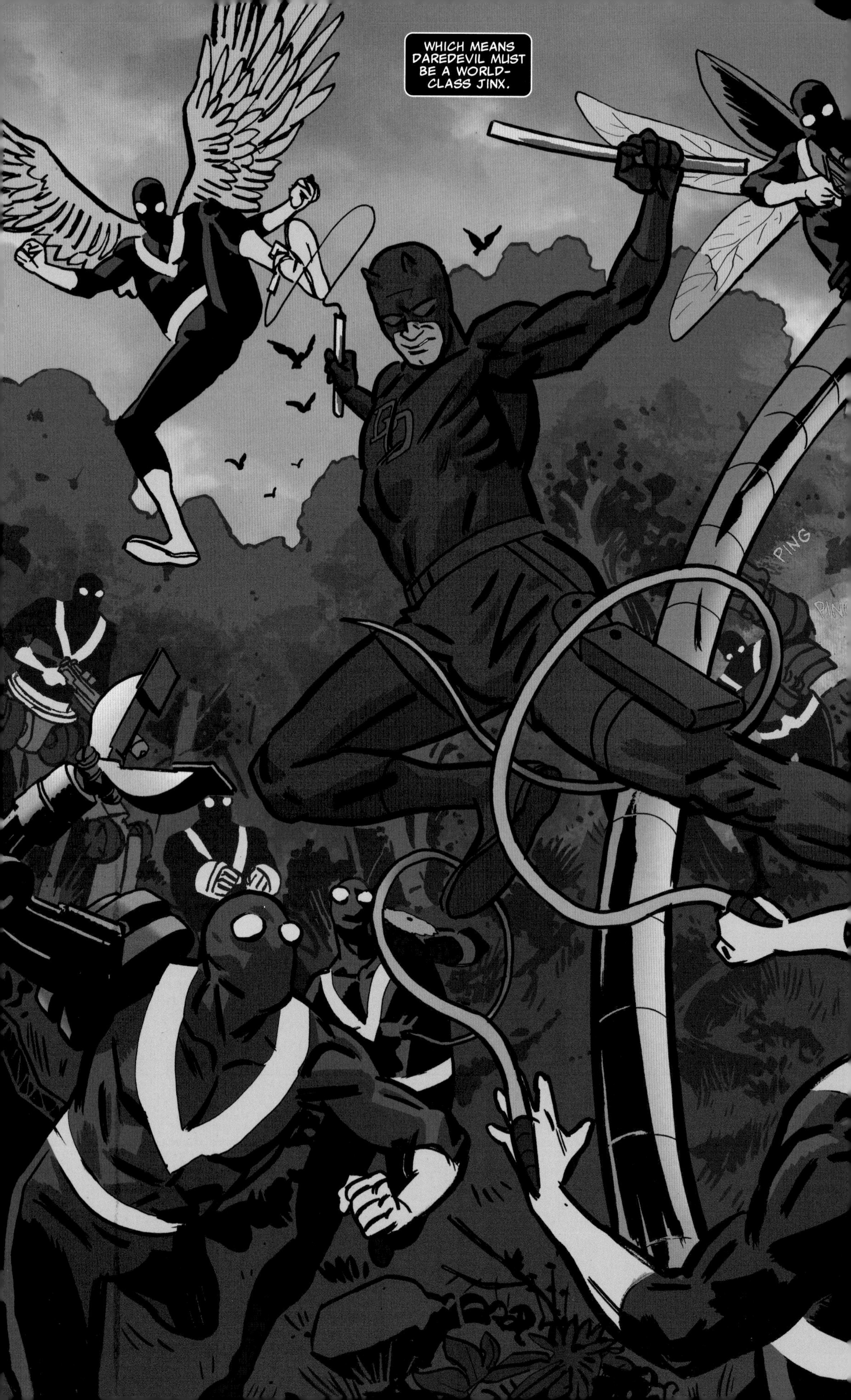
WHICH MEANS DAREDEVIL MUST BE A WORLD-CLASS JINX.
PING
PING

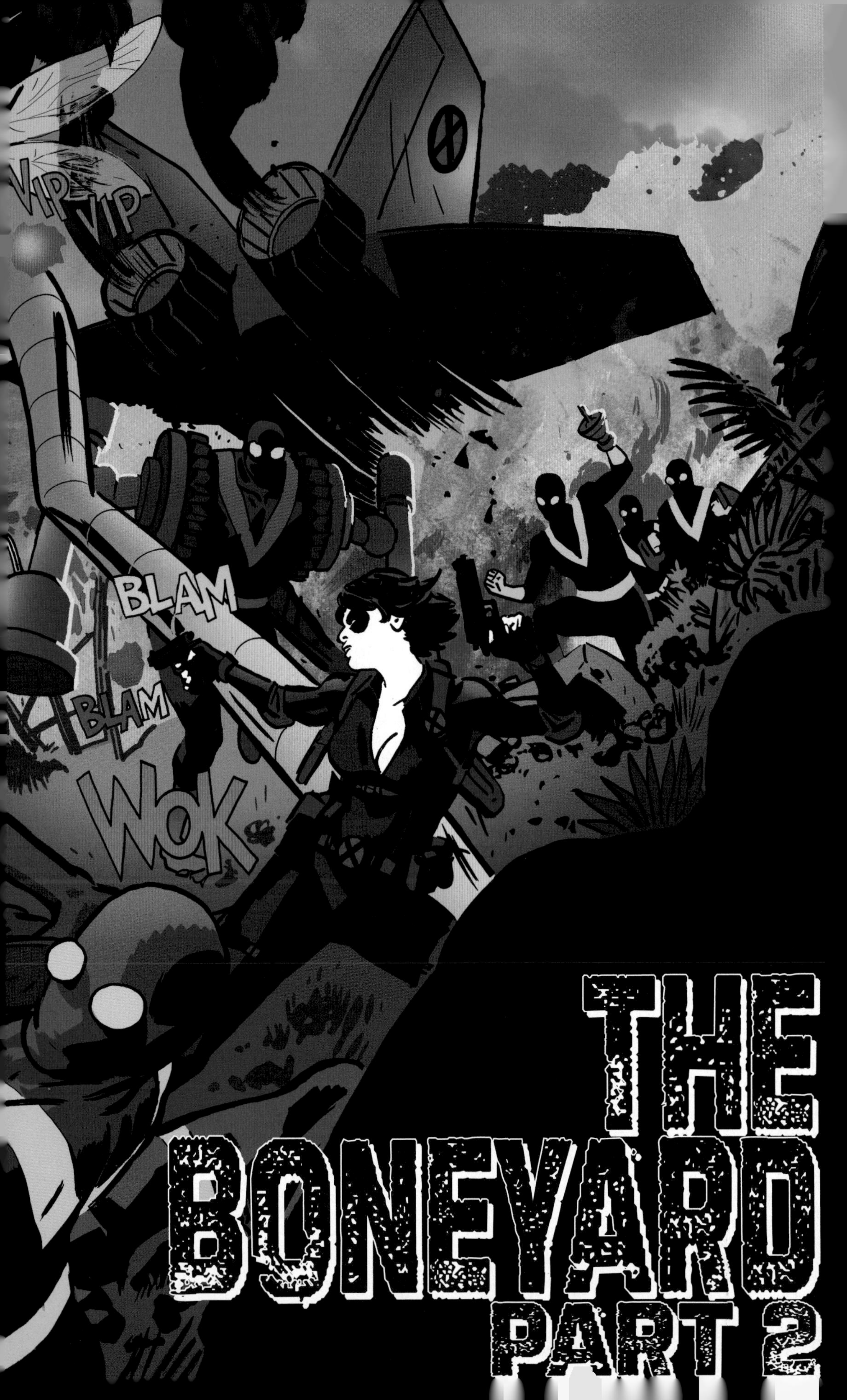
VIP VIP
BLAM
BLAM
WOK
THE BONEYARD
PART 2

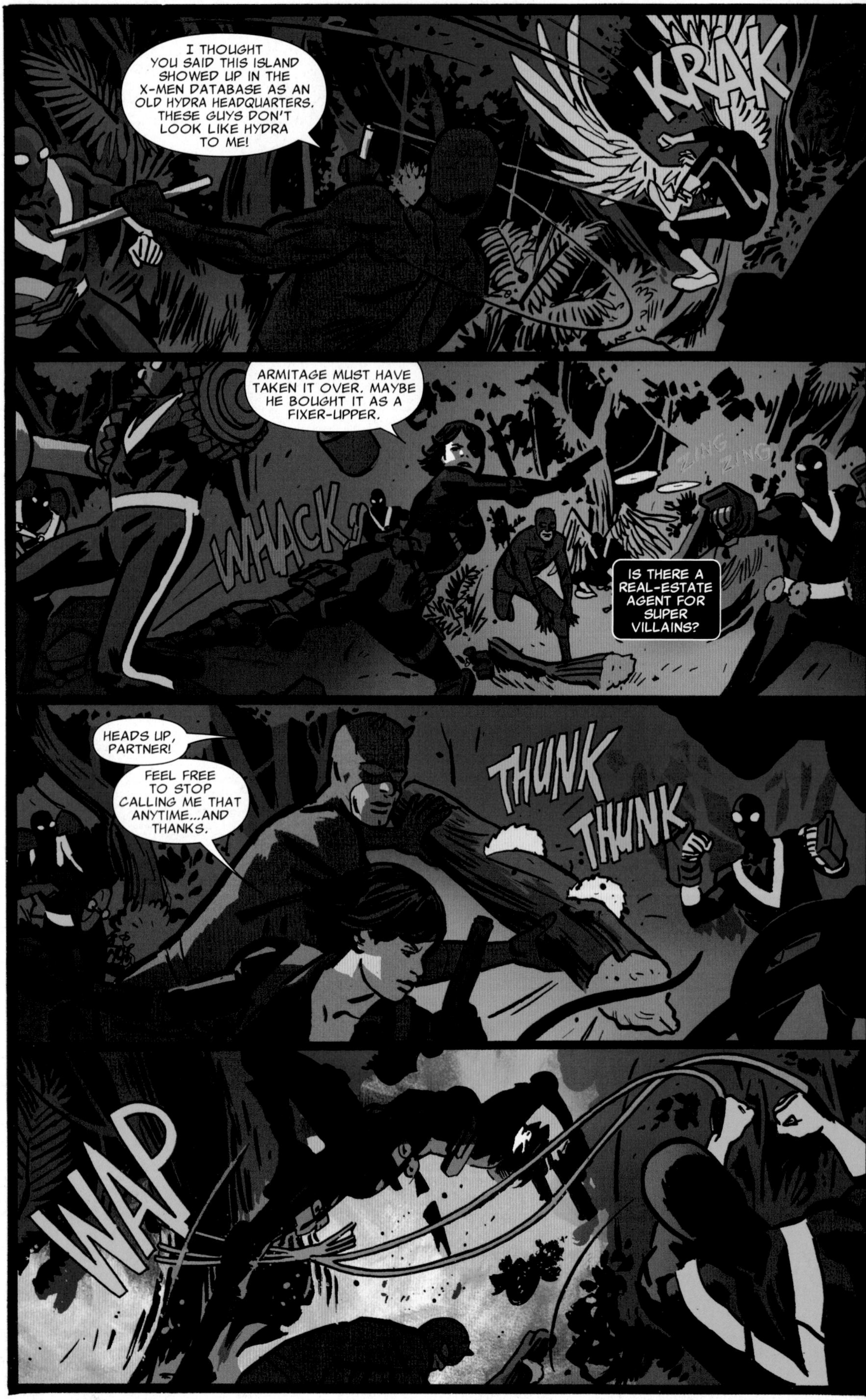
I THOUGHT YOU SAID THIS ISLAND SHOWED UP IN THE X-MEN DATABASE AS AN OLD HYDRA HEADQUARTERS. THESE GUYS DON'T LOOK LIKE HYDRA TO ME!
KRAK
ARMITAGE MUST HAVE TAKEN IT OVER. MAYBE HE BOUGHT IT AS A FIXER-UPPER.
ZING
ZING
WHACK
IS THERE A REAL-ESTATE AGENT FOR SUPER VILLAINS?
HEADS UP, PARTNER!
FEEL FREE TO STOP CALLING ME THAT ANYTIME...AND THANKS.
THUNK
THUNK
WAP

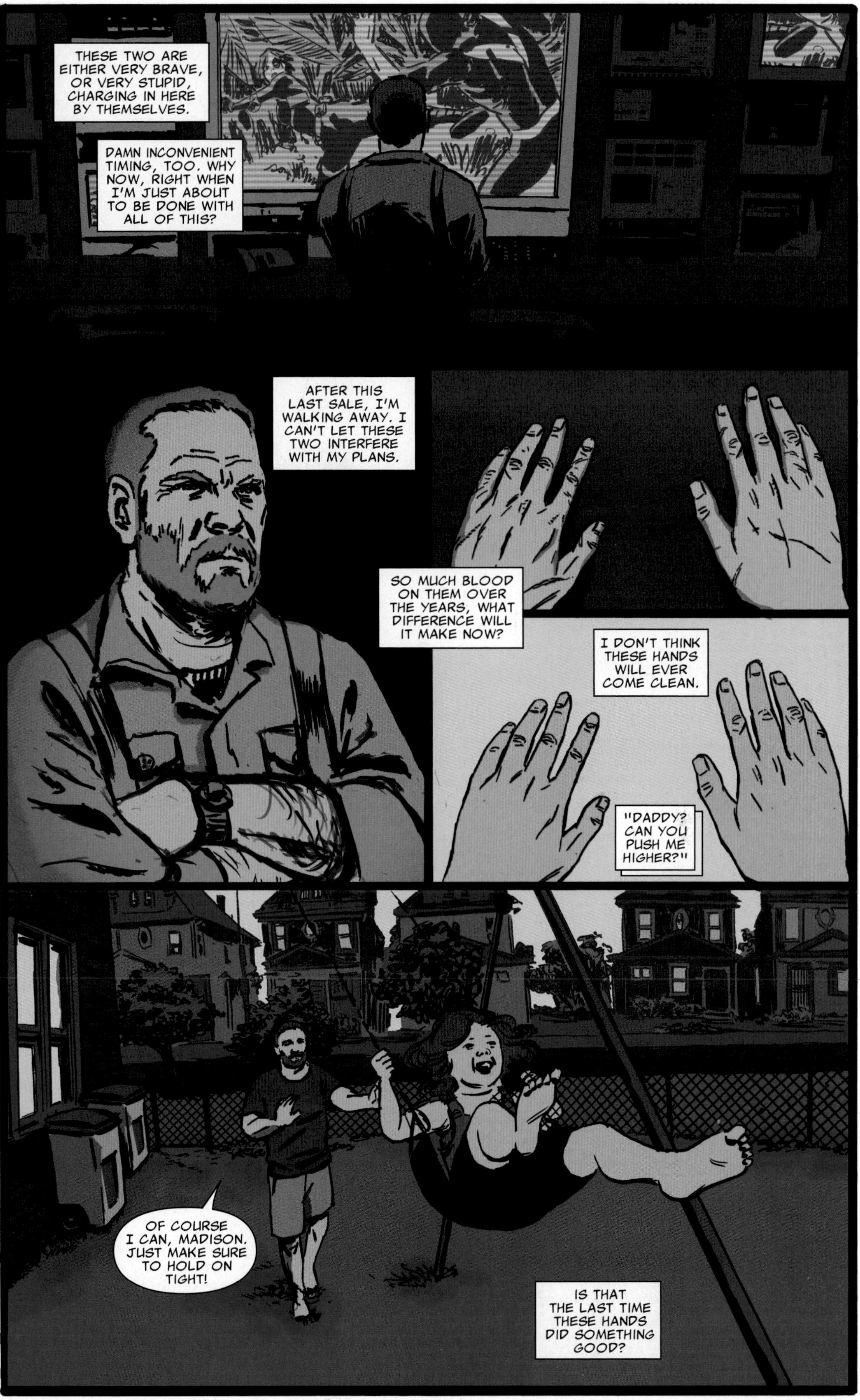
THESE TWO ARE EITHER VERY BRAVE, OR VERY STUPID, CHARGING IN HERE BY THEMSELVES.
DAMN INCONVENIENT TIMING, TOO. WHY NOW, RIGHT WHEN I'M JUST ABOUT TO BE DONE WITH ALL OF THIS?
AFTER THIS LAST SALE, I'M WALKING AWAY. I CAN'T LET THESE TWO INTERFERE WITH MY PLANS.
SO MUCH BLOOD ON THEM OVER THE YEARS, WHAT DIFFERENCE WILL IT MAKE NOW?
I DON'T THINK THESE HANDS WILL EVER COME CLEAN.
"DADDY? CAN YOU PUSH ME HIGHER?"
OF COURSE I CAN, MADISON. JUST MAKE SURE TO HOLD ON TIGHT!
IS THAT THE LAST TIME THESE HANDS DID SOMETHING GOOD?

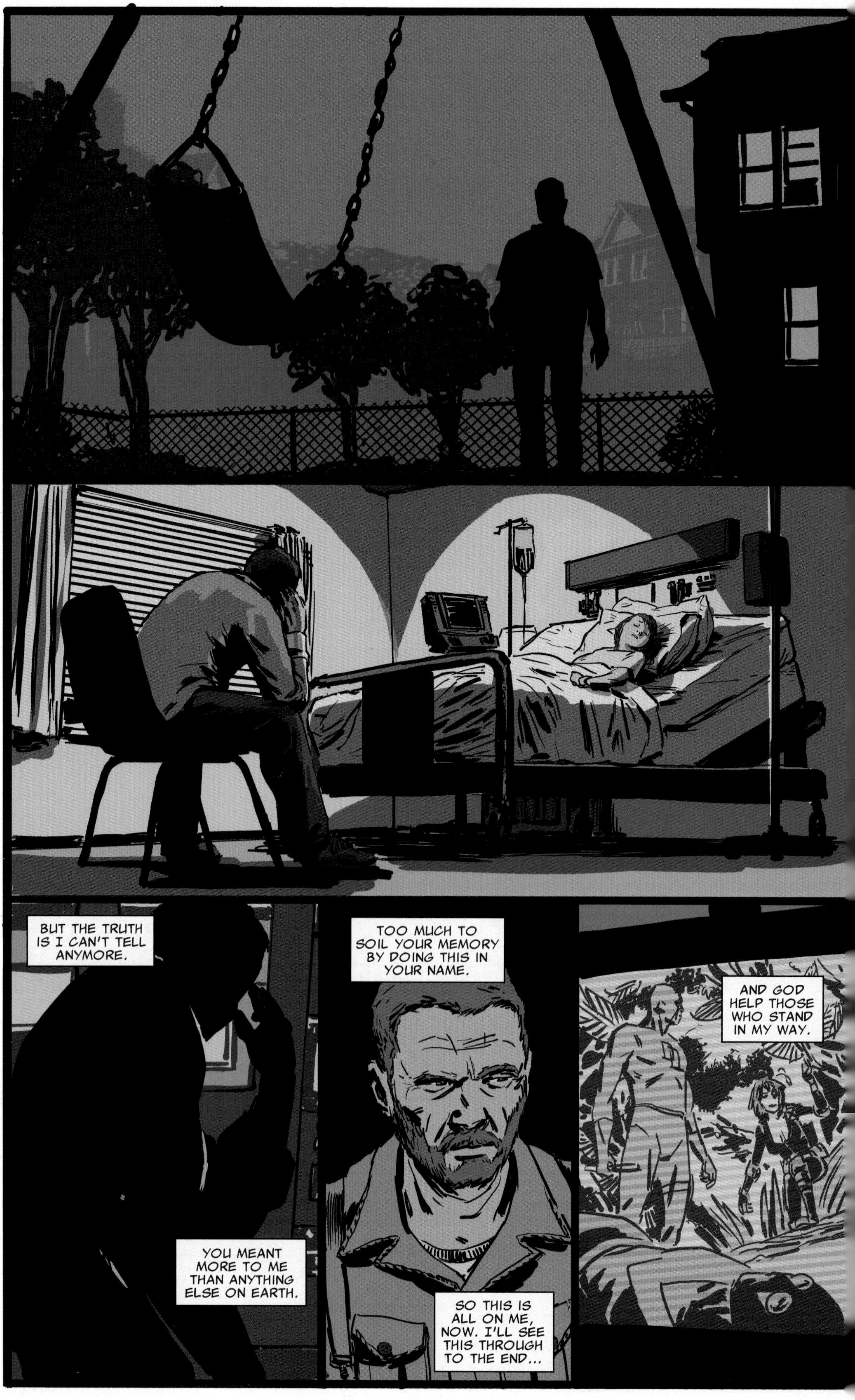
BUT THE TRUTH IS I CAN'T TELL ANYMORE.
YOU MEANT MORE TO ME THAN ANYTHING ELSE ON EARTH.
TOO MUCH TO SOIL YOUR MEMORY BY DOING THIS IN YOUR NAME.
SO THIS IS ALL ON ME, NOW. I'LL SEE THIS THROUGH TO THE END...
AND GOD HELP THOSE WHO STAND IN MY WAY.

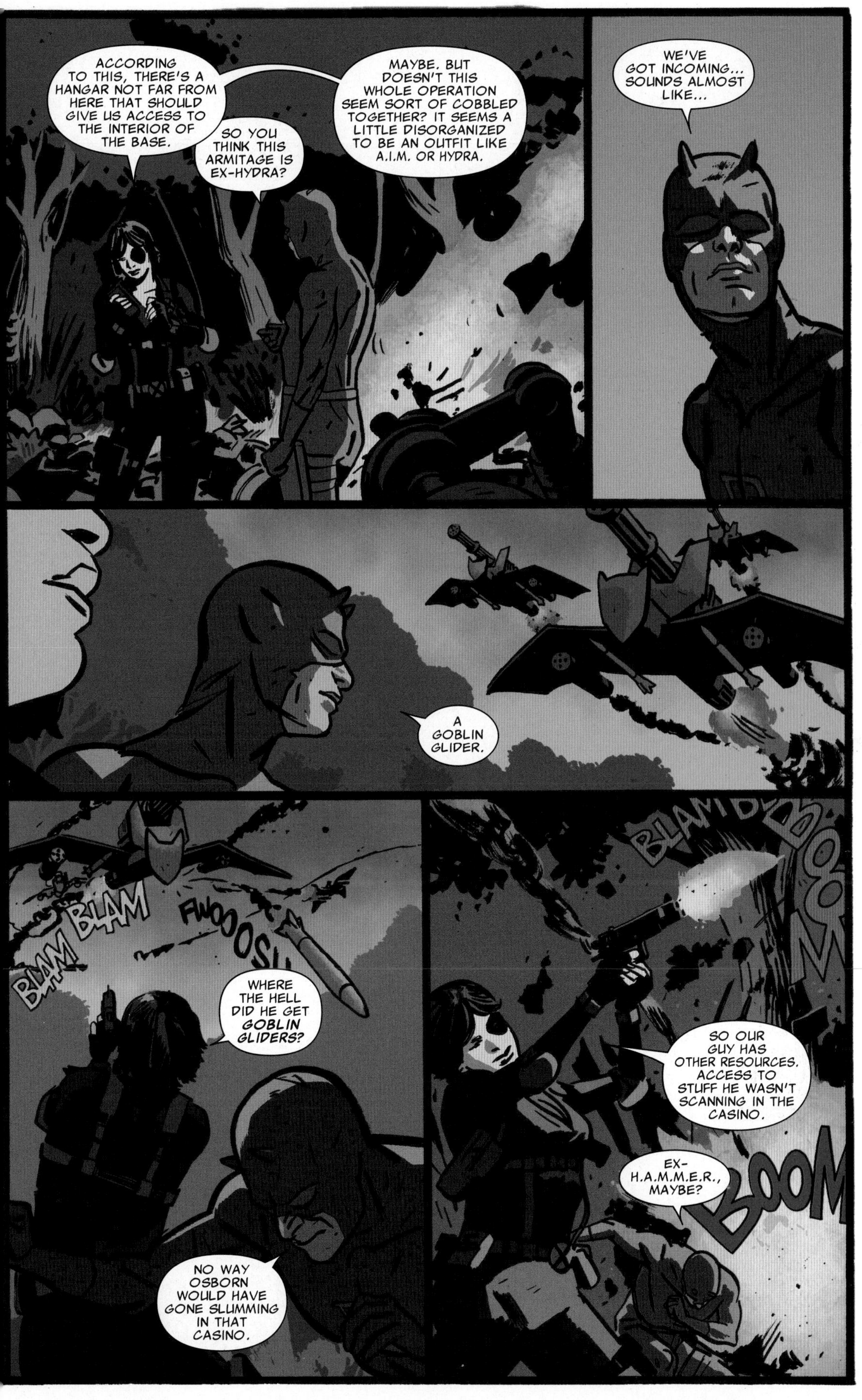
ACCORDING TO THIS, THERE'S A HANGAR NOT FAR FROM HERE THAT SHOULD GIVE US ACCESS TO THE INTERIOR OF THE BASE.
SO YOU THINK THIS ARMITAGE IS EX-HYDRA?
MAYBE. BUT DOESN'T THIS WHOLE OPERATION SEEM SORT OF COBBLED TOGETHER? IT SEEMS A LITTLE DISORGANIZED TO BE AN OUTFIT LIKE A.I.M. OR HYDRA.
WE'VE GOT INCOMING... SOUNDS ALMOST LIKE...
A GOBLIN GLIDER.
BLAM BLAM
BLAM
FWOOOSH
WHERE THE HELL DID HE GET GOBLIN GLIDERS?
NO WAY OSBORN WOULD HAVE GONE SLUMMING IN THAT CASINO.
BLAM BLAM
SO OUR GUY HAS OTHER RESOURCES. ACCESS TO STUFF HE WASN'T SCANNING IN THE CASINO.
EX-H.A.M.M.E.R., MAYBE?
BOOM

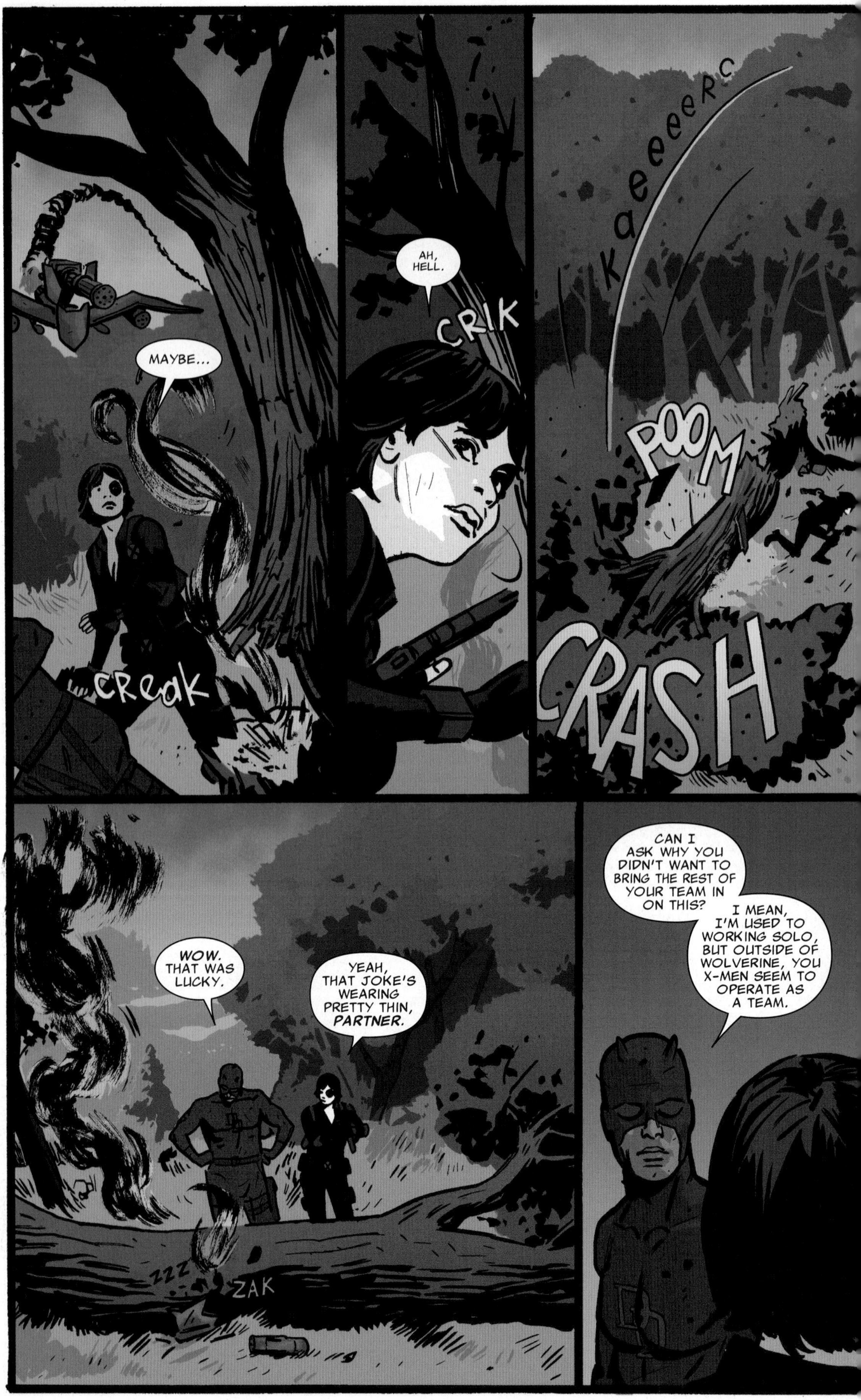
MAYBE...
CREAK
AH, HELL.
CRIK
KAEEEERC
POOM
CRASH
WOW. THAT WAS LUCKY.
YEAH, THAT JOKE'S WEARING PRETTY THIN, PARTNER.
ZZZ
ZAK
CAN I ASK WHY YOU DIDN'T WANT TO BRING THE REST OF YOUR TEAM IN ON THIS?
I MEAN, I'M USED TO WORKING SOLO, BUT OUTSIDE OF WOLVERINE, YOU X-MEN SEEM TO OPERATE AS A TEAM.

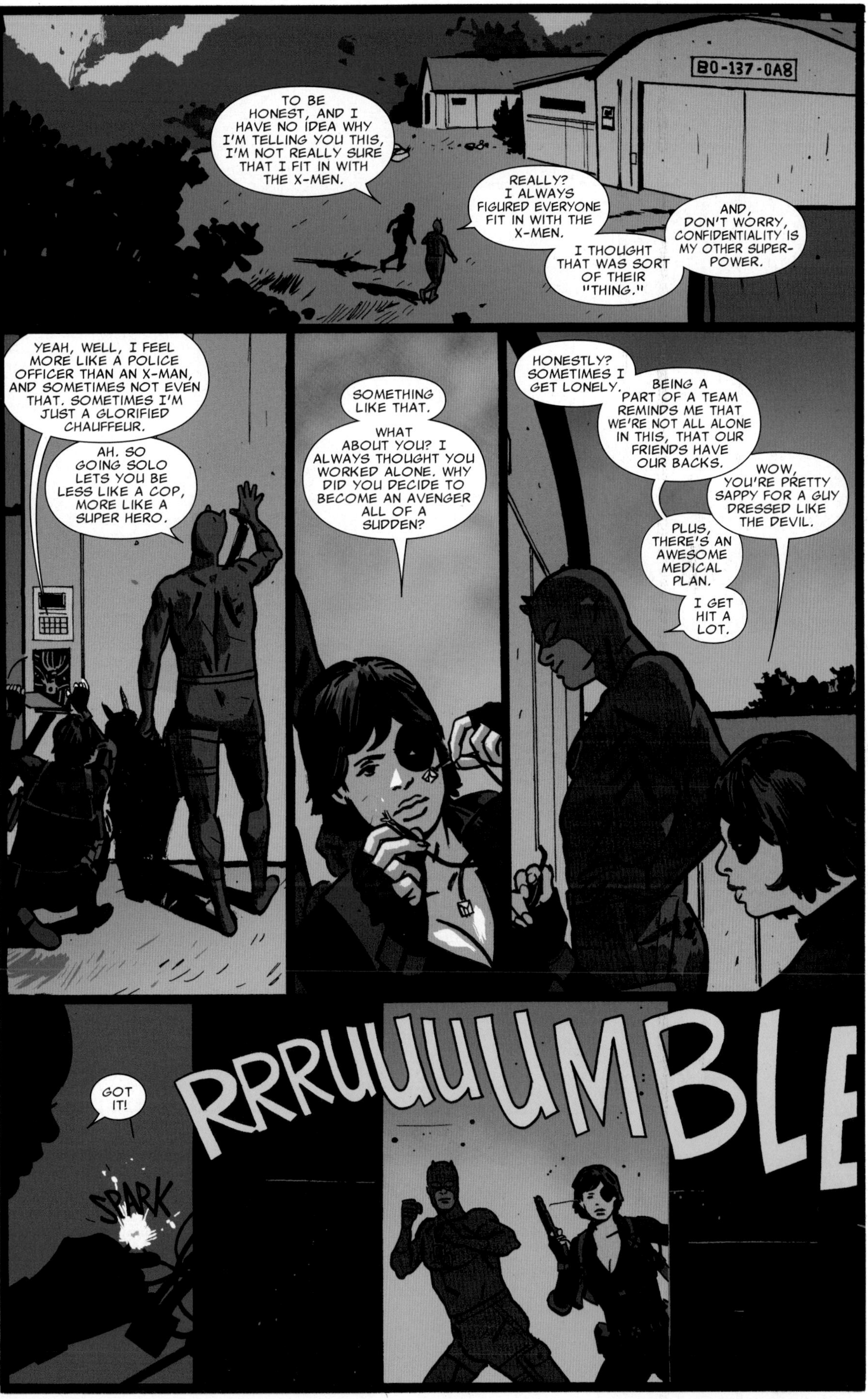
BO-137-0A8
TO BE HONEST, AND I HAVE NO IDEA WHY I'M TELLING YOU THIS, I'M NOT REALLY SURE THAT I FIT IN WITH THE X-MEN.
REALLY? I ALWAYS FIGURED EVERYONE FIT IN WITH THE X-MEN.
I THOUGHT THAT WAS SORT OF THEIR "THING."
AND, DON'T WORRY, CONFIDENTIALITY IS MY OTHER SUPER-POWER.
YEAH, WELL, I FEEL MORE LIKE A POLICE OFFICER THAN AN X-MAN, AND SOMETIMES NOT EVEN THAT. SOMETIMES I'M JUST A GLORIFIED CHAUFFEUR.
AH. SO GOING SOLO LETS YOU BE LESS LIKE A COP, MORE LIKE A SUPER HERO.
SOMETHING LIKE THAT.
WHAT ABOUT YOU? I ALWAYS THOUGHT YOU WORKED ALONE. WHY DID YOU DECIDE TO BECOME AN AVENGER ALL OF A SUDDEN?
HONESTLY? SOMETIMES I GET LONELY.
BEING A PART OF A TEAM REMINDS ME THAT WE'RE NOT ALL ALONE IN THIS, THAT OUR FRIENDS HAVE OUR BACKS.
PLUS, THERE'S AN AWESOME MEDICAL PLAN.
I GET HIT A LOT.
WOW, YOU'RE PRETTY SAPPY FOR A GUY DRESSED LIKE THE DEVIL.
GOT IT!
SPARK
RRRUUUUMBLE

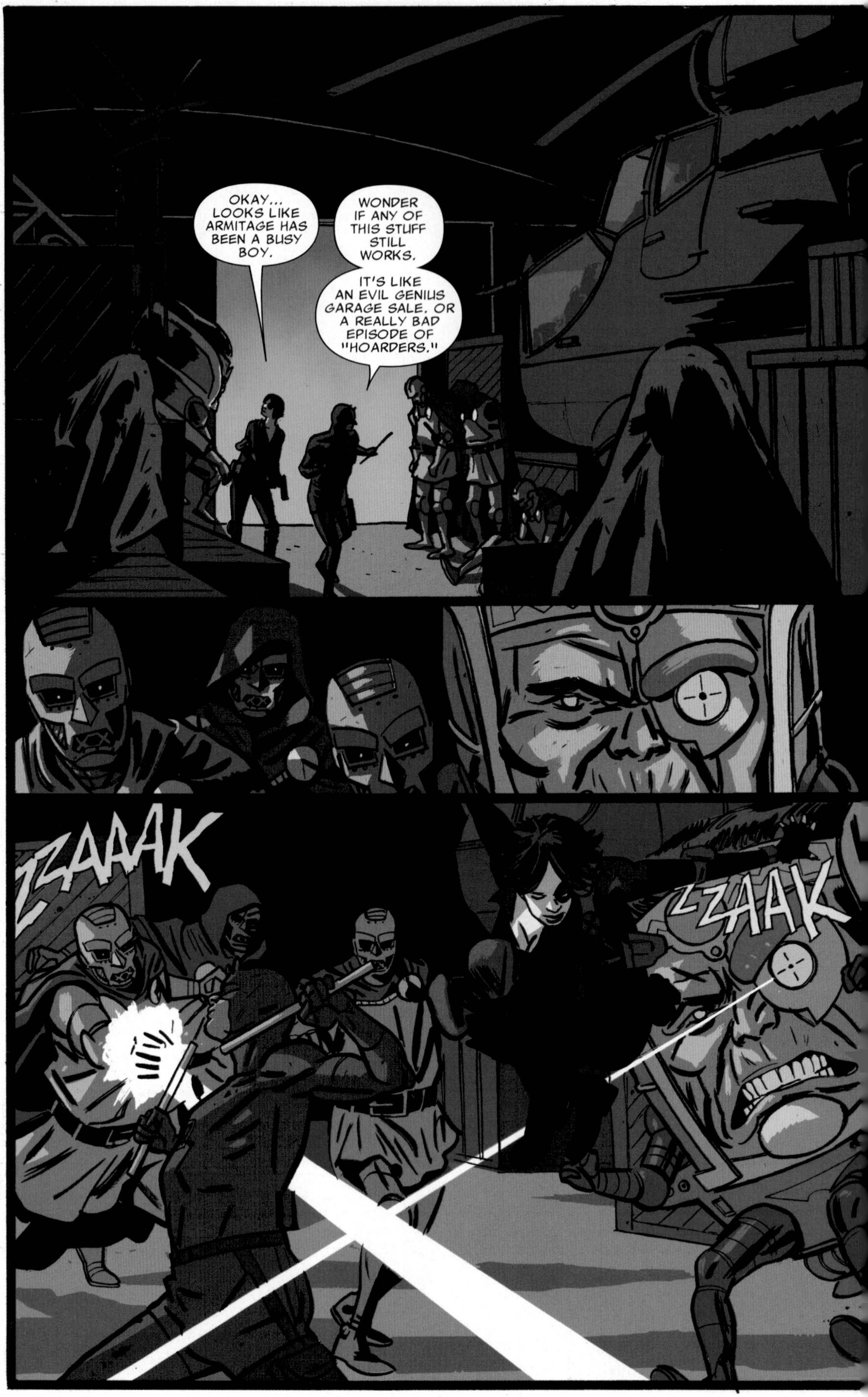
OKAY... LOOKS LIKE ARMITAGE HAS BEEN A BUSY BOY.
WONDER IF ANY OF THIS STUFF STILL WORKS.
IT'S LIKE AN EVIL GENIUS GARAGE SALE. OR A REALLY BAD EPISODE OF "HOARDERS."
ZZAAAK
ZZAAK

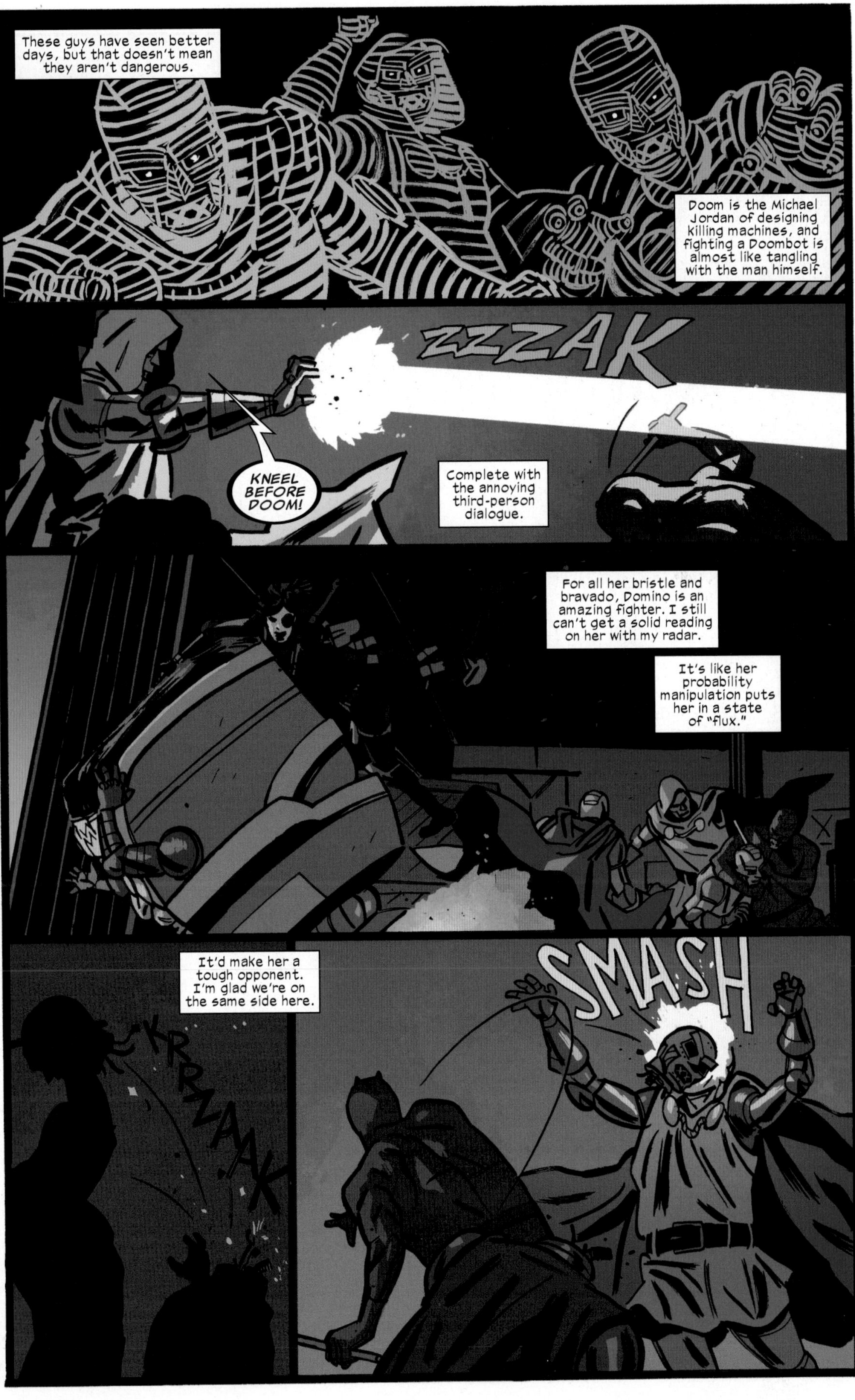
These guys have seen better days, but that doesn't mean they aren't dangerous.
Doom is the Michael Jordan of designing killing machines, and fighting a Doombot is almost like tangling with the man himself.
ZZZAK
KNEEL BEFORE DOOM!
Complete with the annoying third-person dialogue.
For all her bristle and bravado, Domino is an amazing fighter. I still can't get a solid reading on her with my radar.
It's like her probability manipulation puts her in a state of "flux."
It'd make her a tough opponent. I'm glad we're on the same side here.
KRRZAAK
SMASH

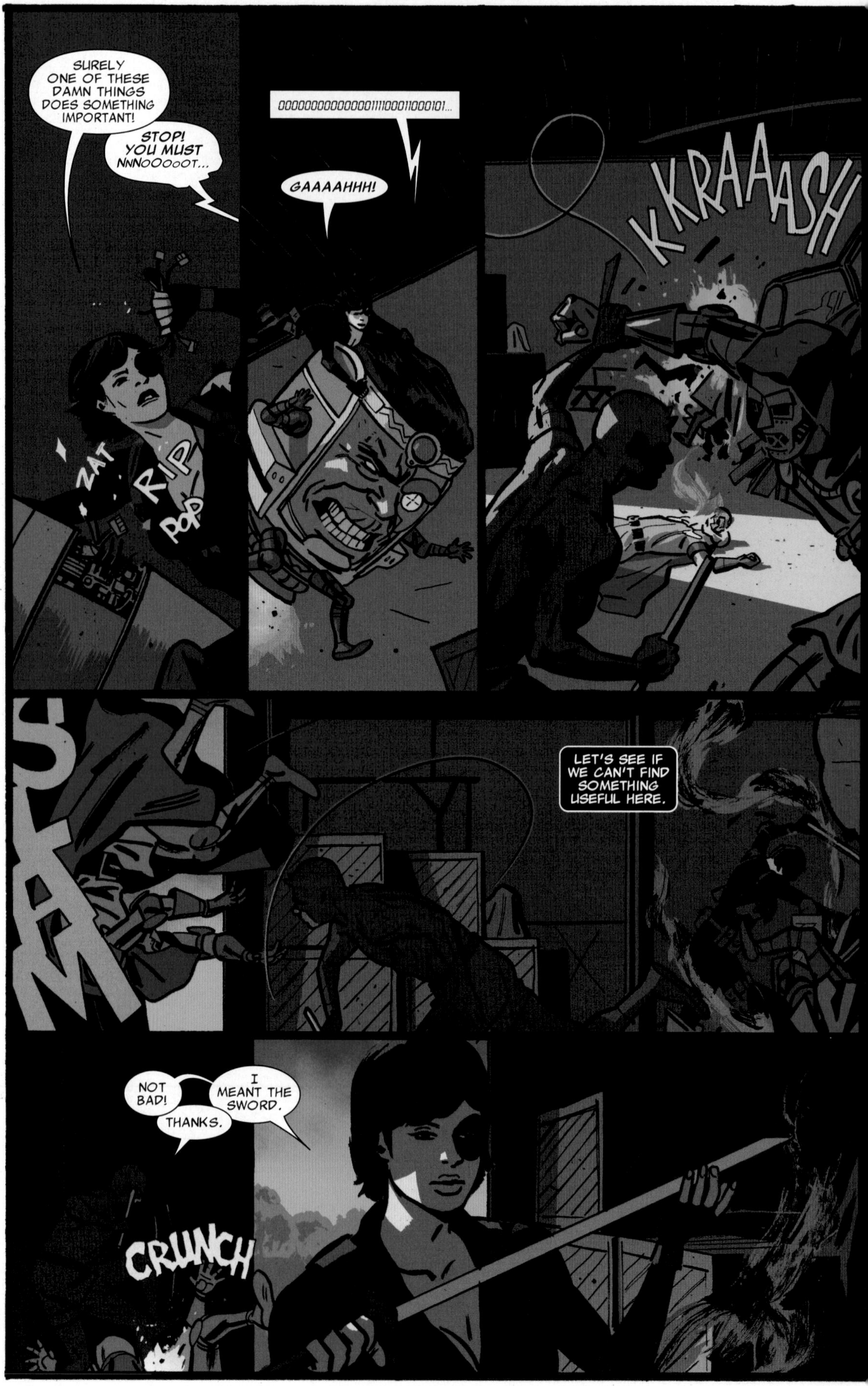
SURELY ONE OF THESE DAMN THINGS DOES SOMETHING IMPORTANT!
STOP! YOU MUST NNNOOOoOT...
ZAT
RIP
POP
0000000000000000111100001100001 01...
GAAAAHHH!
KKRAAAASH
SLAM
LET'S SEE IF WE CAN'T FIND SOMETHING USEFUL HERE.
NOT BAD!
THANKS.
I MEANT THE SWORD.
CRUNCH

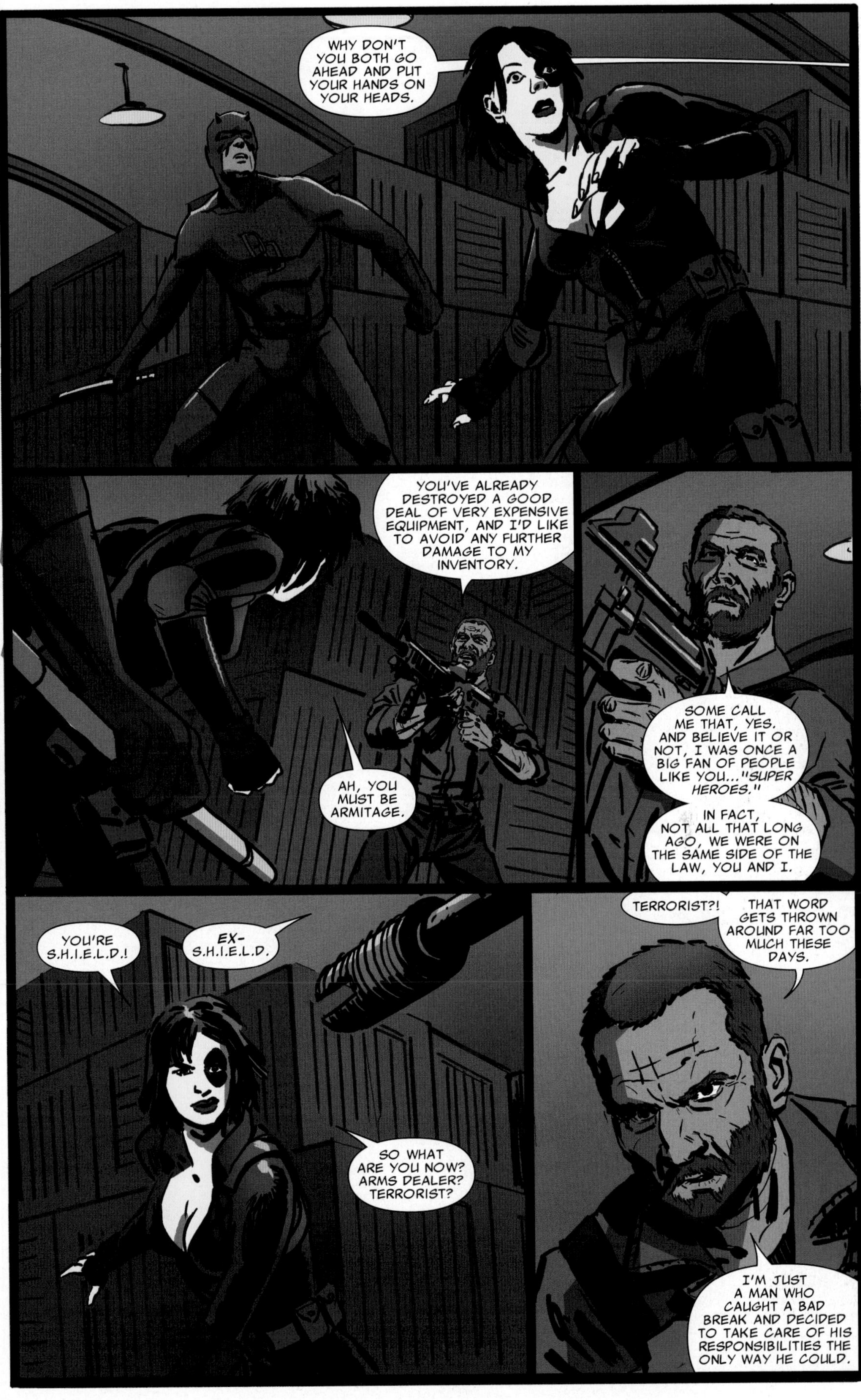
WHY DON'T YOU BOTH GO AHEAD AND PUT YOUR HANDS ON YOUR HEADS.
YOU'VE ALREADY DESTROYED A GOOD DEAL OF VERY EXPENSIVE EQUIPMENT, AND I'D LIKE TO AVOID ANY FURTHER DAMAGE TO MY INVENTORY.
AH, YOU MUST BE ARMITAGE.
SOME CALL ME THAT, YES. AND BELIEVE IT OR NOT, I WAS ONCE A BIG FAN OF PEOPLE LIKE YOU..."SUPER HEROES."
IN FACT, NOT ALL THAT LONG AGO, WE WERE ON THE SAME SIDE OF THE LAW, YOU AND I.
YOU'RE S.H.I.E.L.D.!
EX-S.H.I.E.L.D.
SO WHAT ARE YOU NOW? ARMS DEALER? TERRORIST?
TERRORIST?!
THAT WORD GETS THROWN AROUND FAR TOO MUCH THESE DAYS.
I'M JUST A MAN WHO CAUGHT A BAD BREAK AND DECIDED TO TAKE CARE OF HIS RESPONSIBILITIES THE ONLY WAY HE COULD.

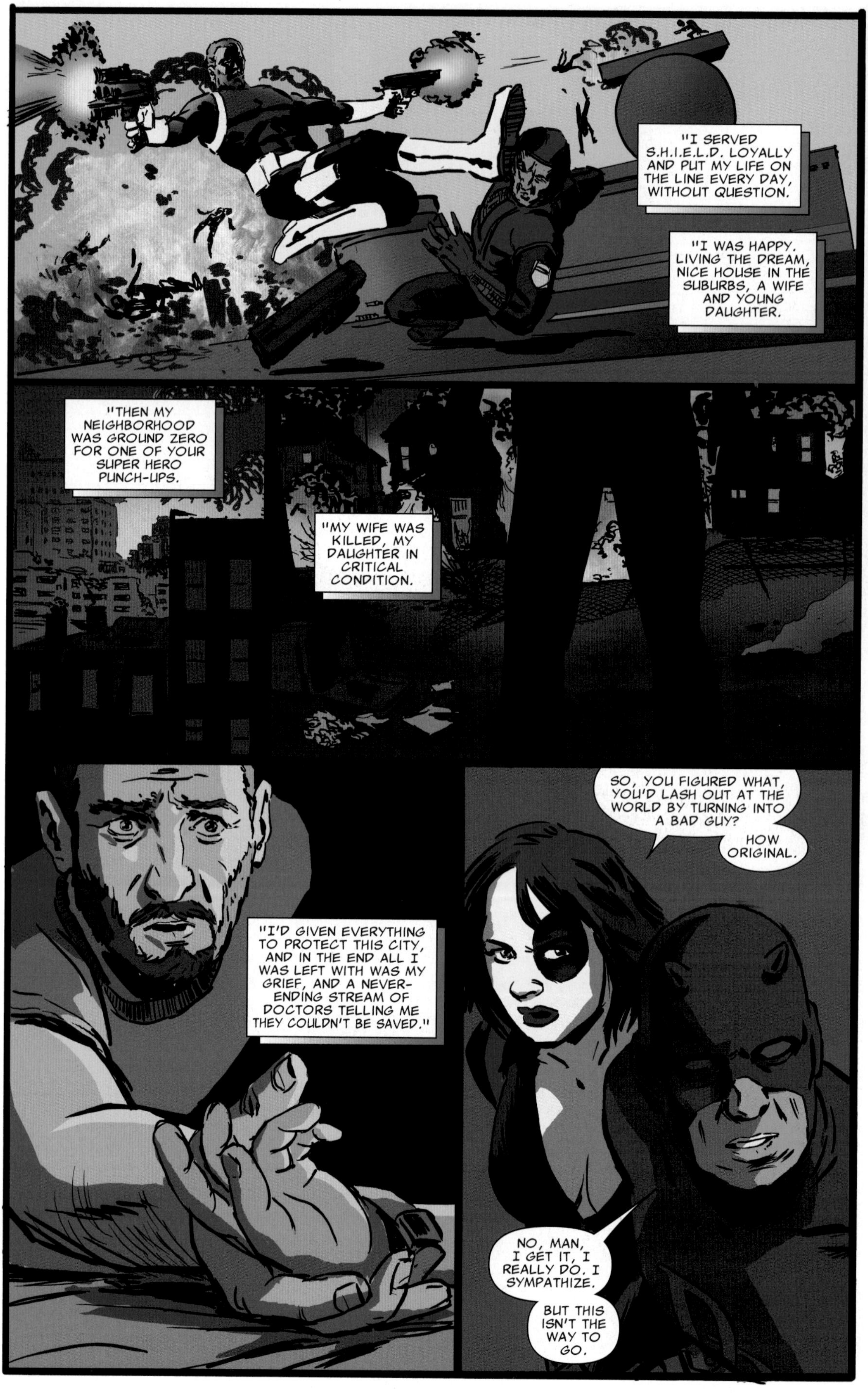
"I SERVED S.H.I.E.L.D. LOYALLY AND PUT MY LIFE ON THE LINE EVERY DAY, WITHOUT QUESTION.
"I WAS HAPPY. LIVING THE DREAM, NICE HOUSE IN THE SUBURBS, A WIFE AND YOUNG DAUGHTER.
"THEN MY NEIGHBORHOOD WAS GROUND ZERO FOR ONE OF YOUR SUPER HERO PUNCH-UPS.
"MY WIFE WAS KILLED, MY DAUGHTER IN CRITICAL CONDITION.
"I'D GIVEN EVERYTHING TO PROTECT THIS CITY, AND IN THE END ALL I WAS LEFT WITH WAS MY GRIEF, AND A NEVER-ENDING STREAM OF DOCTORS TELLING ME THEY COULDN'T BE SAVED."
SO, YOU FIGURED WHAT, YOU'D LASH OUT AT THE WORLD BY TURNING INTO A BAD GUY?
HOW ORIGINAL.
NO, MAN, I GET IT, I REALLY DO. I SYMPATHIZE.
BUT THIS ISN'T THE WAY TO GO.

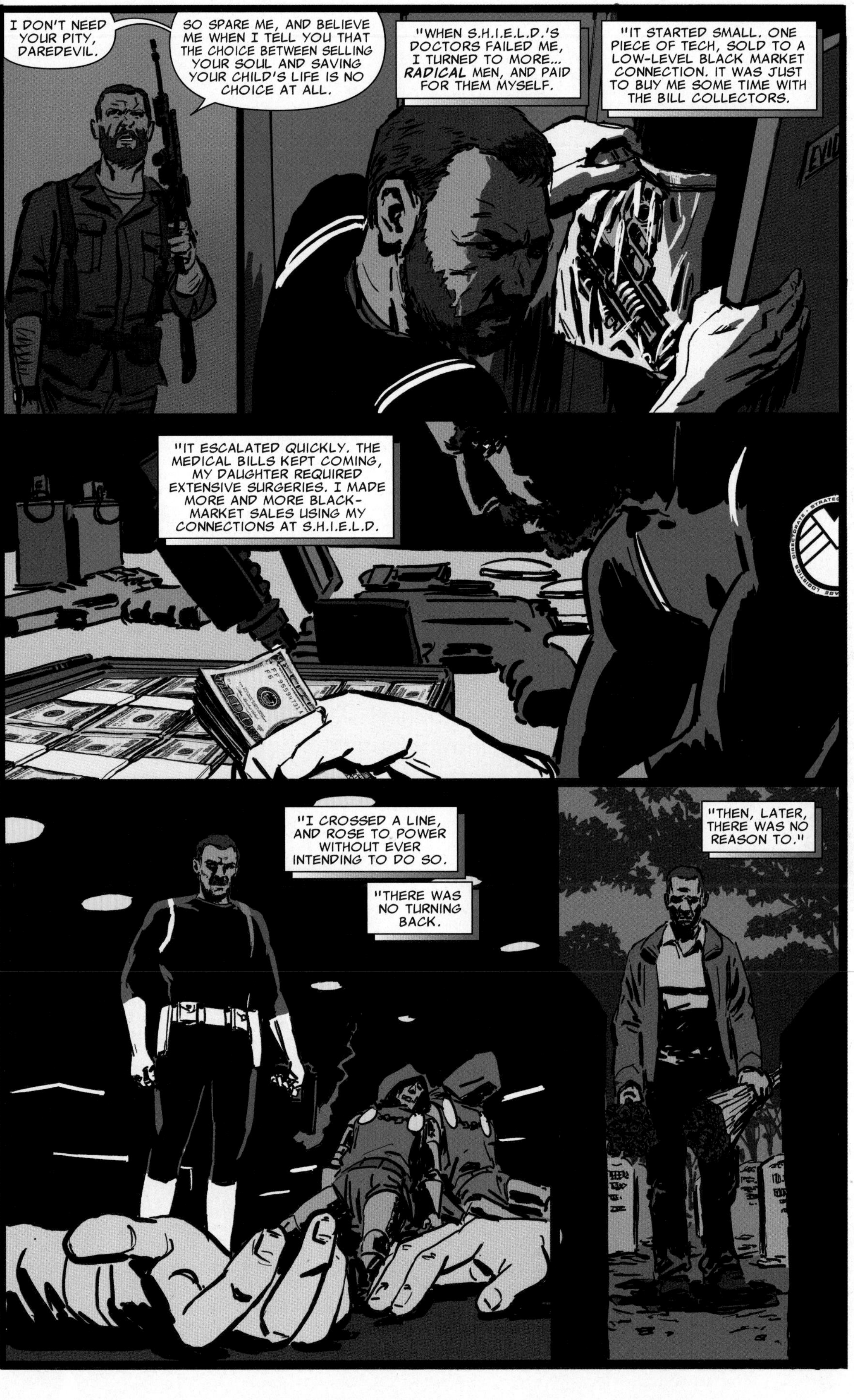
I DON'T NEED YOUR PITY, DAREDEVIL.
SO SPARE ME, AND BELIEVE ME WHEN I TELL YOU THAT THE CHOICE BETWEEN SELLING YOUR SOUL AND SAVING YOUR CHILD'S LIFE IS NO CHOICE AT ALL.
"WHEN S.H.I.E.L.D.'S DOCTORS FAILED ME, I TURNED TO MORE... *RADICAL* MEN, AND PAID FOR THEM MYSELF.
"IT STARTED SMALL. ONE PIECE OF TECH, SOLD TO A LOW-LEVEL BLACK MARKET CONNECTION. IT WAS JUST TO BUY ME SOME TIME WITH THE BILL COLLECTORS.
"IT ESCALATED QUICKLY. THE MEDICAL BILLS KEPT COMING, MY DAUGHTER REQUIRED EXTENSIVE SURGERIES. I MADE MORE AND MORE BLACK-MARKET SALES USING MY CONNECTIONS AT S.H.I.E.L.D.
"I CROSSED A LINE, AND ROSE TO POWER WITHOUT EVER INTENDING TO DO SO.
"THERE WAS NO TURNING BACK.
"THEN, LATER, THERE WAS NO REASON TO."

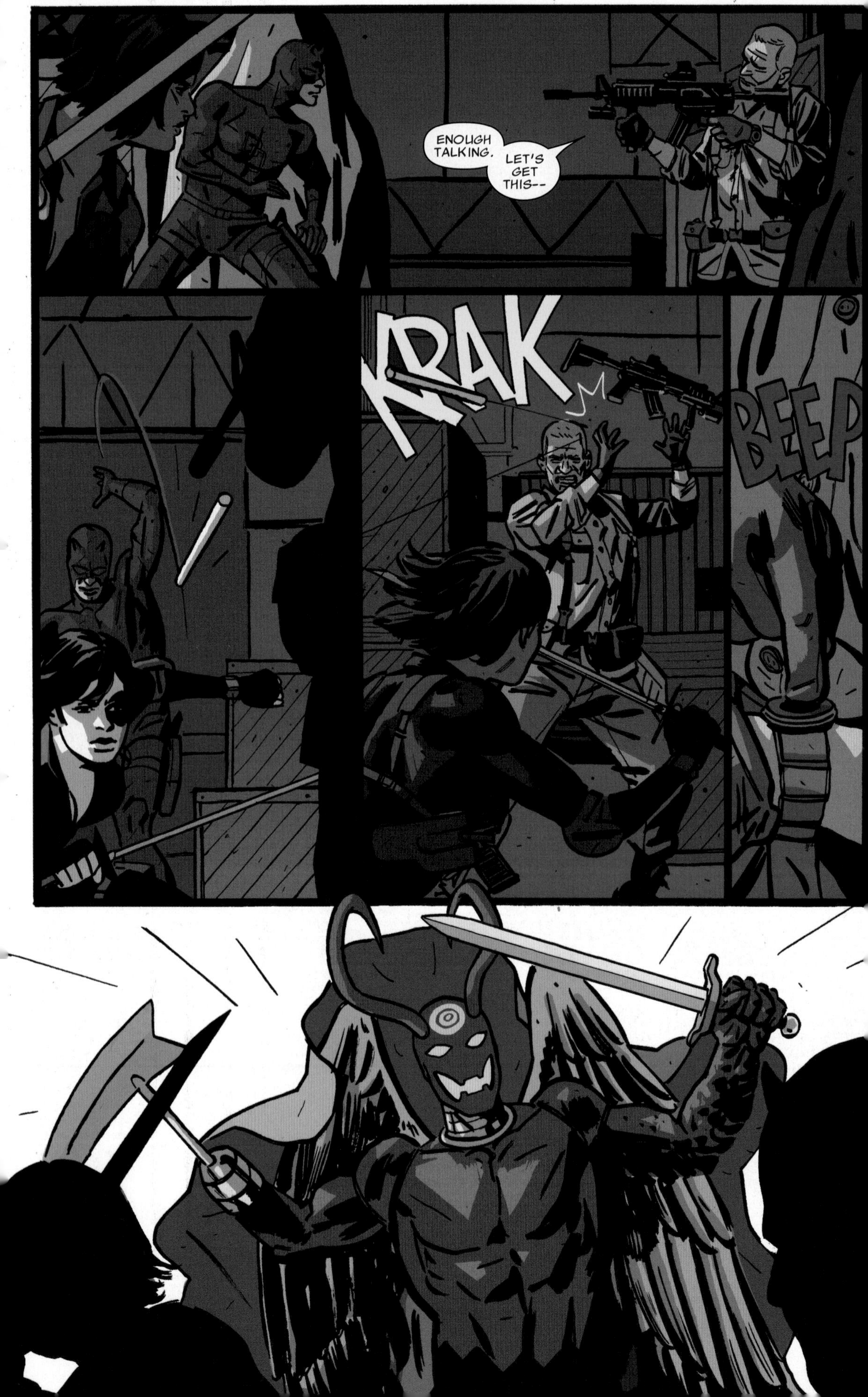
ENOUGH TALKING.
LET'S GET THIS--
KRAK
BEEP

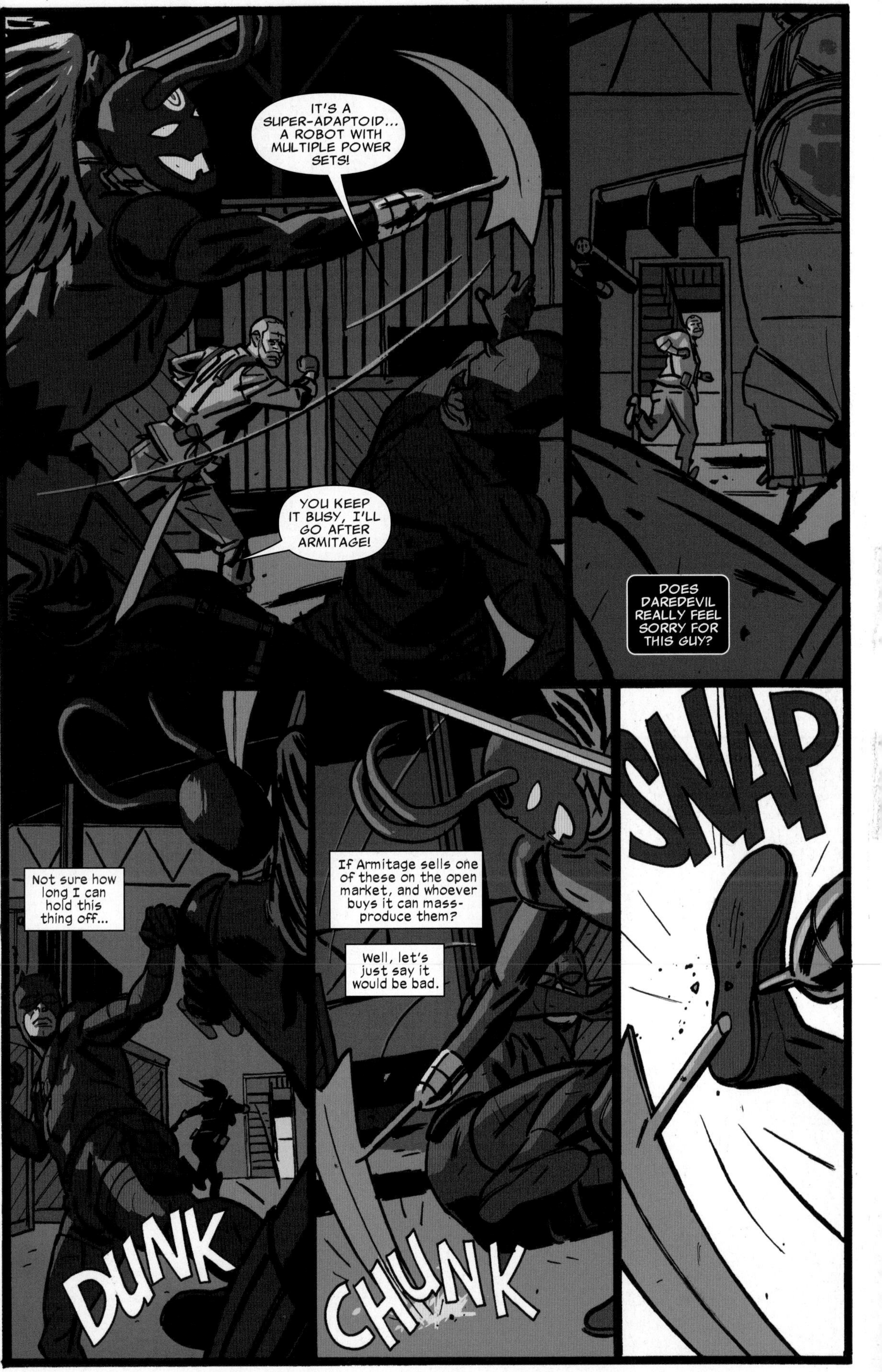
IT'S A SUPER-ADAPTOID... A ROBOT WITH MULTIPLE POWER SETS!
YOU KEEP IT BUSY, I'LL GO AFTER ARMITAGE!
DOES DAREDEVIL REALLY FEEL SORRY FOR THIS GUY?
Not sure how long I can hold this thing off...
DUNK
If Armitage sells one of these on the open market, and whoever buys it can mass-produce them?
Well, let's just say it would be bad.
CHUNK
SNAP

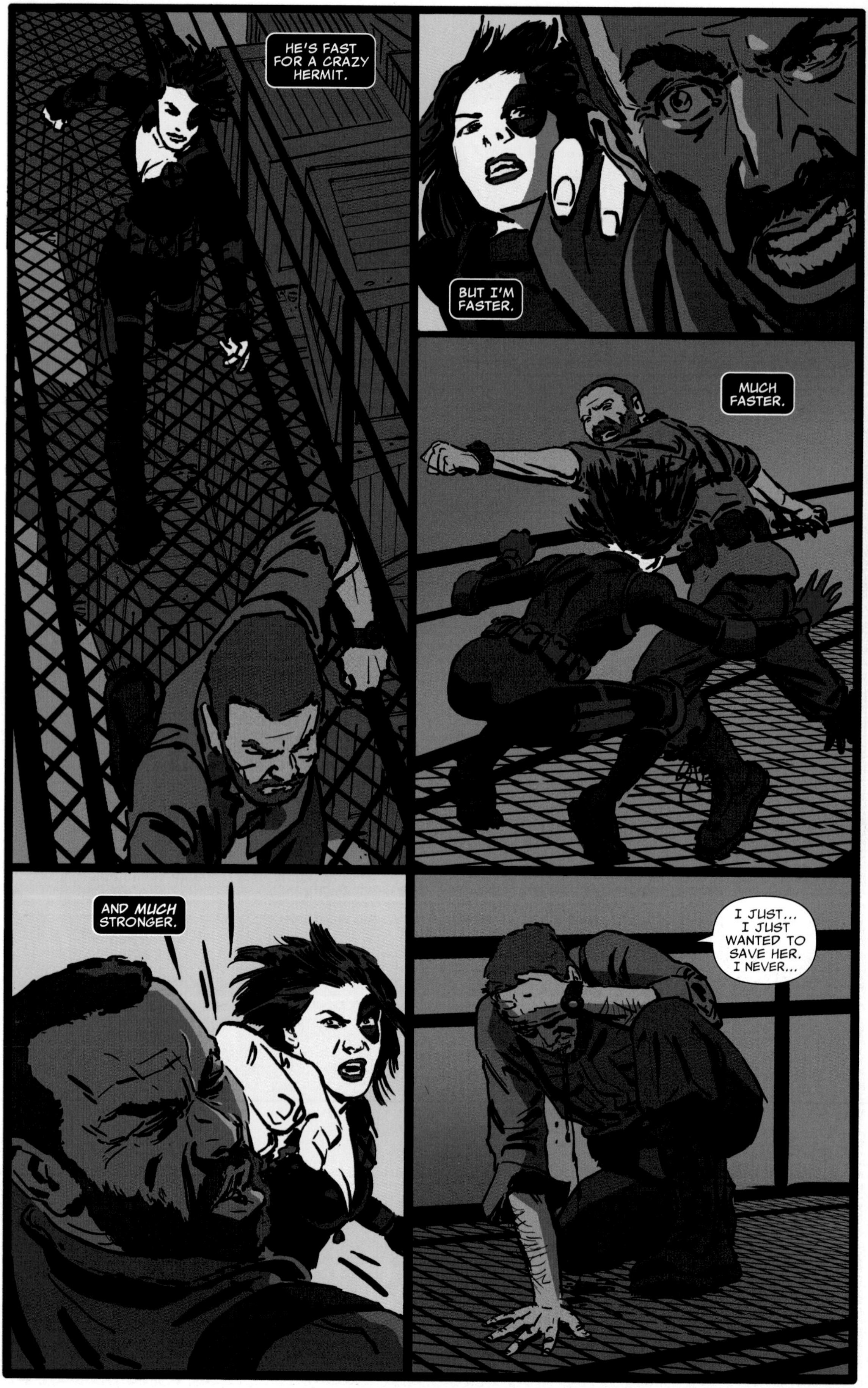
HE'S FAST FOR A CRAZY HERMIT.
BUT I'M FASTER.
MUCH FASTER.
AND MUCH STRONGER.
I JUST... I JUST WANTED TO SAVE HER. I NEVER...

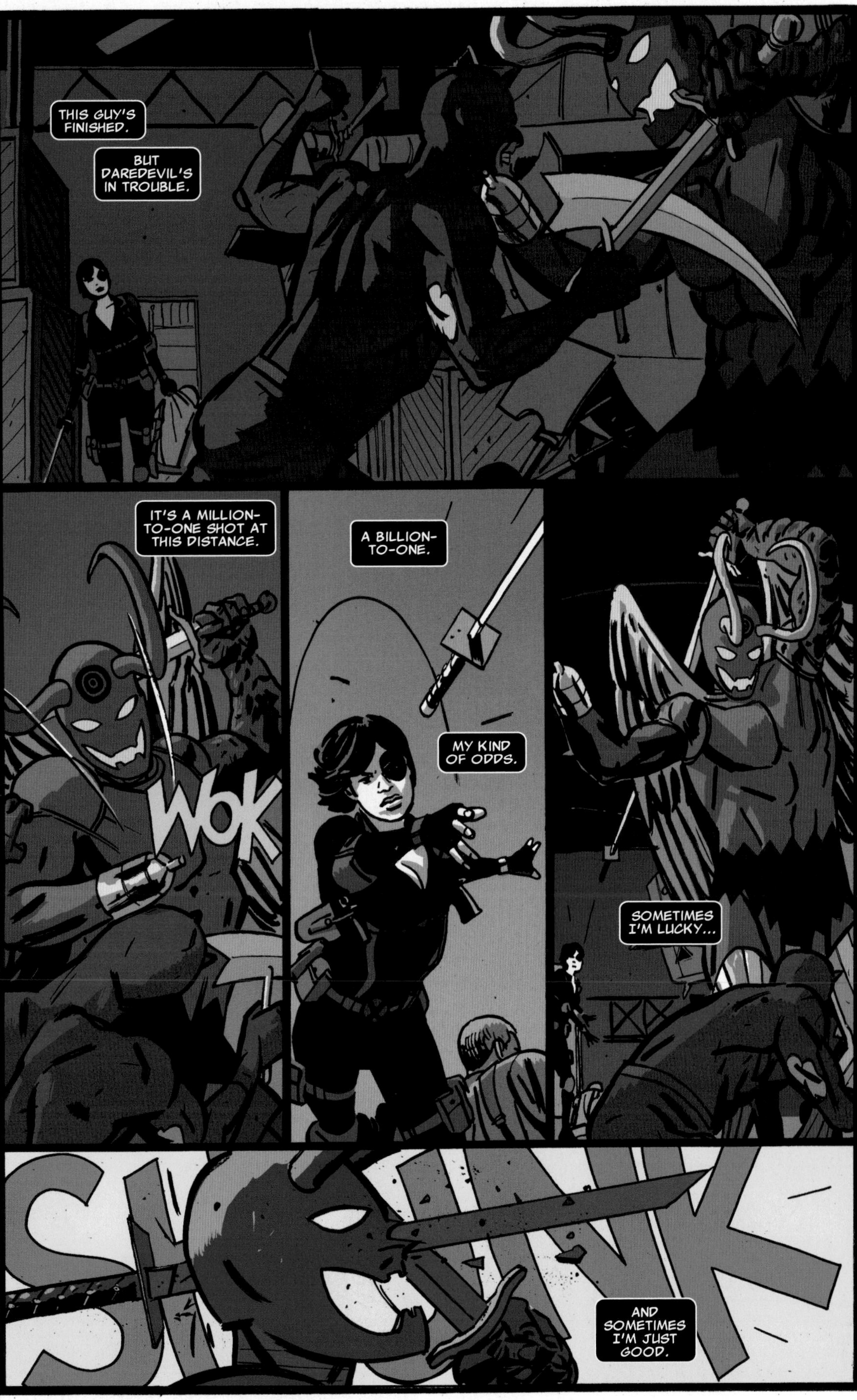
THIS GUY'S FINISHED.
BUT DAREDEVIL'S IN TROUBLE.
IT'S A MILLION-TO-ONE SHOT AT THIS DISTANCE.
WOK
A BILLION-TO-ONE.
MY KIND OF ODDS.
SOMETIMES I'M LUCKY...
AND SOMETIMES I'M JUST GOOD.

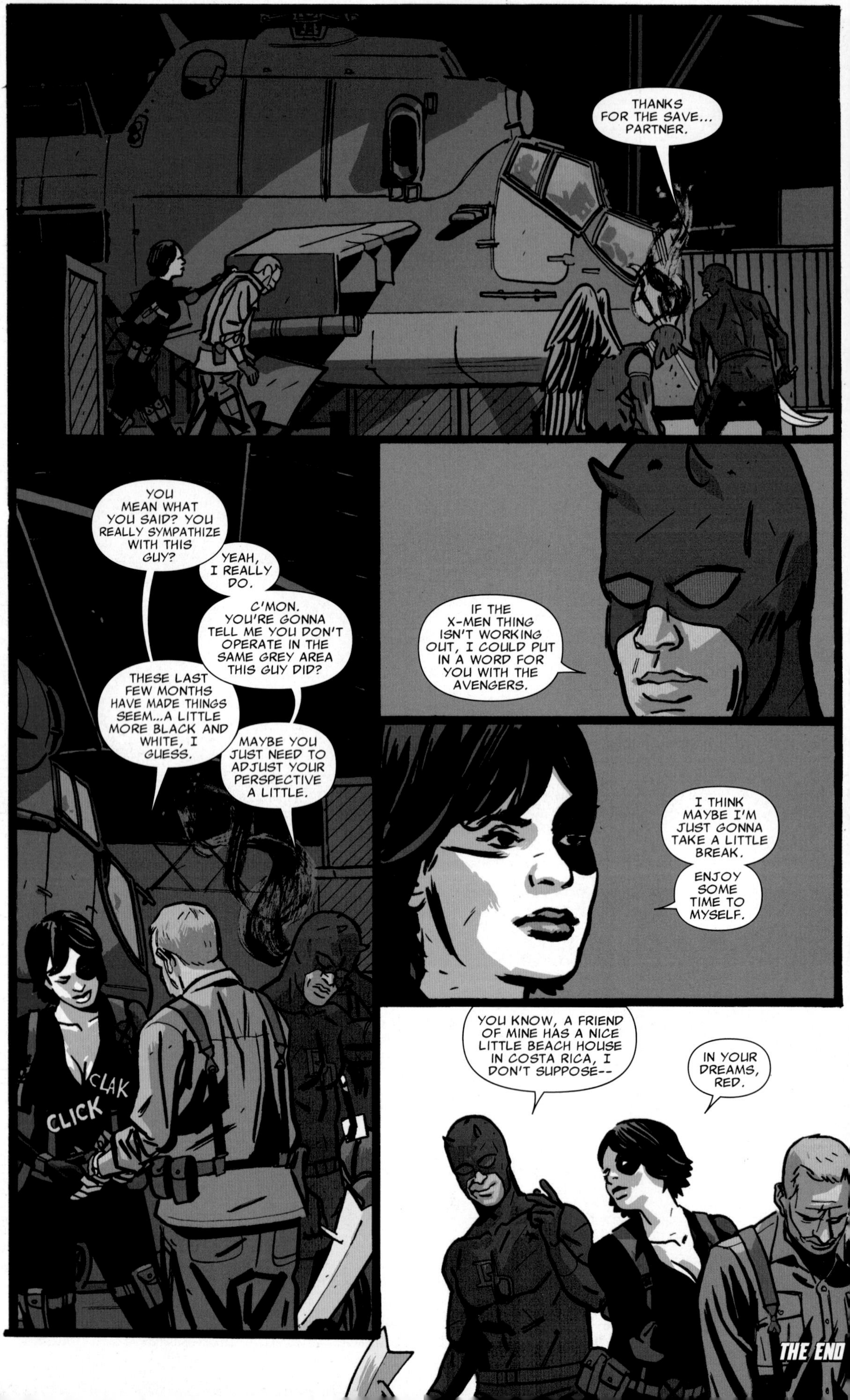
THANKS FOR THE SAVE... PARTNER.
YOU MEAN WHAT YOU SAID? YOU REALLY SYMPATHIZE WITH THIS GUY?
YEAH, I REALLY DO.
C'MON. YOU'RE GONNA TELL ME YOU DON'T OPERATE IN THE SAME GREY AREA THIS GUY DID?
THESE LAST FEW MONTHS HAVE MADE THINGS SEEM...A LITTLE MORE BLACK AND WHITE, I GUESS.
MAYBE YOU JUST NEED TO ADJUST YOUR PERSPECTIVE A LITTLE.
CLAK
CLICK
IF THE X-MEN THING ISN'T WORKING OUT, I COULD PUT IN A WORD FOR YOU WITH THE AVENGERS.
I THINK MAYBE I'M JUST GONNA TAKE A LITTLE BREAK.
ENJOY SOME TIME TO MYSELF.
YOU KNOW, A FRIEND OF MINE HAS A NICE LITTLE BEACH HOUSE IN COSTA RICA, I DON'T SUPPOSE--
IN YOUR DREAMS, RED.
THE END

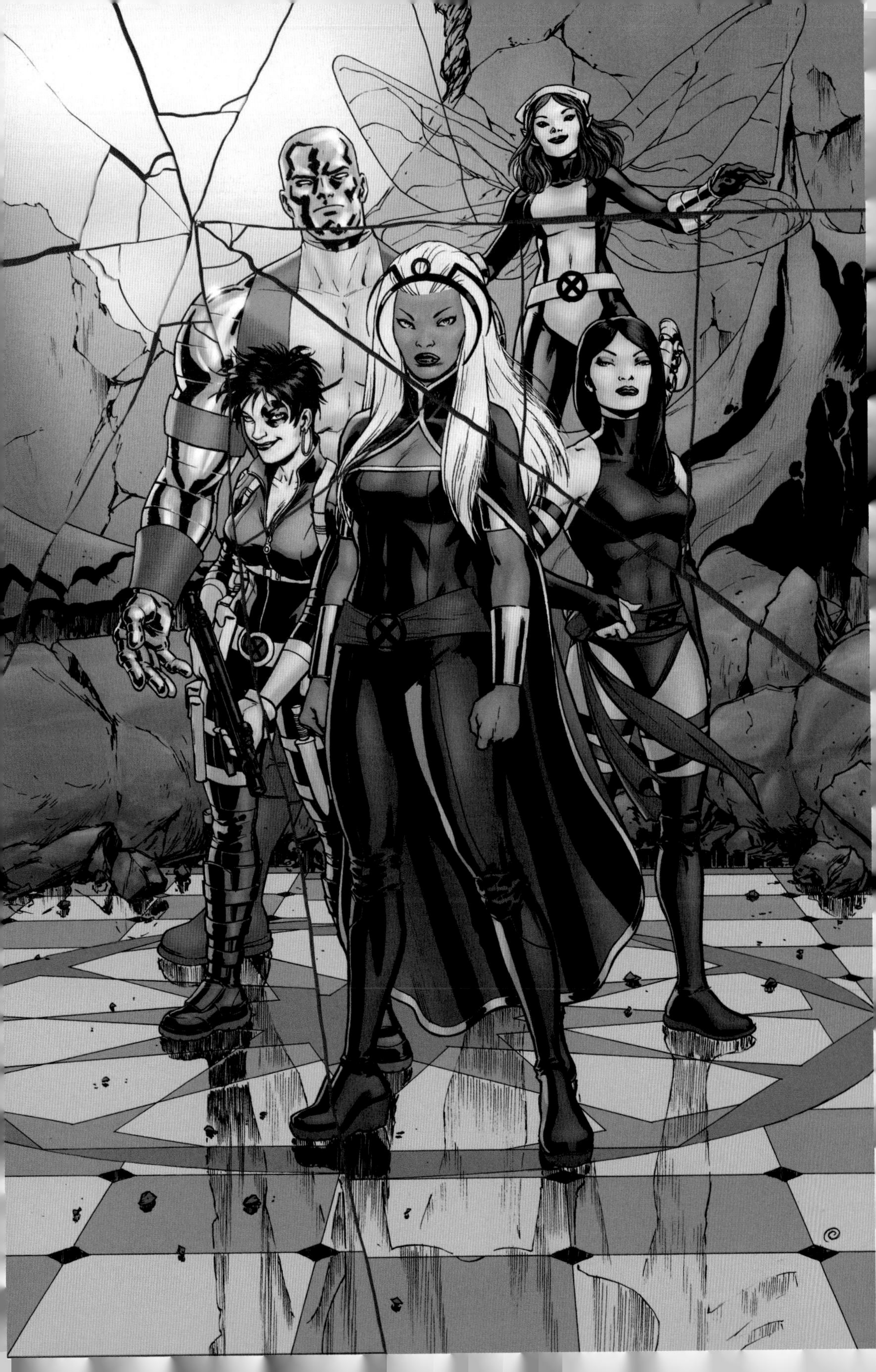

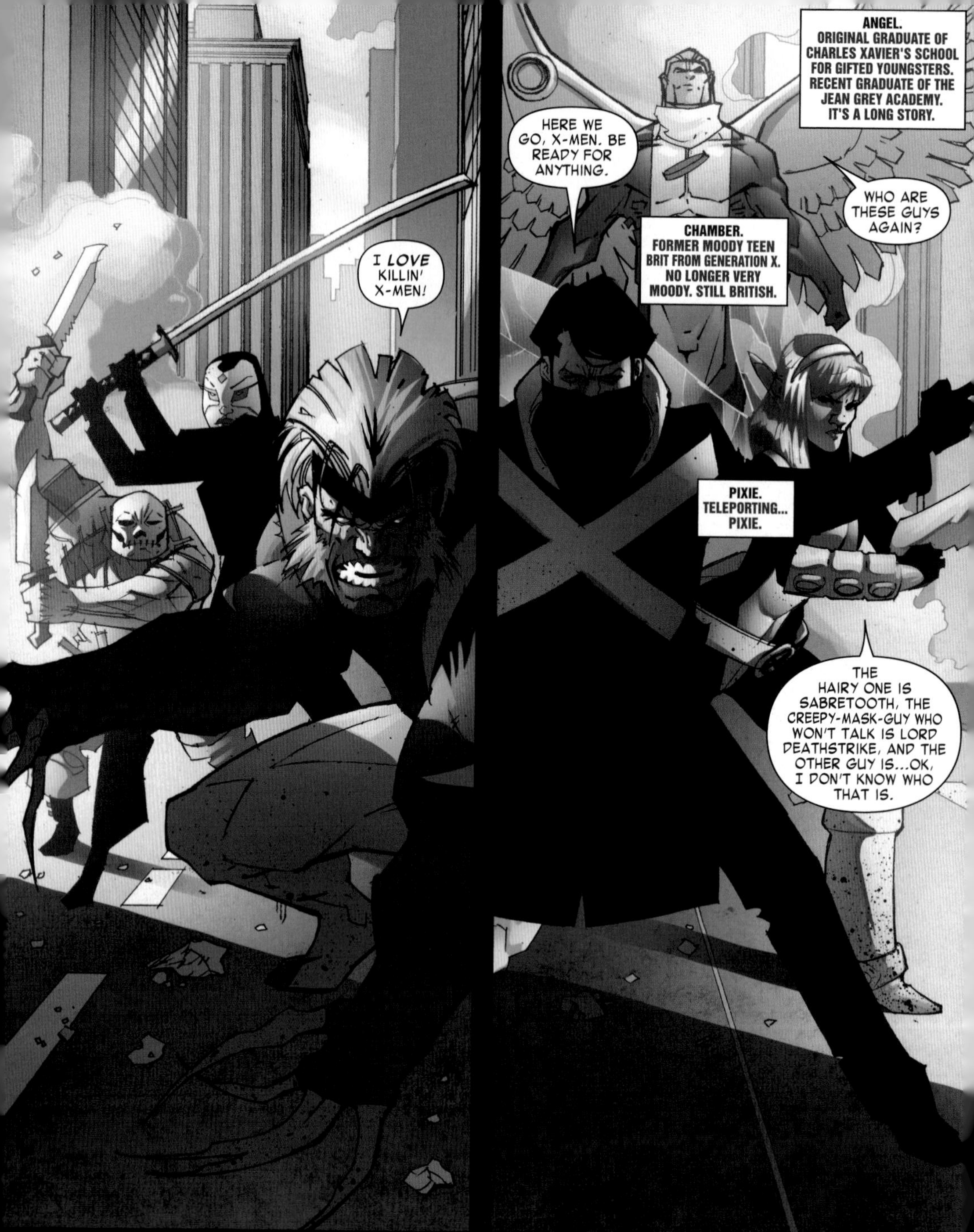
I LOVE KILLIN' X-MEN!
HERE WE GO, X-MEN. BE READY FOR ANYTHING.
ANGEL. ORIGINAL GRADUATE OF CHARLES XAVIER'S SCHOOL FOR GIFTED YOUNGSTERS. RECENT GRADUATE OF THE JEAN GREY ACADEMY. IT'S A LONG STORY.
CHAMBER. FORMER MOODY TEEN BRIT FROM GENERATION X. NO LONGER VERY MOODY. STILL BRITISH.
WHO ARE THESE GUYS AGAIN?
PIXIE. TELEPORTING... PIXIE.
THE HAIRY ONE IS SABRETOOTH, THE CREEPY-MASK-GUY WHO WON'T TALK IS LORD DEATHSTRIKE, AND THE OTHER GUY IS...OK, I DON'T KNOW WHO THAT IS.
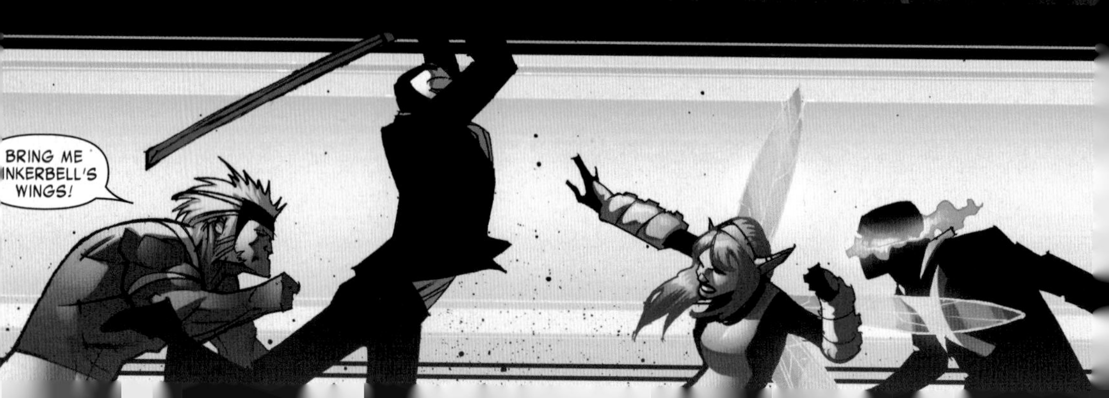
BRING ME INKERBELL'S WINGS!

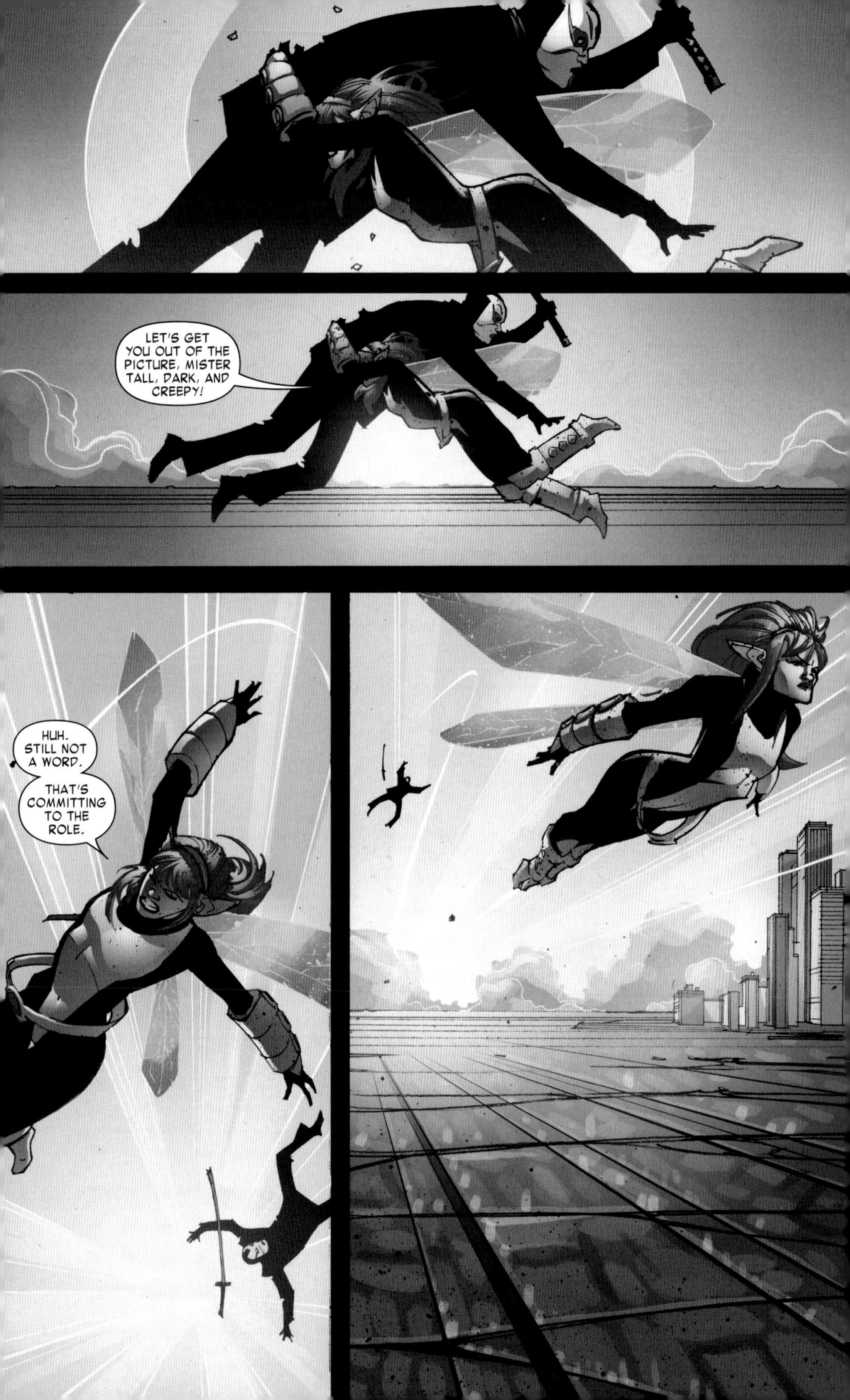
LET'S GET YOU OUT OF THE PICTURE, MISTER TALL, DARK, AND CREEPY!
HUH. STILL NOT A WORD.
THAT'S COMMITTING TO THE ROLE.

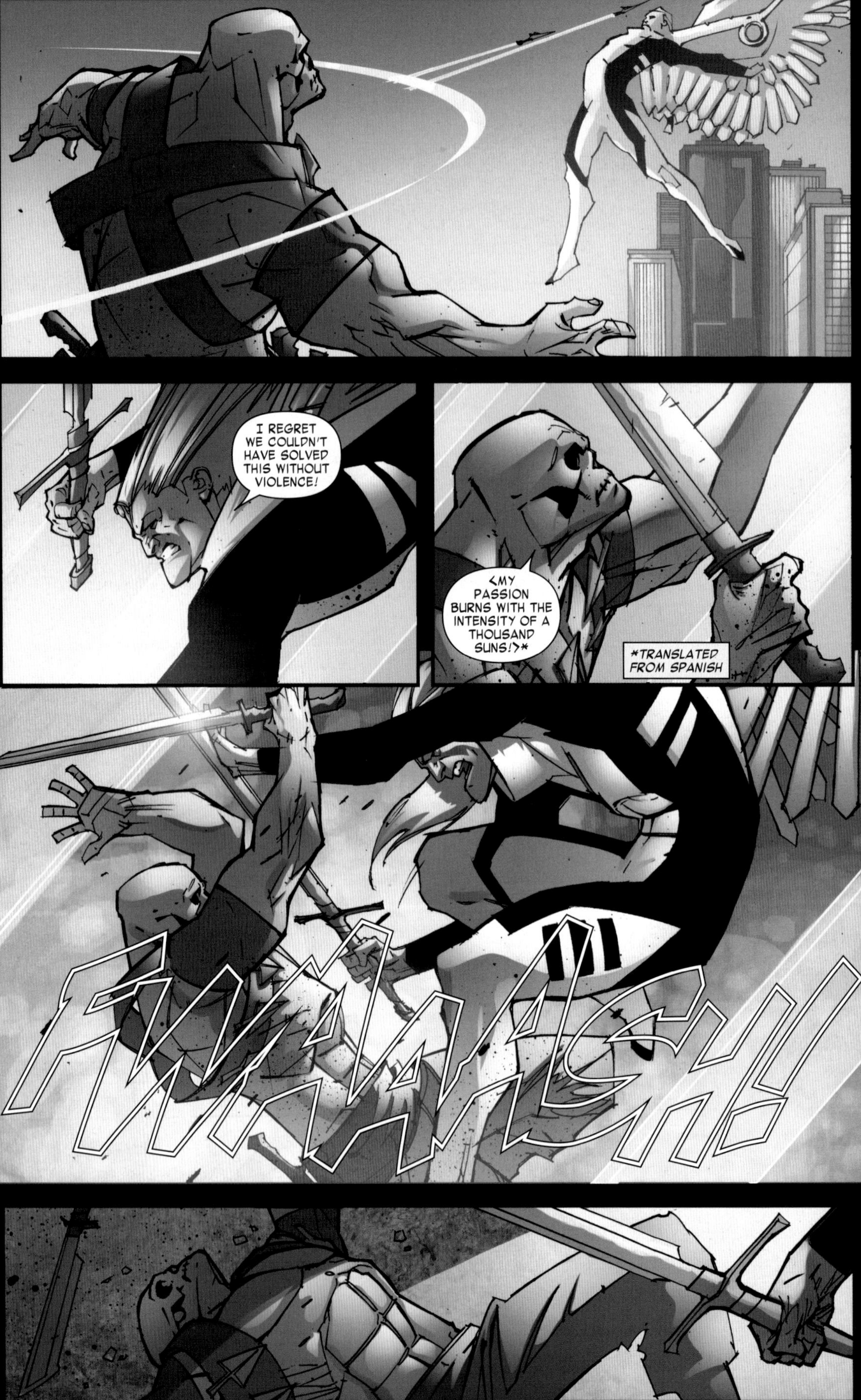
I REGRET WE COULDN'T HAVE SOLVED THIS WITHOUT VIOLENCE!
<MY PASSION BURNS WITH THE INTENSITY OF A THOUSAND SUNS!>*
*TRANSLATED FROM SPANISH

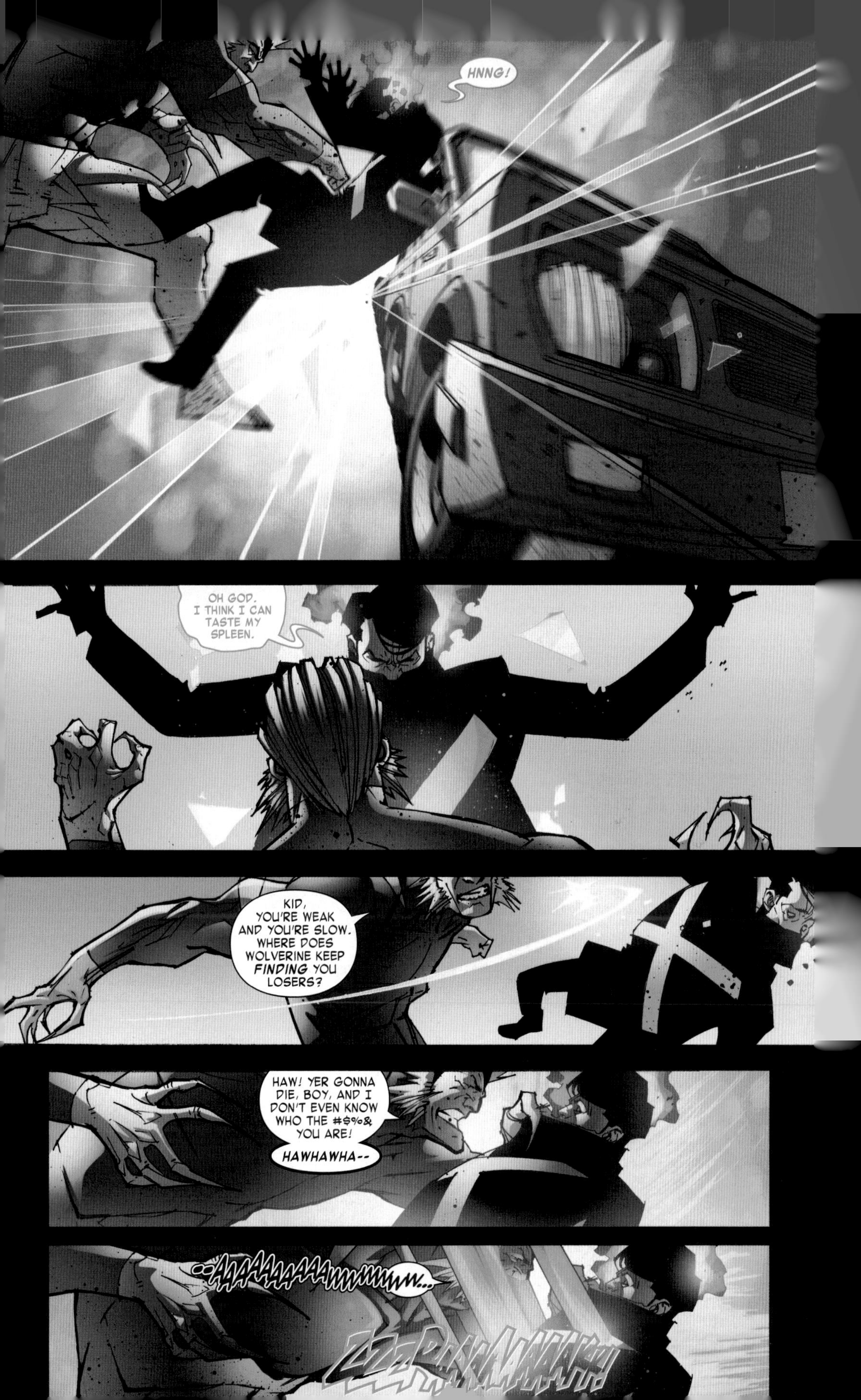
HNNG!
OH GOD. I THINK I CAN TASTE MY SPLEEN.
KID, YOU'RE WEAK AND YOU'RE SLOW. WHERE DOES WOLVERINE KEEP *FINDING* YOU LOSERS?
HAW! YER GONNA DIE, BOY, AND I DON'T EVEN KNOW WHO THE #$%& YOU ARE!
HAWHAWHA--
--AAAAAAAAAAWWWWWWW...

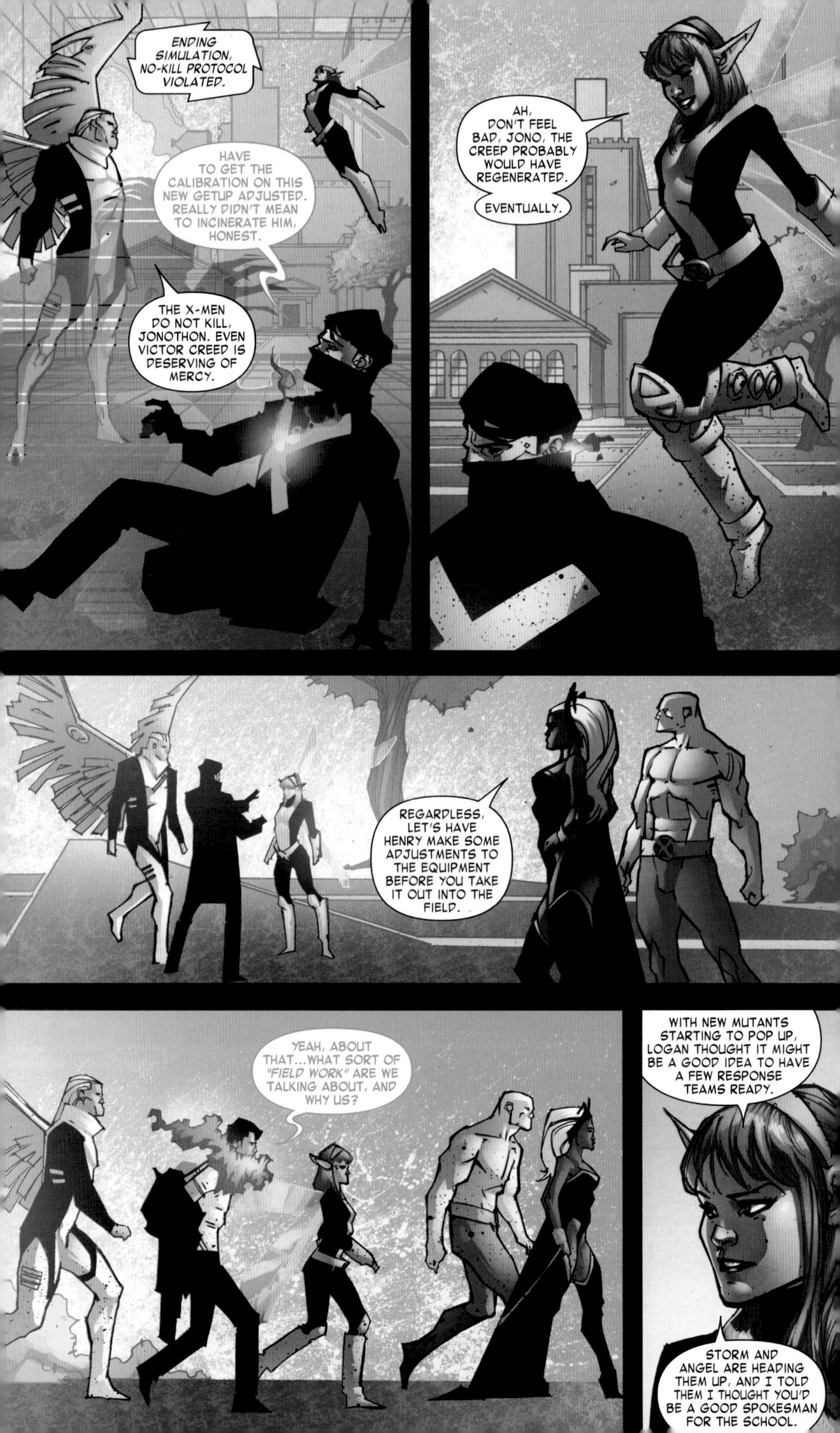
ENDING SIMULATION, NO-KILL PROTOCOL VIOLATED.
HAVE TO GET THE CALIBRATION ON THIS NEW GETUP ADJUSTED. REALLY DIDN'T MEAN TO INCINERATE HIM, HONEST.
THE X-MEN DO NOT KILL, JONOTHON. EVEN VICTOR CREED IS DESERVING OF MERCY.
AH, DON'T FEEL BAD, JONO, THE CREEP PROBABLY WOULD HAVE REGENERATED.
EVENTUALLY.
REGARDLESS, LET'S HAVE HENRY MAKE SOME ADJUSTMENTS TO THE EQUIPMENT BEFORE YOU TAKE IT OUT INTO THE FIELD.
YEAH, ABOUT THAT...WHAT SORT OF "FIELD WORK" ARE WE TALKING ABOUT, AND WHY US?
WITH NEW MUTANTS STARTING TO POP UP, LOGAN THOUGHT IT MIGHT BE A GOOD IDEA TO HAVE A FEW RESPONSE TEAMS READY.
STORM AND ANGEL ARE HEADING THEM UP, AND I TOLD THEM I THOUGHT YOU'D BE A GOOD SPOKESMAN FOR THE SCHOOL.

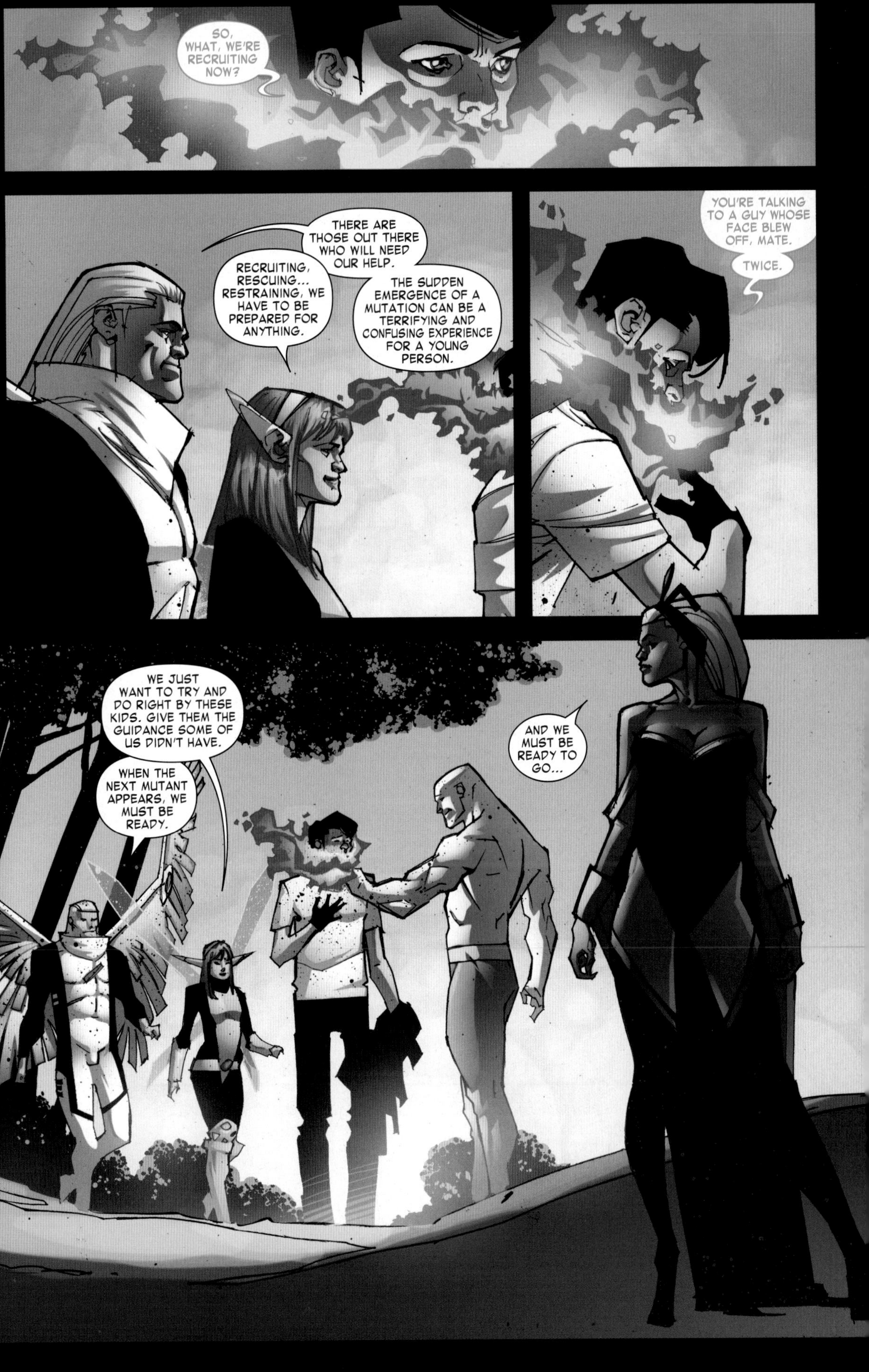
SO, WHAT, WE'RE RECRUITING NOW?
RECRUITING, RESCUING... RESTRAINING, WE HAVE TO BE PREPARED FOR ANYTHING.
THERE ARE THOSE OUT THERE WHO WILL NEED OUR HELP.
THE SUDDEN EMERGENCE OF A MUTATION CAN BE A TERRIFYING AND CONFUSING EXPERIENCE FOR A YOUNG PERSON.
YOU'RE TALKING TO A GUY WHOSE FACE BLEW OFF, MATE.
TWICE.
WE JUST WANT TO TRY AND DO RIGHT BY THESE KIDS. GIVE THEM THE GUIDANCE SOME OF US DIDN'T HAVE.
WHEN THE NEXT MUTANT APPEARS, WE MUST BE READY.
AND WE MUST BE READY TO GO...

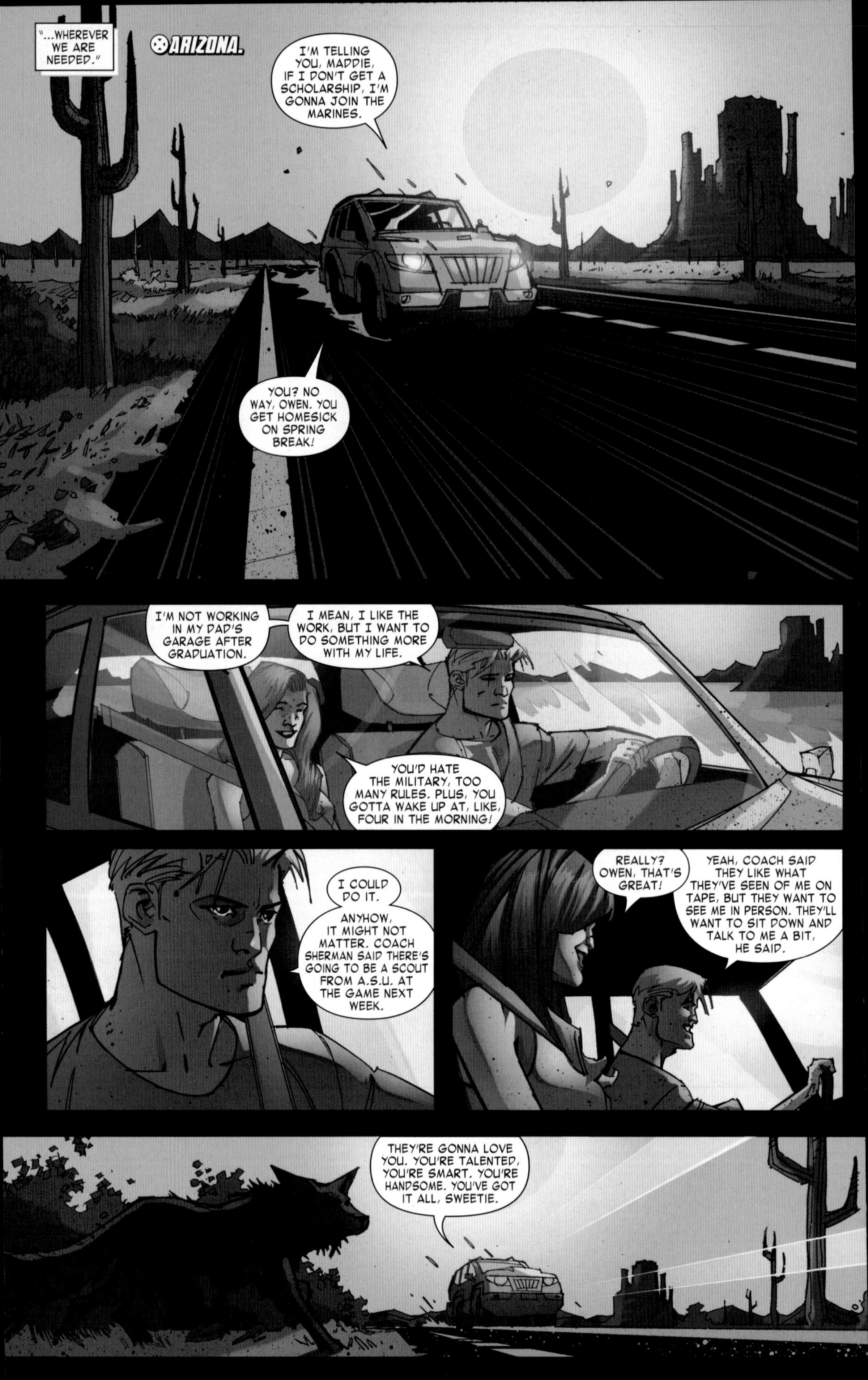
"...WHEREVER WE ARE NEEDED."
ARIZONA.
I'M TELLING YOU, MADDIE, IF I DON'T GET A SCHOLARSHIP, I'M GONNA JOIN THE MARINES.
YOU? NO WAY, OWEN. YOU GET HOMESICK ON SPRING BREAK!
I'M NOT WORKING IN MY DAD'S GARAGE AFTER GRADUATION.
I MEAN, I LIKE THE WORK, BUT I WANT TO DO SOMETHING MORE WITH MY LIFE.
YOU'D HATE THE MILITARY, TOO MANY RULES. PLUS, YOU GOTTA WAKE UP AT, LIKE, FOUR IN THE MORNING!
I COULD DO IT.
ANYHOW, IT MIGHT NOT MATTER. COACH SHERMAN SAID THERE'S GOING TO BE A SCOUT FROM A.S.U. AT THE GAME NEXT WEEK.
REALLY? OWEN, THAT'S GREAT!
YEAH, COACH SAID THEY LIKE WHAT THEY'VE SEEN OF ME ON TAPE, BUT THEY WANT TO SEE ME IN PERSON. THEY'LL WANT TO SIT DOWN AND TALK TO ME A BIT, HE SAID.
THEY'RE GONNA LOVE YOU. YOU'RE TALENTED, YOU'RE SMART. YOU'RE HANDSOME. YOU'VE GOT IT ALL, SWEETIE.

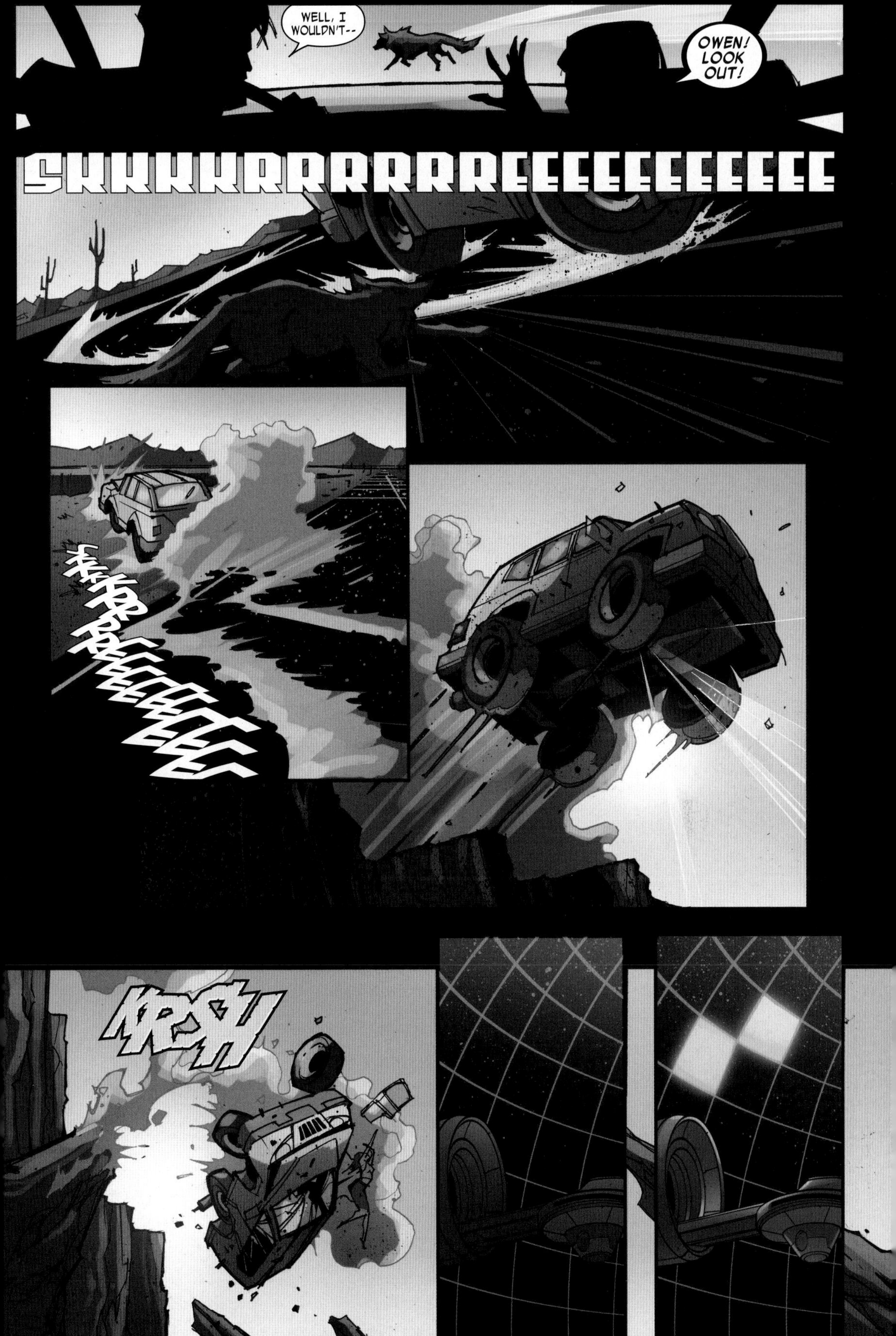
WELL, I WOULDN'T--
OWEN! LOOK OUT!
SKKKKRRRRRREEEEEEEEEE
KRSH

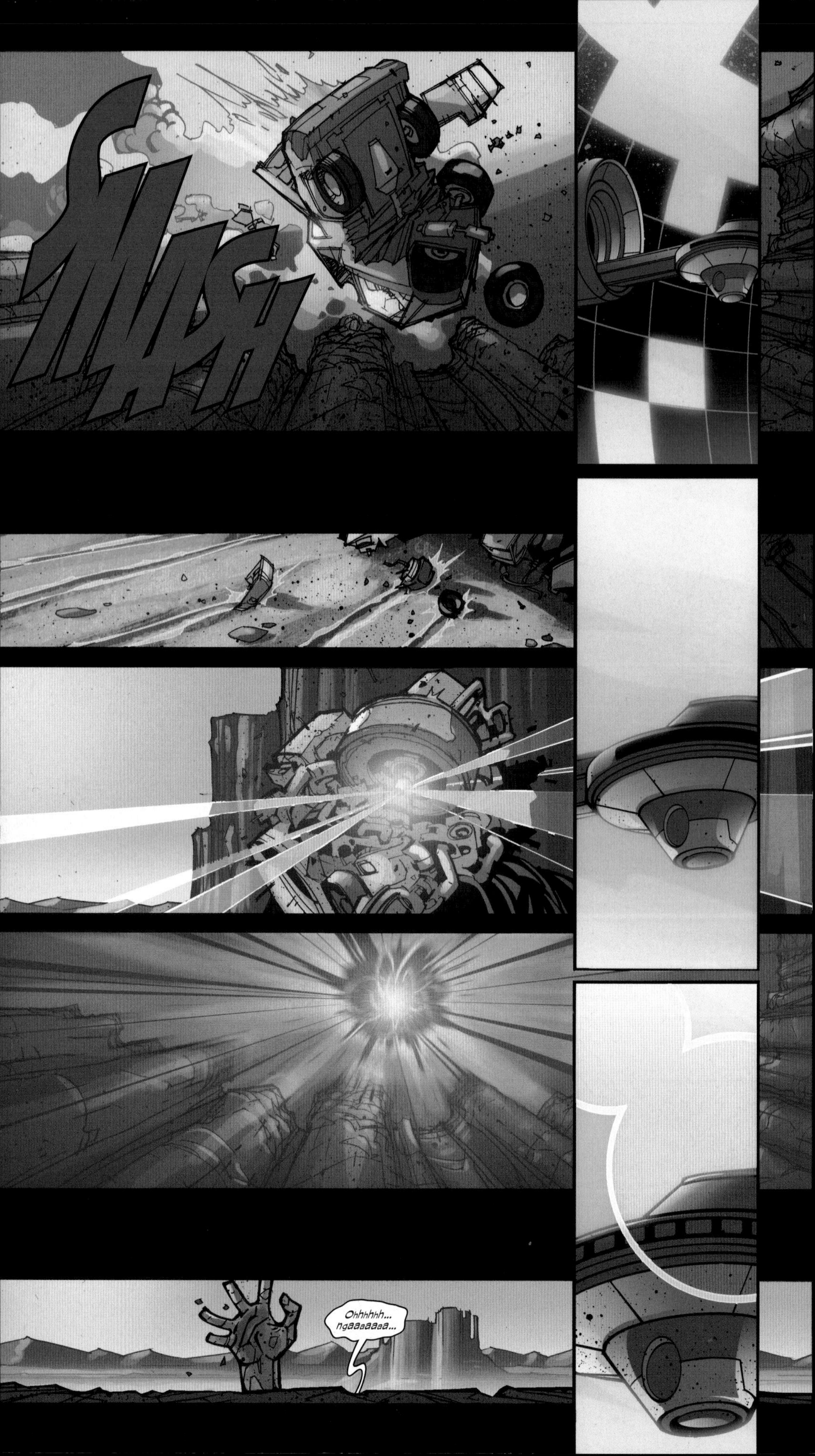
SMASH
Ohhhhhh... ngaaaaaaa...

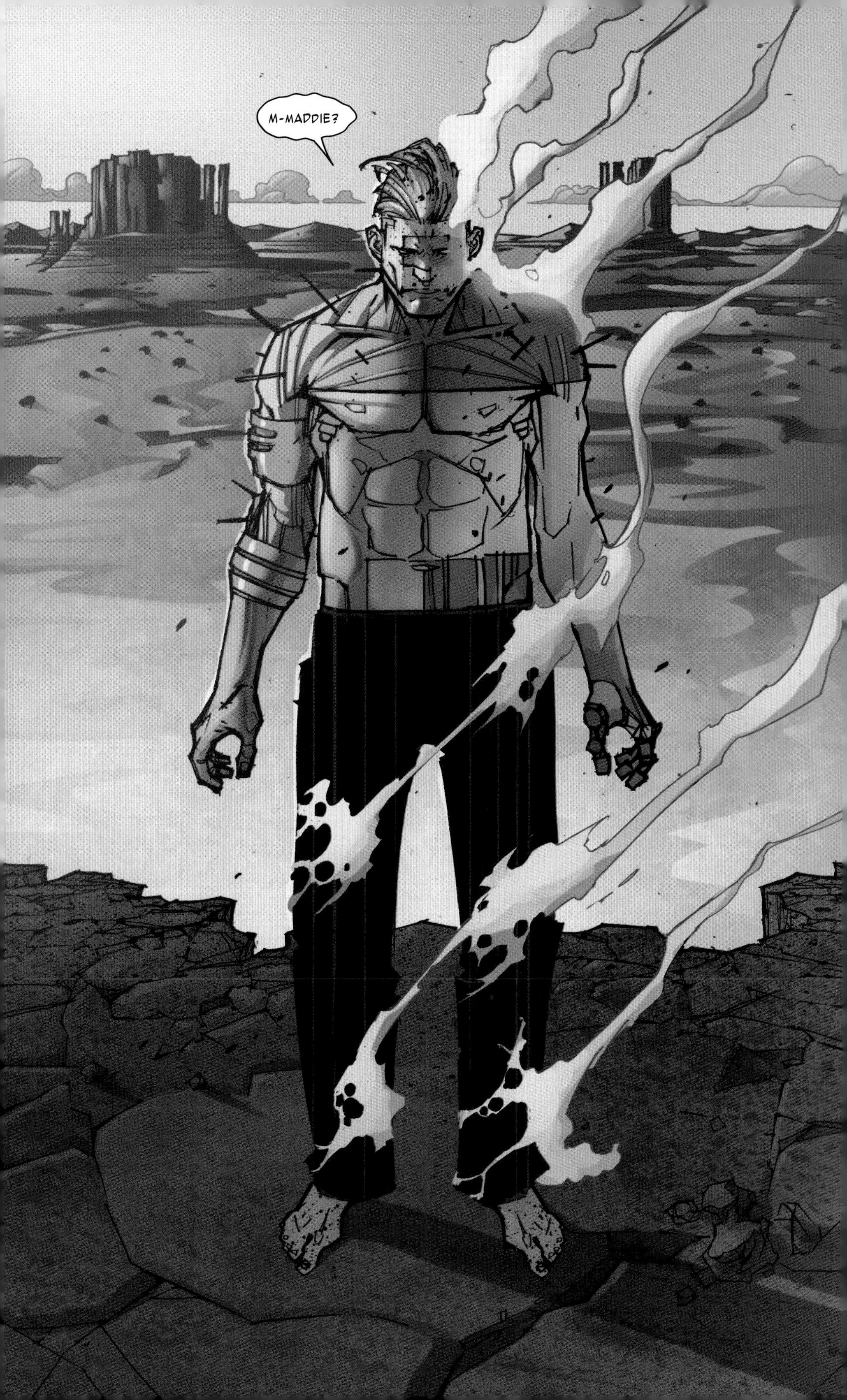
M-MADDIE?

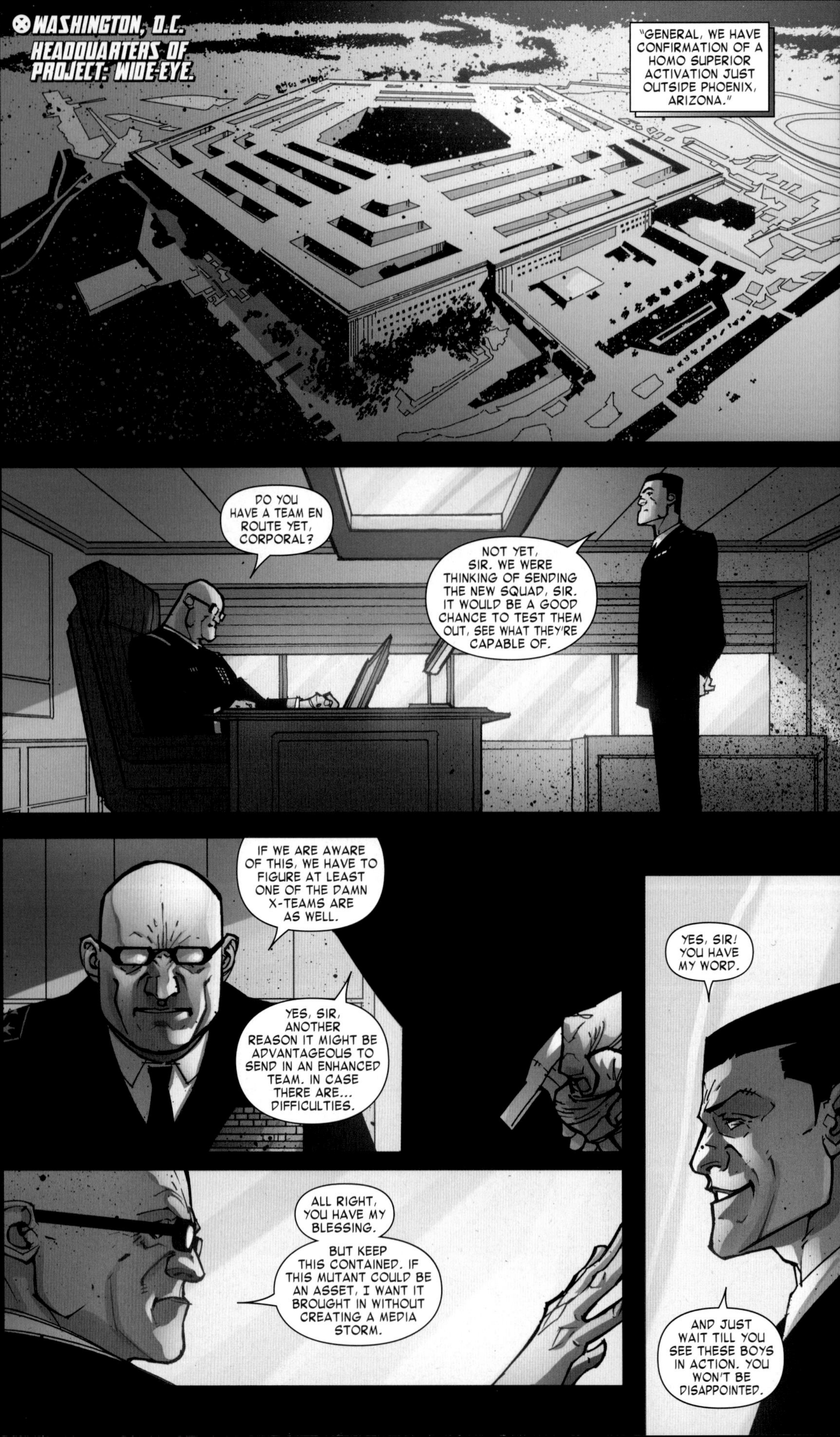
WASHINGTON, D.C.
HEADQUARTERS OF PROJECT: WIDE-EYE.
"GENERAL, WE HAVE CONFIRMATION OF A HOMO SUPERIOR ACTIVATION JUST OUTSIDE PHOENIX, ARIZONA."
DO YOU HAVE A TEAM EN ROUTE YET, CORPORAL?
NOT YET, SIR. WE WERE THINKING OF SENDING THE NEW SQUAD, SIR. IT WOULD BE A GOOD CHANCE TO TEST THEM OUT, SEE WHAT THEY'RE CAPABLE OF.
IF WE ARE AWARE OF THIS, WE HAVE TO FIGURE AT LEAST ONE OF THE DAMN X-TEAMS ARE AS WELL.
YES, SIR, ANOTHER REASON IT MIGHT BE ADVANTAGEOUS TO SEND IN AN ENHANCED TEAM. IN CASE THERE ARE... DIFFICULTIES.
ALL RIGHT, YOU HAVE MY BLESSING.
BUT KEEP THIS CONTAINED. IF THIS MUTANT COULD BE AN ASSET, I WANT IT BROUGHT IN WITHOUT CREATING A MEDIA STORM.
YES, SIR! YOU HAVE MY WORD.
AND JUST WAIT TILL YOU SEE THESE BOYS IN ACTION. YOU WON'T BE DISAPPOINTED.

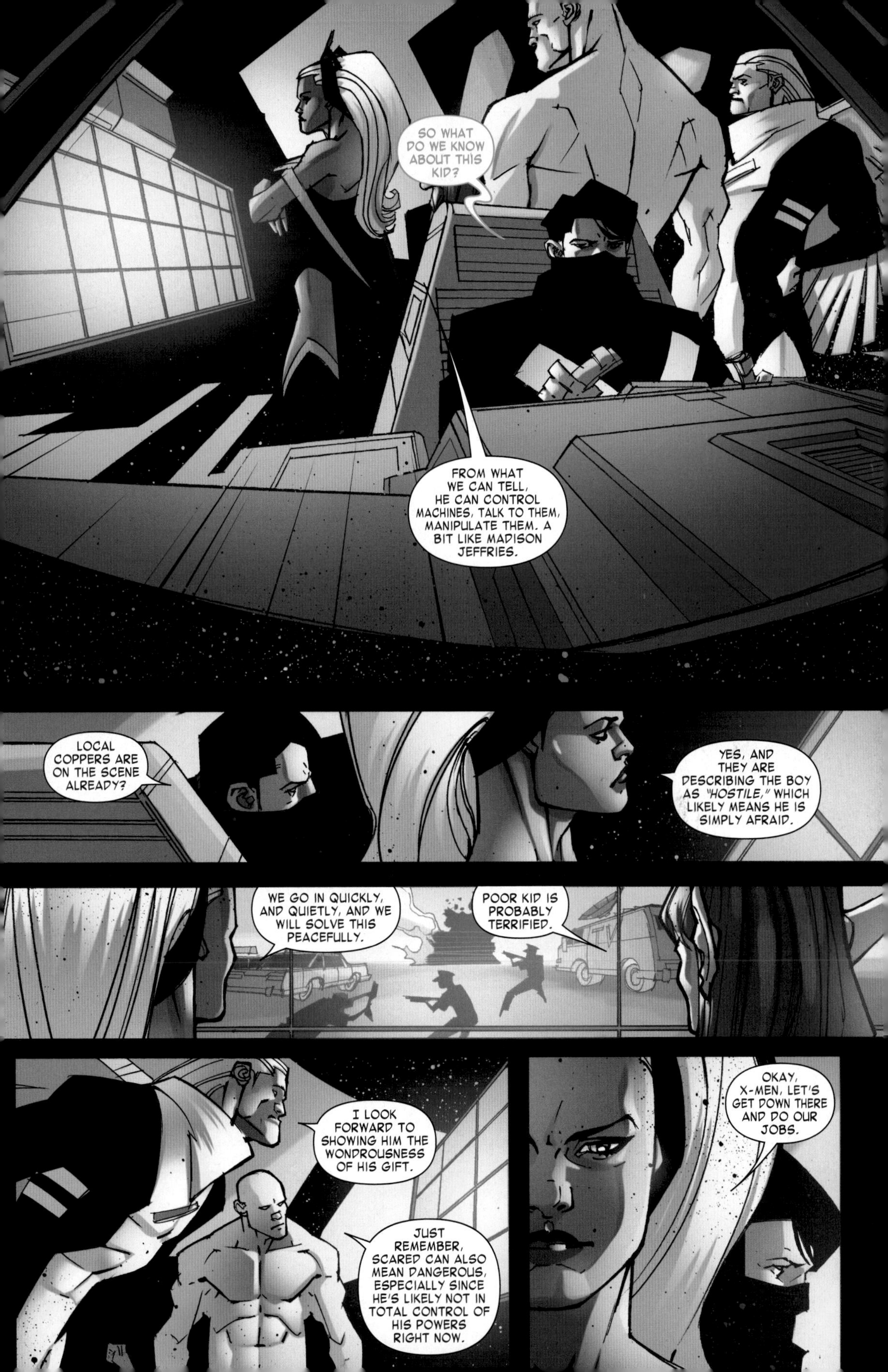
SO WHAT DO WE KNOW ABOUT THIS KID?
FROM WHAT WE CAN TELL, HE CAN CONTROL MACHINES, TALK TO THEM, MANIPULATE THEM. A BIT LIKE MADISON JEFFRIES.
LOCAL COPPERS ARE ON THE SCENE ALREADY?
YES, AND THEY ARE DESCRIBING THE BOY AS "HOSTILE," WHICH LIKELY MEANS HE IS SIMPLY AFRAID.
WE GO IN QUICKLY, AND QUIETLY, AND WE WILL SOLVE THIS PEACEFULLY.
POOR KID IS PROBABLY TERRIFIED.
TV
I LOOK FORWARD TO SHOWING HIM THE WONDROUSNESS OF HIS GIFT.
JUST REMEMBER, SCARED CAN ALSO MEAN DANGEROUS, ESPECIALLY SINCE HE'S LIKELY NOT IN TOTAL CONTROL OF HIS POWERS RIGHT NOW.
OKAY, X-MEN, LET'S GET DOWN THERE AND DO OUR JOBS.

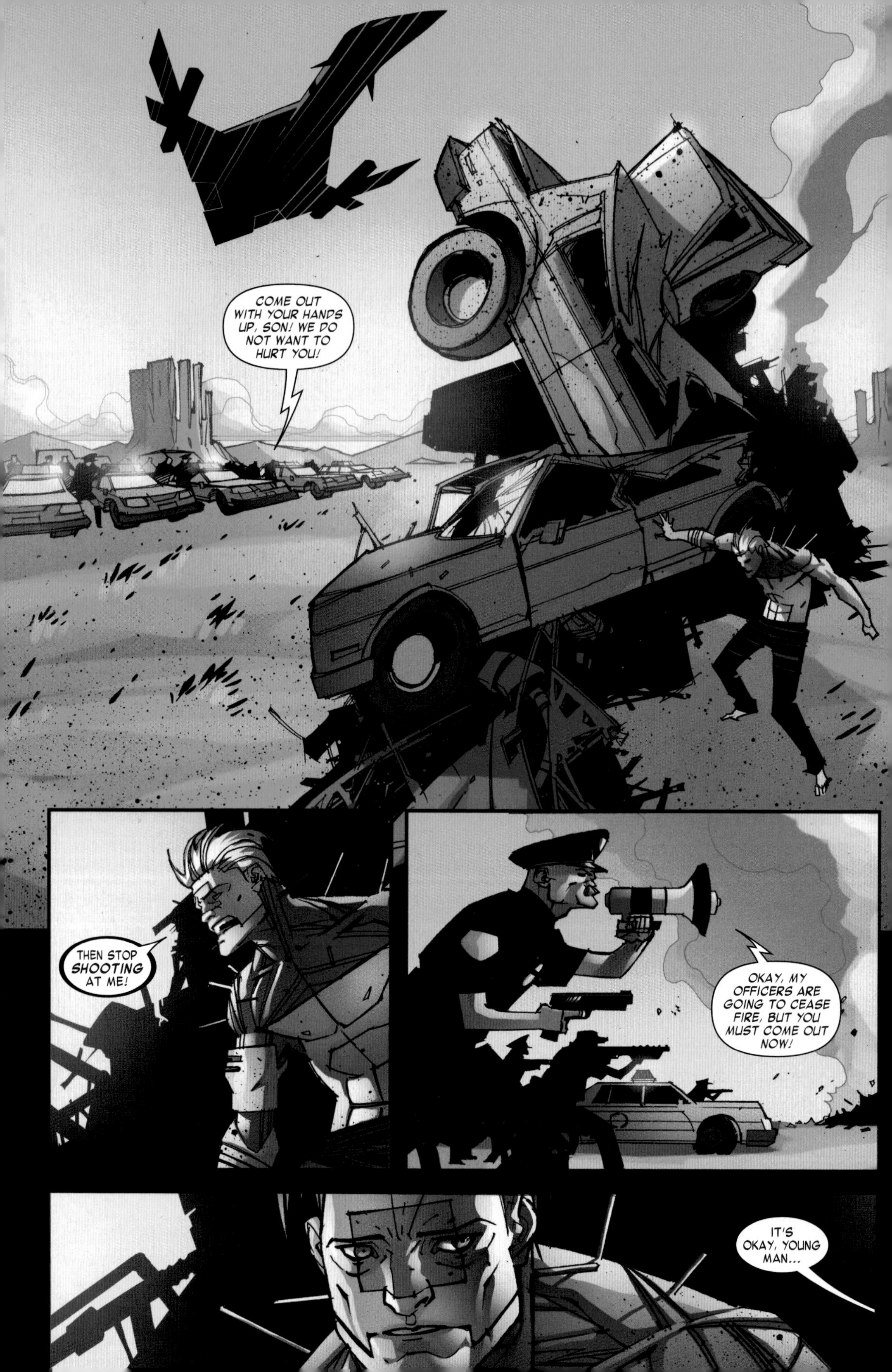
COME OUT WITH YOUR HANDS UP, SON! WE DO NOT WANT TO HURT YOU!
THEN STOP SHOOTING AT ME!
OKAY, MY OFFICERS ARE GOING TO CEASE FIRE, BUT YOU MUST COME OUT NOW!
IT'S OKAY, YOUNG MAN...

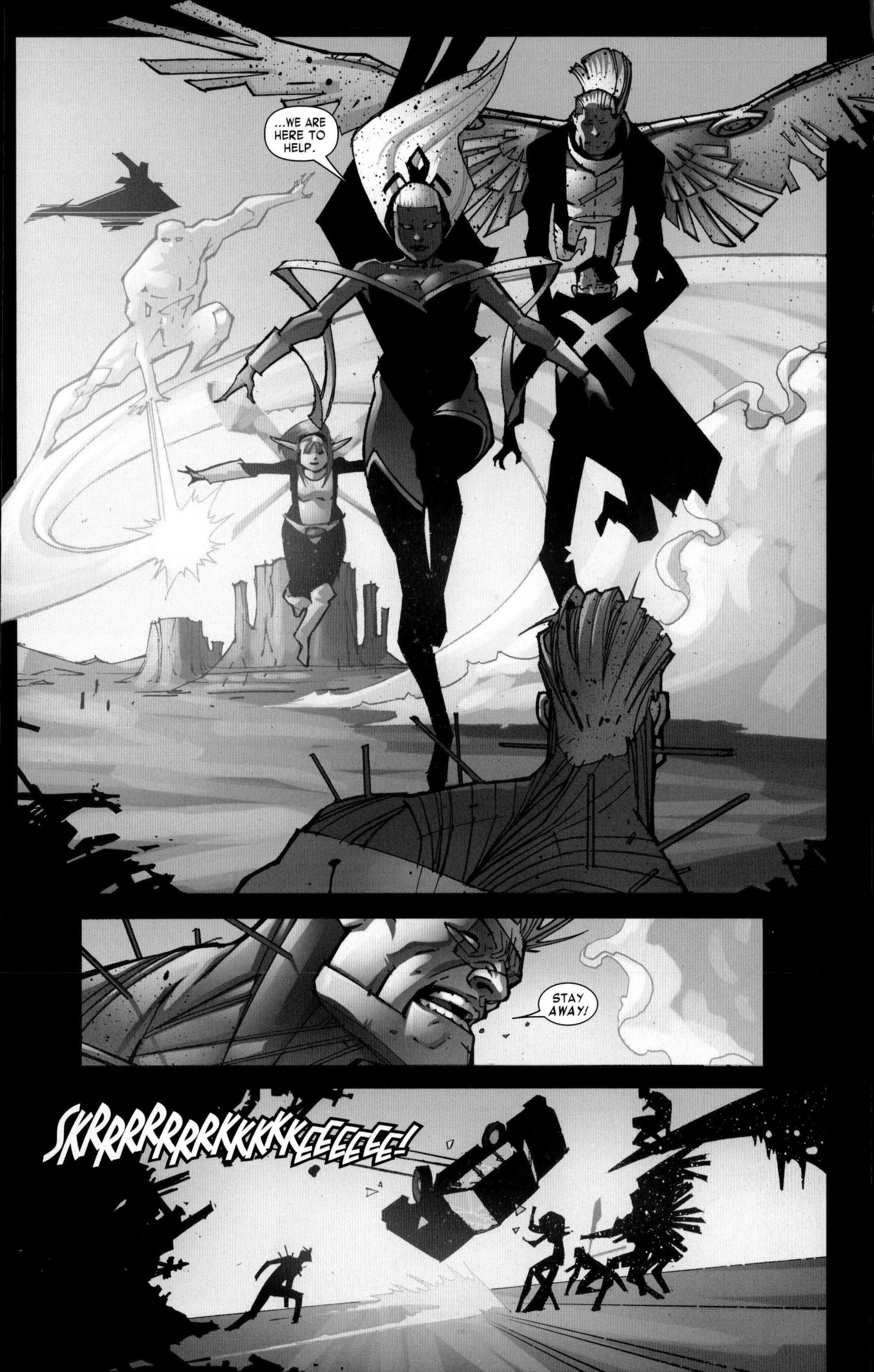
...WE ARE HERE TO HELP.
STAY AWAY!
SKRRRRRRRKKKKKEEEEEE!

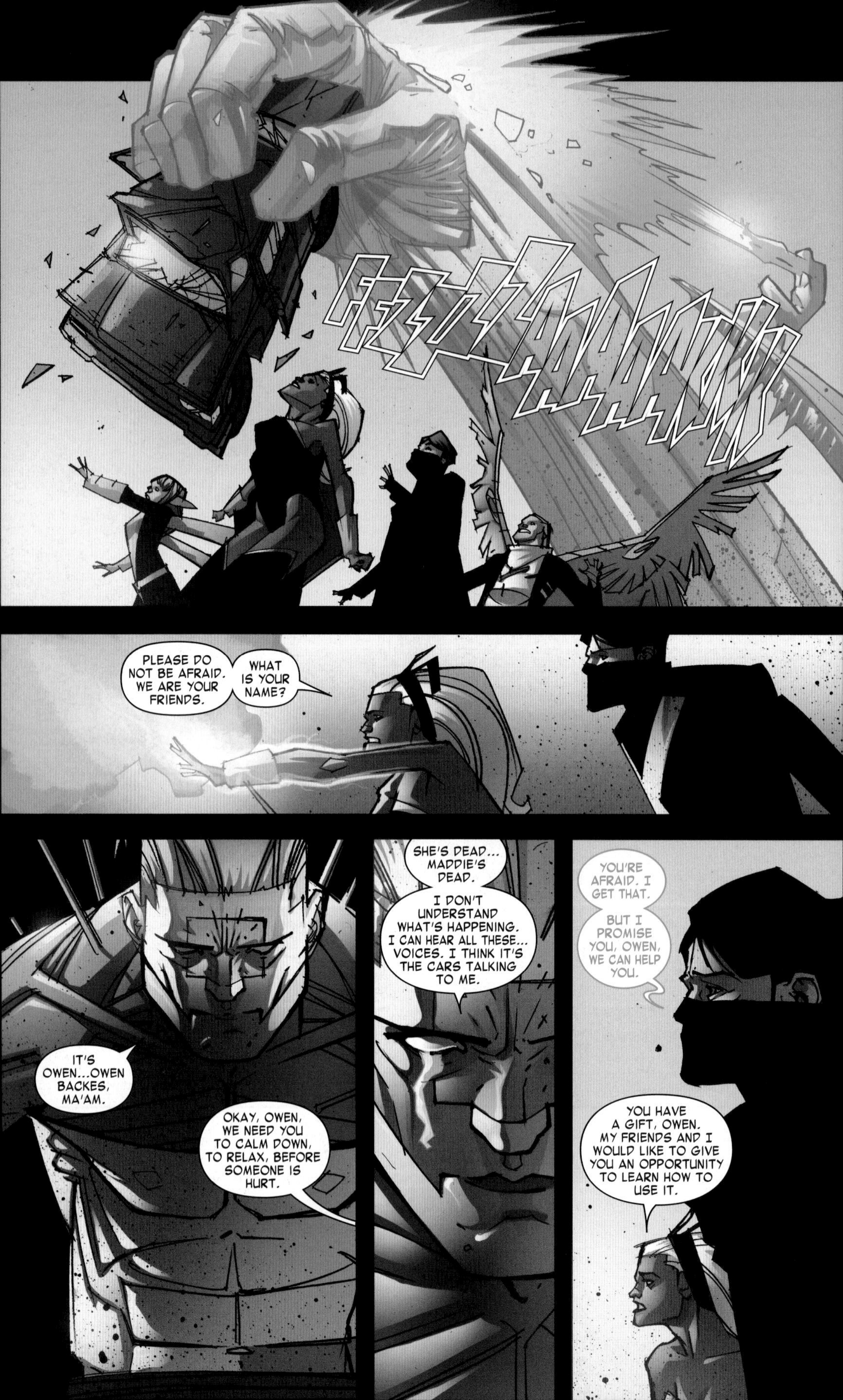
PLEASE DO NOT BE AFRAID. WE ARE YOUR FRIENDS.
WHAT IS YOUR NAME?
IT'S OWEN...OWEN BACKES, MA'AM.
OKAY, OWEN, WE NEED YOU TO CALM DOWN, TO RELAX, BEFORE SOMEONE IS HURT.
SHE'S DEAD... MADDIE'S DEAD.
I DON'T UNDERSTAND WHAT'S HAPPENING. I CAN HEAR ALL THESE... VOICES. I THINK IT'S THE CARS TALKING TO ME.
YOU'RE AFRAID. I GET THAT.
BUT I PROMISE YOU, OWEN, WE CAN HELP YOU.
YOU HAVE A GIFT, OWEN. MY FRIENDS AND I WOULD LIKE TO GIVE YOU AN OPPORTUNITY TO LEARN HOW TO USE IT.

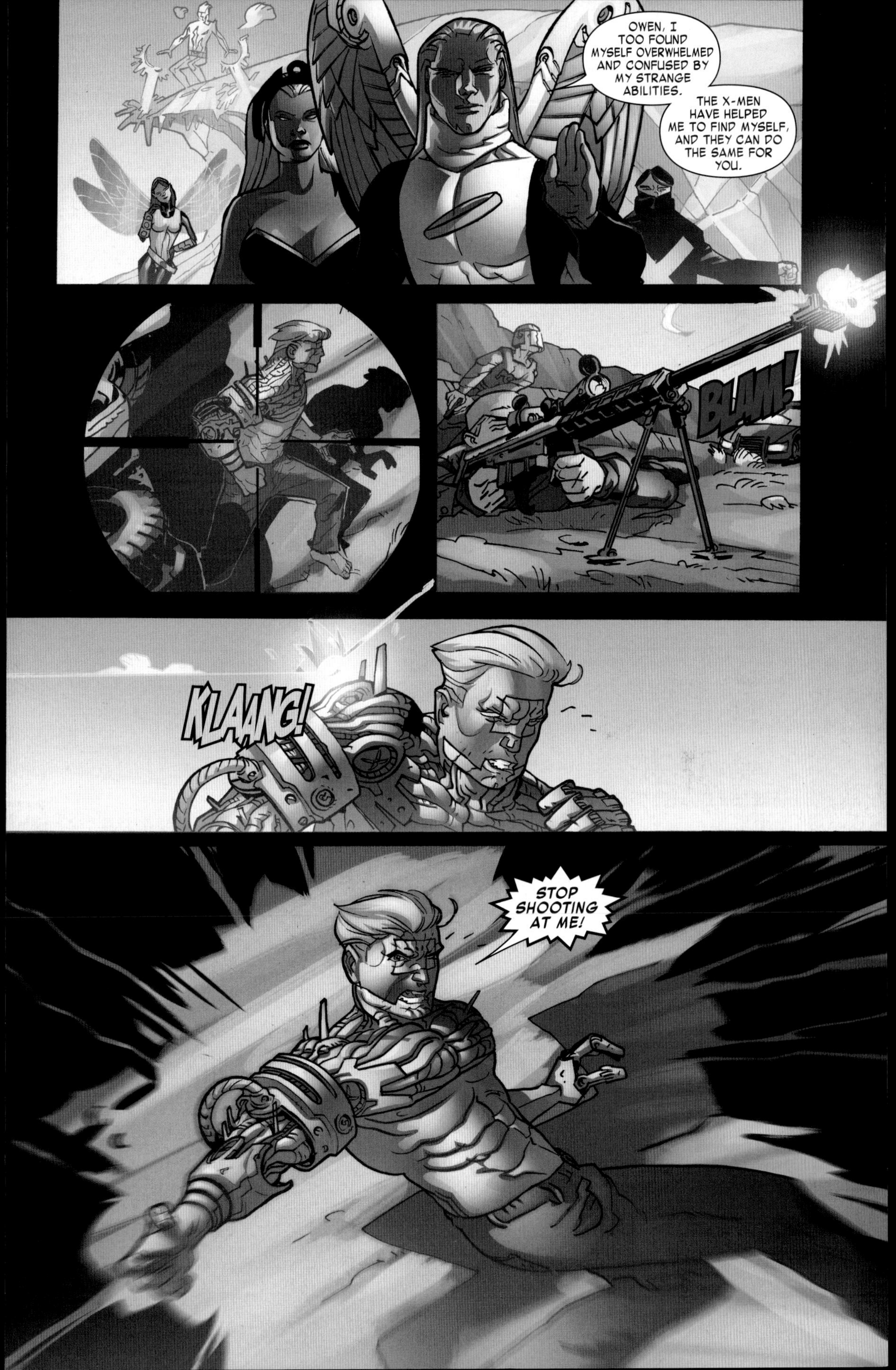
OWEN, I TOO FOUND MYSELF OVERWHELMED AND CONFUSED BY MY STRANGE ABILITIES.
THE X-MEN HAVE HELPED ME TO FIND MYSELF, AND THEY CAN DO THE SAME FOR YOU.
BLAM!
KLAANG!
STOP SHOOTING AT ME!

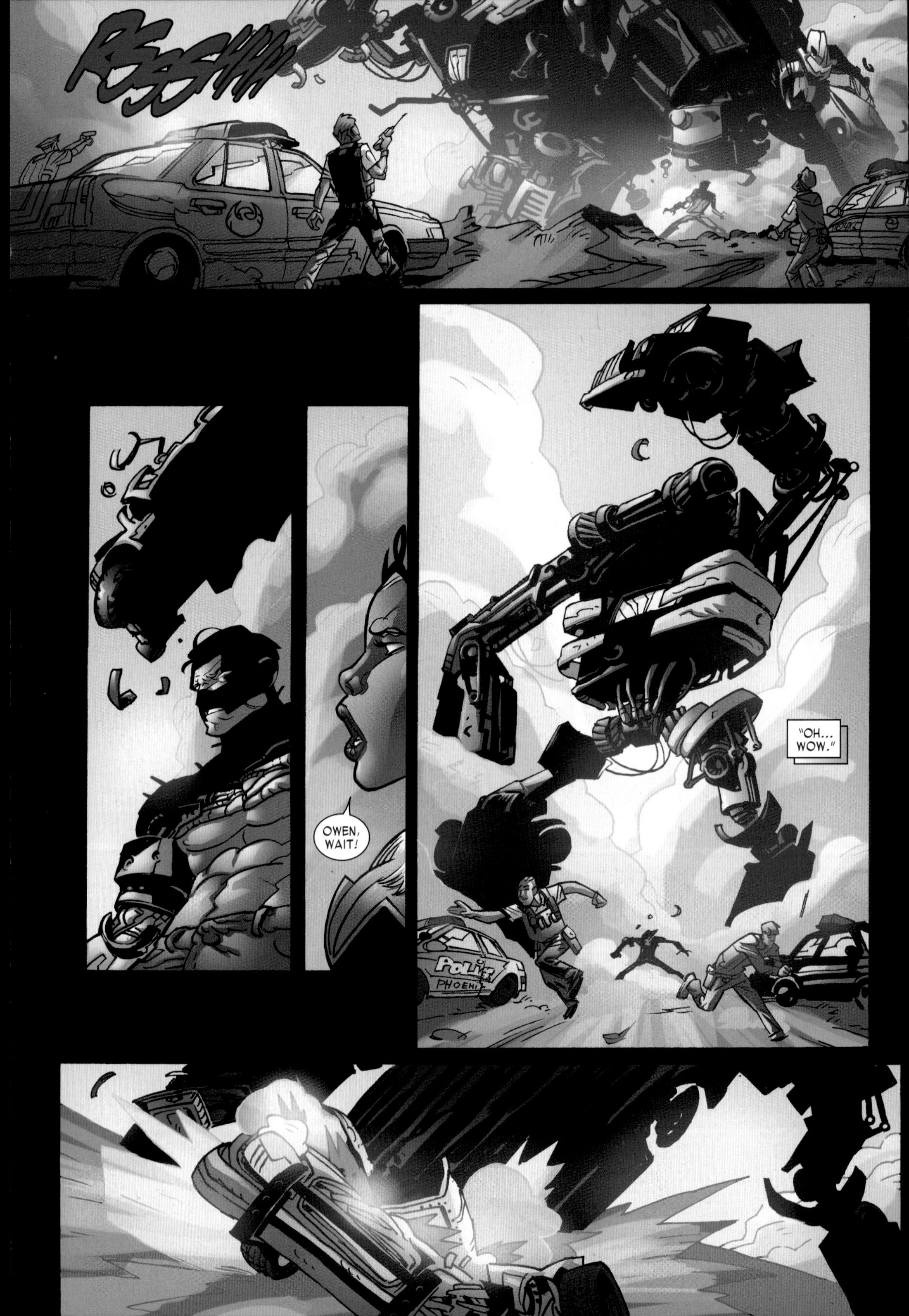
RSSSHHH
OWEN, WAIT!
"OH... WOW."

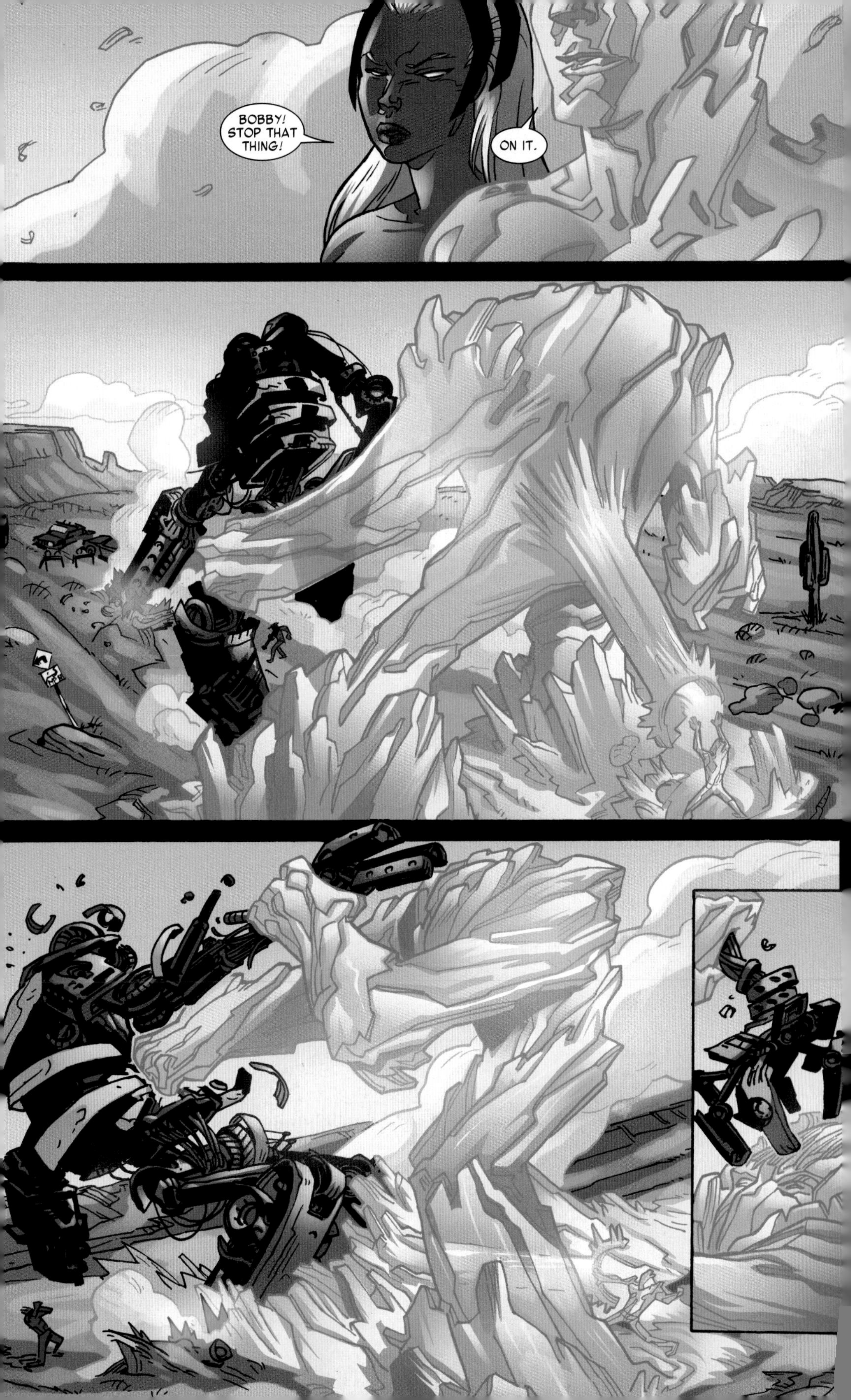
BOBBY! STOP THAT THING!
ON IT.

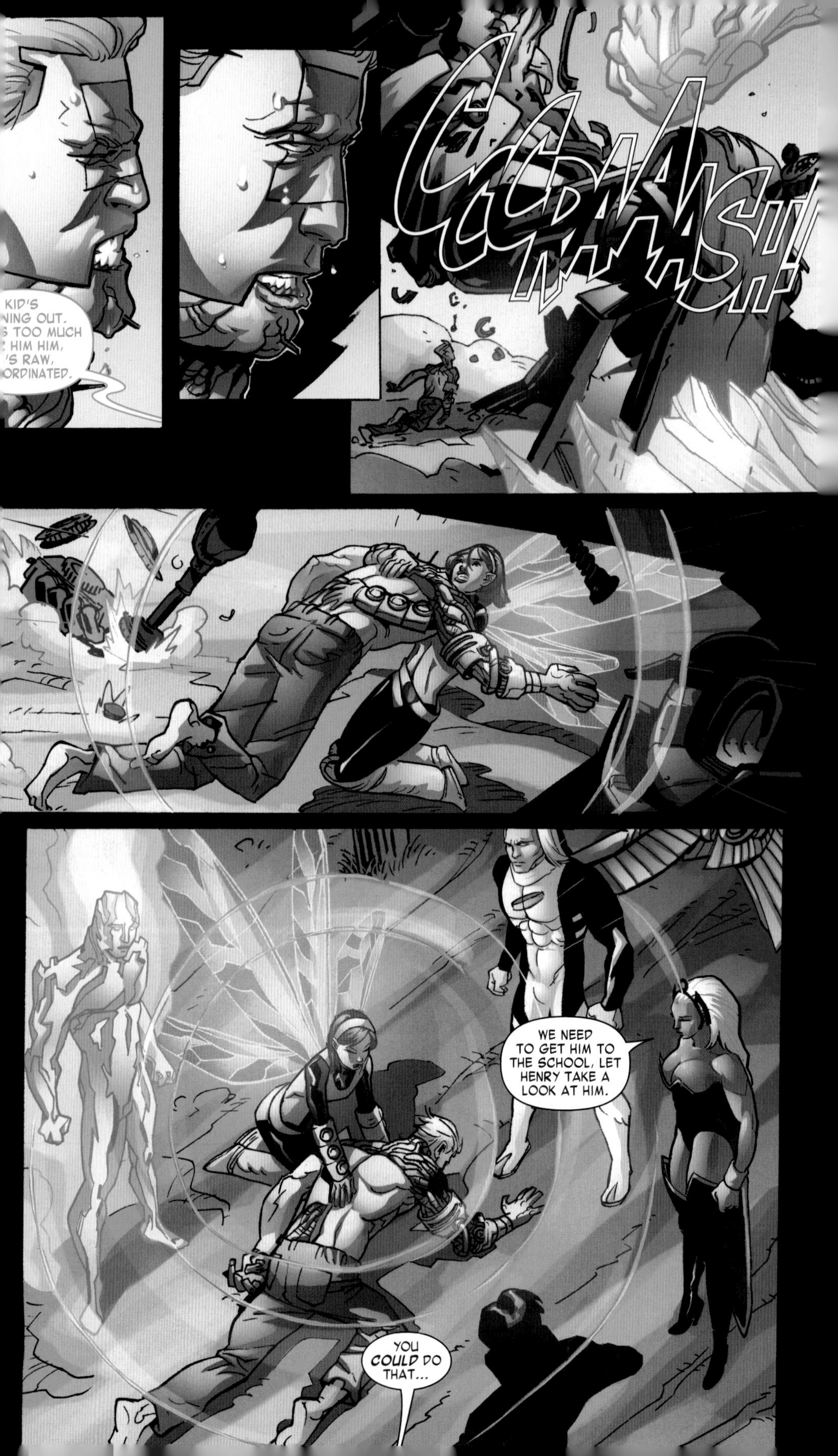
KID'S
NING OUT.
S TOO MUCH
HIM HIM,
'S RAW,
ORDINATED.
WE NEED TO GET HIM TO THE SCHOOL, LET HENRY TAKE A LOOK AT HIM.
YOU COULD DO THAT...

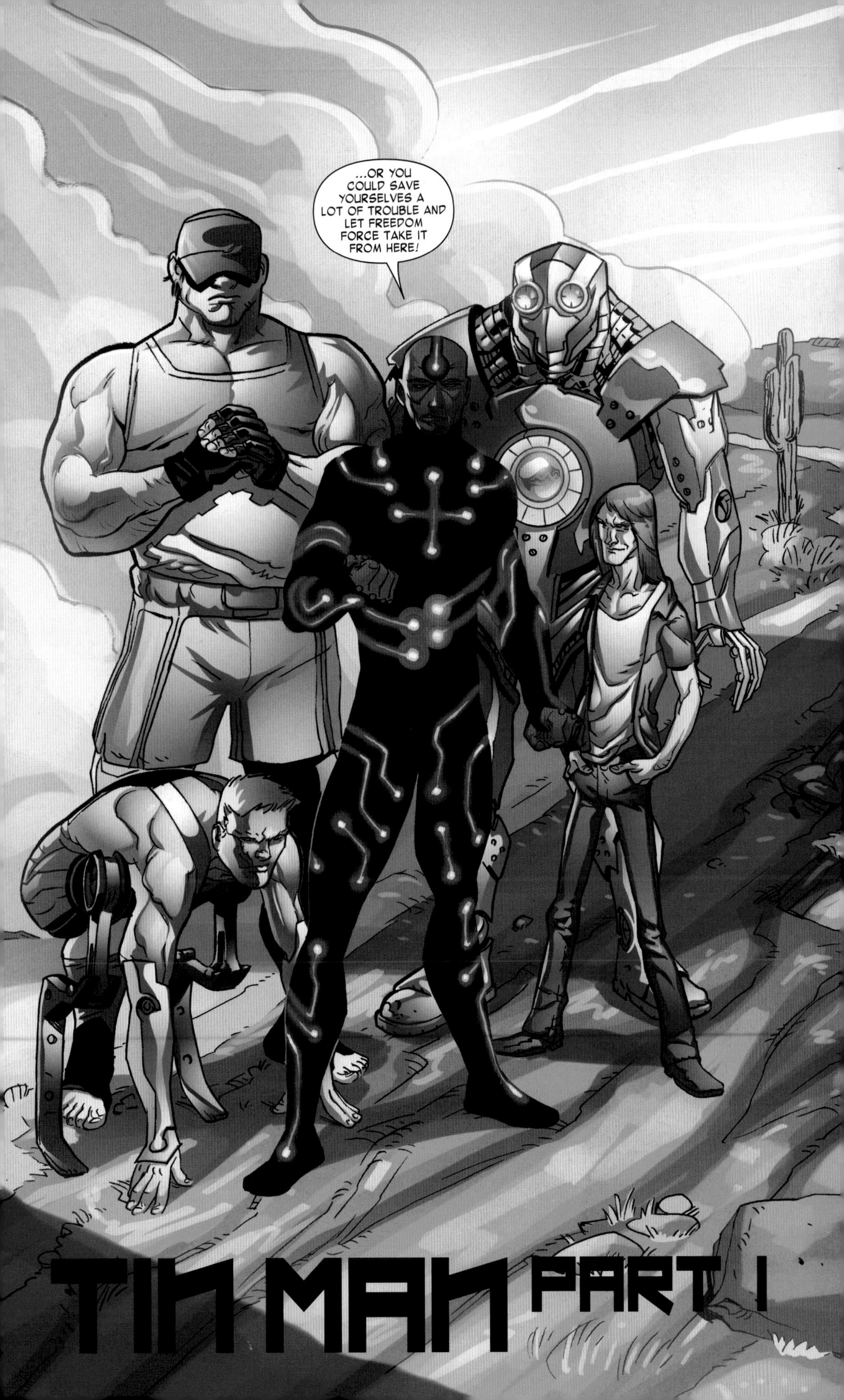
...OR YOU COULD SAVE YOURSELVES A LOT OF TROUBLE AND LET FREEDOM FORCE TAKE IT FROM HERE!
TIN MAN PART I

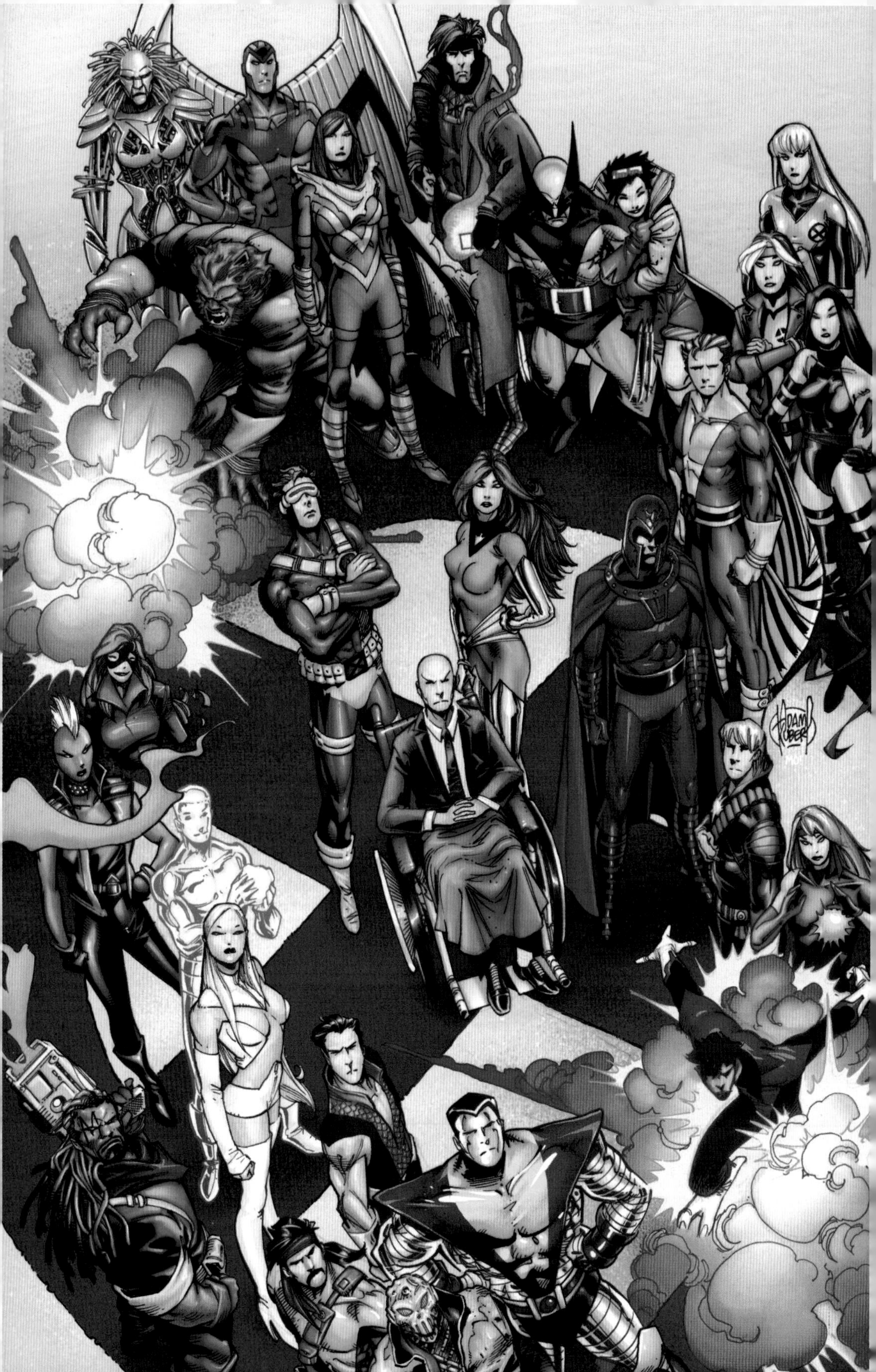

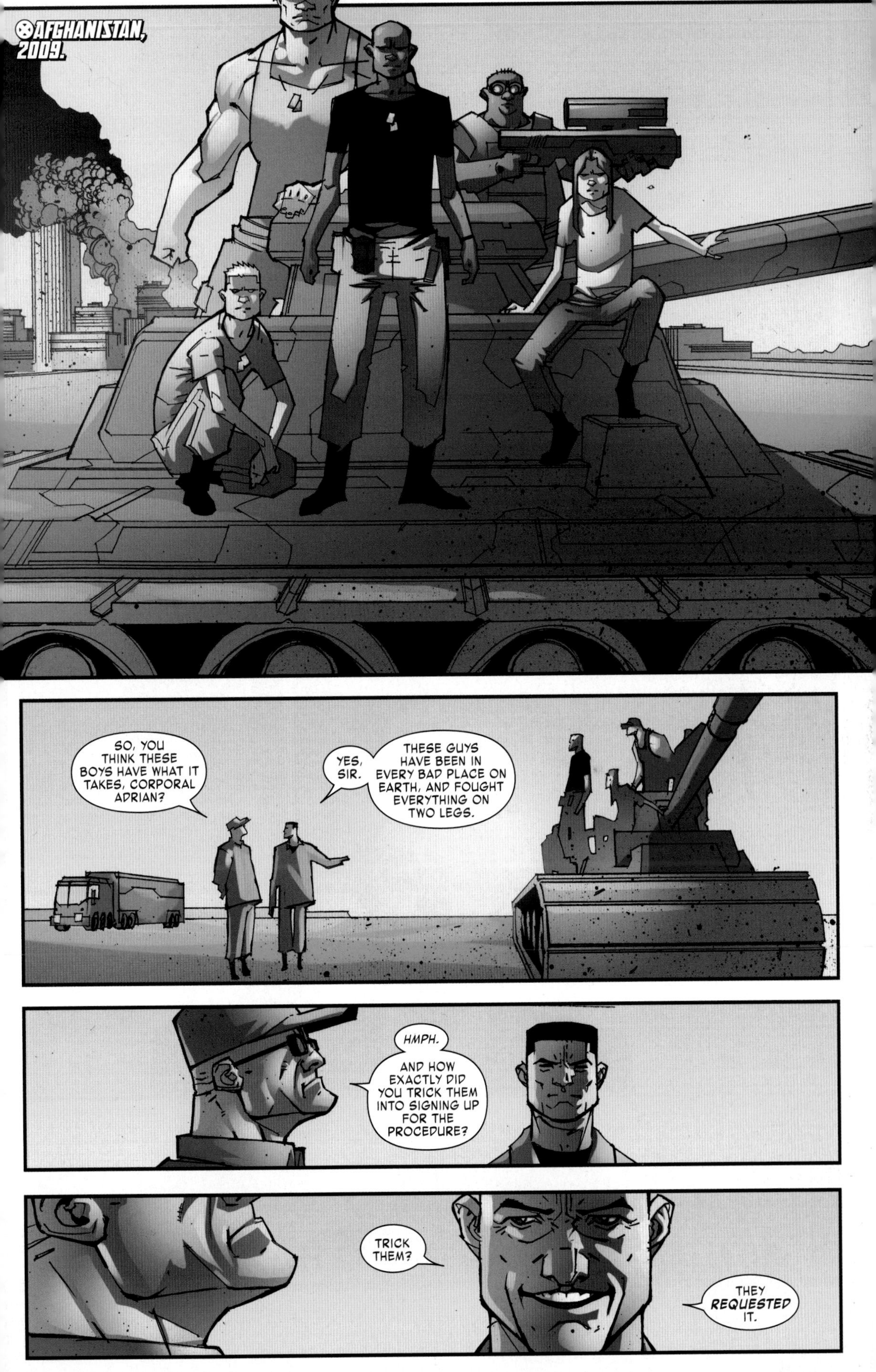
AFGHANISTAN, 2009.
SO, YOU THINK THESE BOYS HAVE WHAT IT TAKES, CORPORAL ADRIAN?
YES, SIR.
THESE GUYS HAVE BEEN IN EVERY BAD PLACE ON EARTH, AND FOUGHT EVERYTHING ON TWO LEGS.
HMPH.
AND HOW EXACTLY DID YOU TRICK THEM INTO SIGNING UP FOR THE PROCEDURE?
TRICK THEM?
THEY REQUESTED IT.

SIX MONTHS POST-OP, AND NOT ONE OF THEM HAS REJECTED THE IMPLANTS.

OKAY, YOU WERE RIGHT.

NOW, STOP GLOATING AND TELL ME JUST EXACTLY WHAT IT IS THE AMERICAN CITIZENS HAVE SPENT THEIR HARD-EARNED TAXES ON.

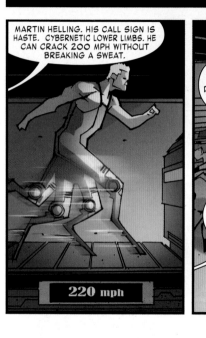

MARTIN HELLING. HIS CALL SIGN IS HASTE. CYBERNETIC LOWER LIMBS. HE CAN CRACK 200 MPH WITHOUT BREAKING A SWEAT.

220 mph

THAT'S JAMES COLE. WE CALL HIM "BRAWL". SUB-DERMAL FORCE FIELDS MAKE HIM INVULNERABLE.

THE FACT THAT HE KNOWS SEVENTEEN DIFFERENT HAND-TO-HAND COMBAT STYLES MAKES HIM SCARY.

THAT ONE DOESN'T LOOK LIKE MUCH.

AH, THAT'S "MASS."

AND LOOKS CAN BE DECEIVING. WATCH.

SMASH!

DENSITY CONTROL. HE CAN INCREASE HIS WEIGHT A HUNDRED-FOLD. ALSO MAKES HIM PRACTICALLY BULLETPROOF.

HUH. NICE.

THE ONE-MAN-ARMY THERE IS CRIMSON COMMANDO.

I'M TOLD THAT THERE IS AT LEAST *PART* OF A MAN IN THERE, BUT I CAN'T SAY HOW MUCH FOR CERTAIN.

WELL, THEY ARE... IMPRESSIVE.

BUT WEREN'T THERE FIVE? I'M PRETTY SURE I PAID FOR FIVE.

AH, YES...

THAT'S VERY ASTUTE OF YOU, SIR.

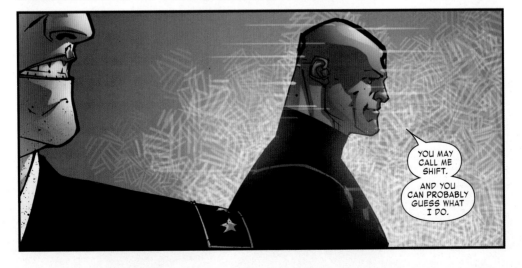

YOU MAY CALL ME SHIFT.

AND YOU CAN PROBABLY GUESS WHAT I DO.

TIN MAN PART 2

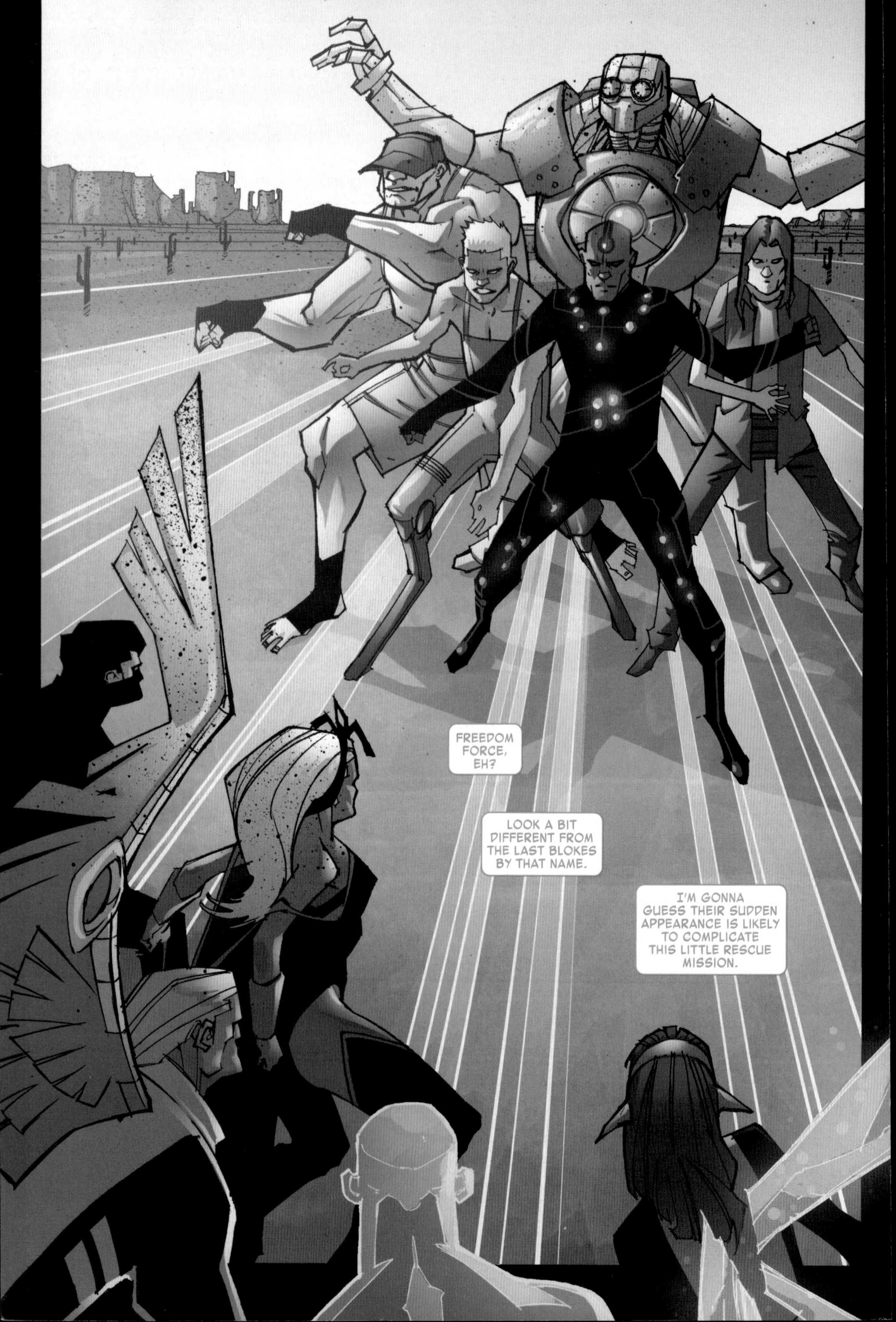
FREEDOM FORCE, EH?
LOOK A BIT DIFFERENT FROM THE LAST BLOKES BY THAT NAME.
I'M GONNA GUESS THEIR SUDDEN APPEARANCE IS LIKELY TO COMPLICATE THIS LITTLE RESCUE MISSION.

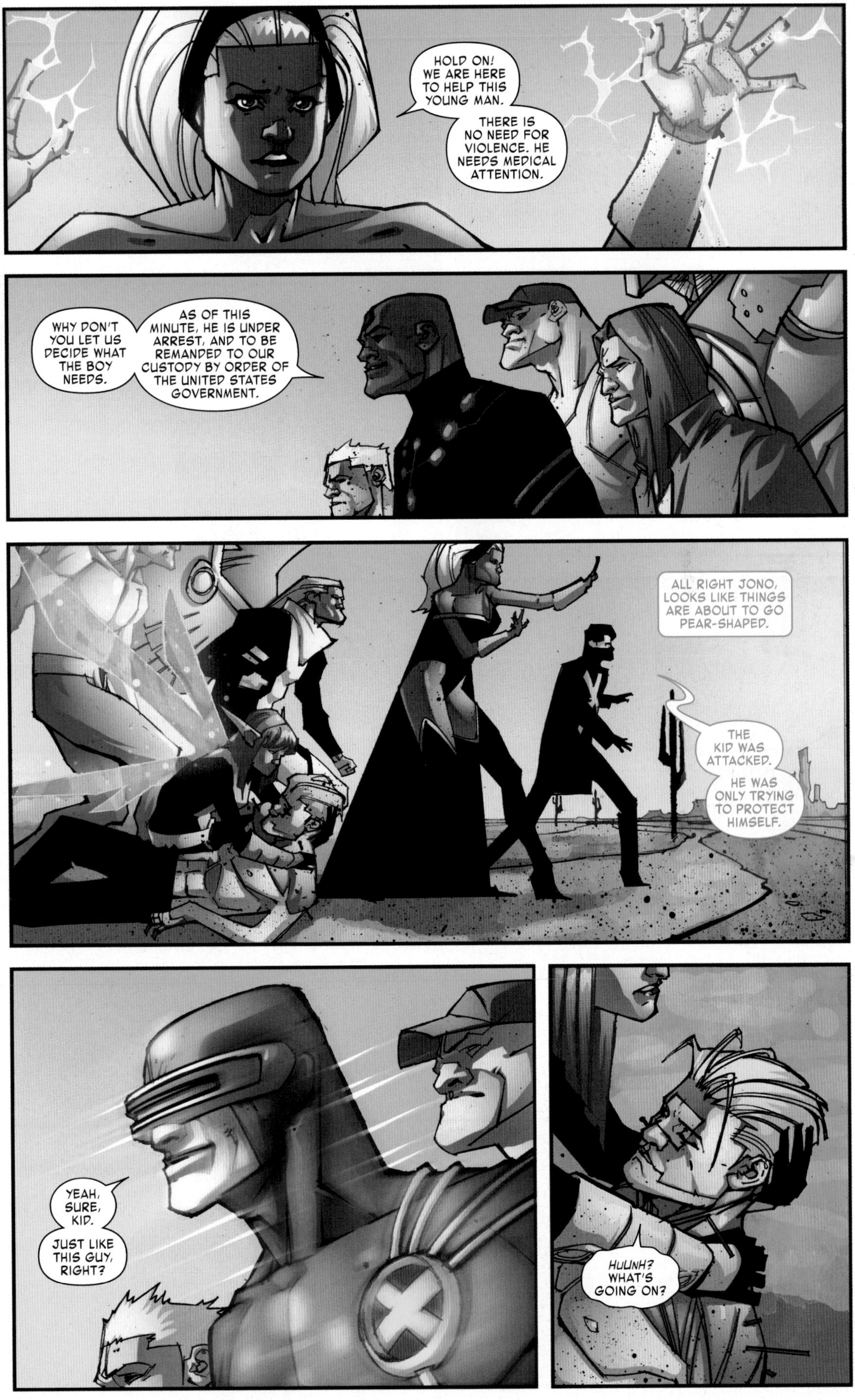
HOLD ON! WE ARE HERE TO HELP THIS YOUNG MAN.
THERE IS NO NEED FOR VIOLENCE. HE NEEDS MEDICAL ATTENTION.
WHY DON'T YOU LET US DECIDE WHAT THE BOY NEEDS.
AS OF THIS MINUTE, HE IS UNDER ARREST, AND TO BE REMANDED TO OUR CUSTODY BY ORDER OF THE UNITED STATES GOVERNMENT.
ALL RIGHT JONO, LOOKS LIKE THINGS ARE ABOUT TO GO PEAR-SHAPED.
THE KID WAS ATTACKED.
HE WAS ONLY TRYING TO PROTECT HIMSELF.
YEAH, SURE, KID.
JUST LIKE THIS GUY, RIGHT?
HUUNH? WHAT'S GOING ON?

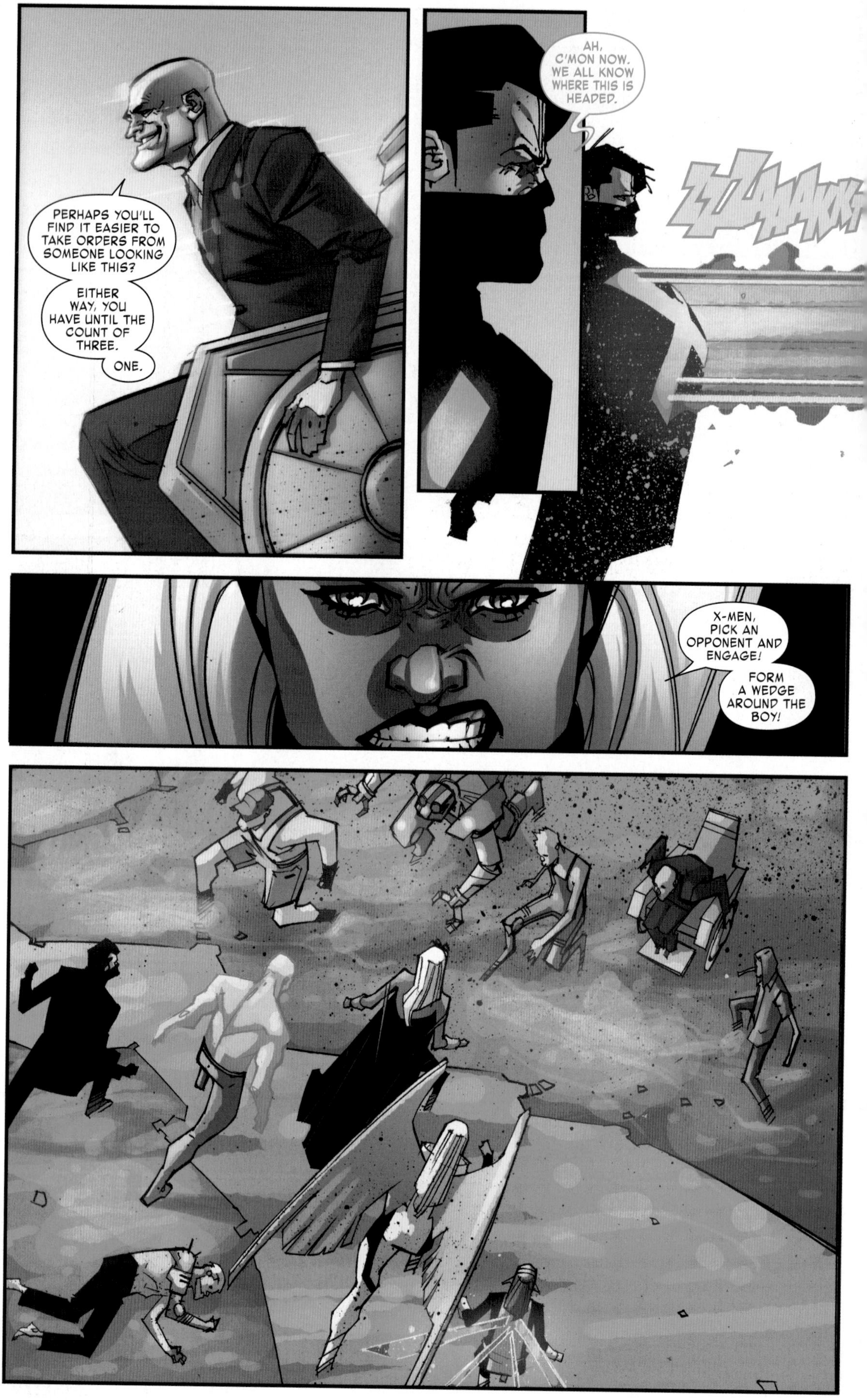
PERHAPS YOU'LL FIND IT EASIER TO TAKE ORDERS FROM SOMEONE LOOKING LIKE THIS?
EITHER WAY, YOU HAVE UNTIL THE COUNT OF THREE.
ONE.
AH, C'MON NOW. WE ALL KNOW WHERE THIS IS HEADED.
ZZZAAAKK
X-MEN, PICK AN OPPONENT AND ENGAGE!
FORM A WEDGE AROUND THE BOY!

UH, CHIEF? SHOULD WE...DO SOMETHING?
ARE YOU KIDDING, THOMPSON?
I THINK WE MIGHT BE OUT OF OUR ELEMENT HERE.
INITIATING COMBAT SEQUENCE. TARGET ACQUIRED.
CHUT CHUT CHUT CHUT CHUT CHUT!
SERIOUSLY? THAT'S THE BEST YOU CAN DO?
THE OLD CRIMSON COMMANDO WAS A LOT SCARIER.
AND HE WAS, LIKE, A THOUSAND YEARS OLD!
TARGET IS COMPRISED OF ORGANIC ICE.
SWITCHING TO LINAC COHERENT LIGHT SOURCE ARRAY.
WARMING UP...
VMMMMMMMMMMM

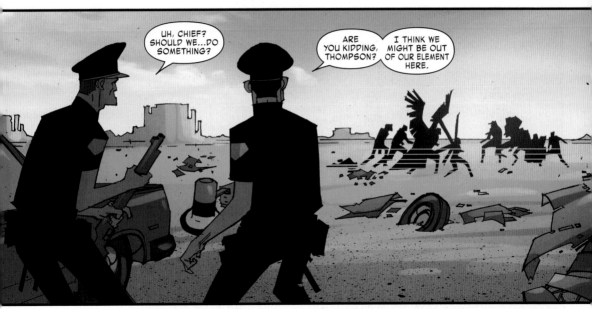

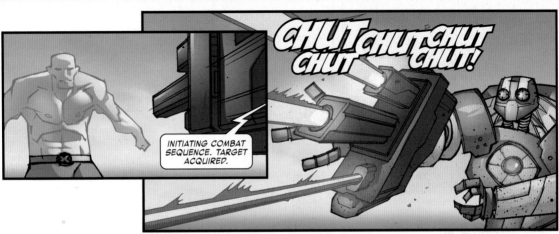

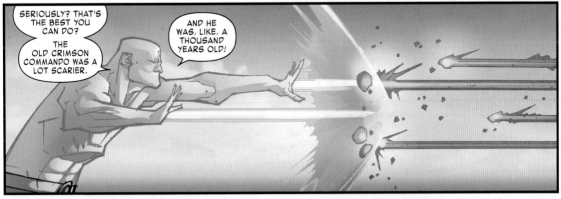

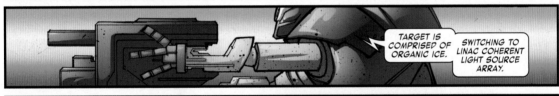

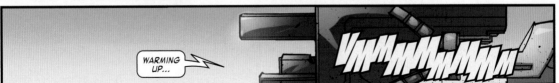

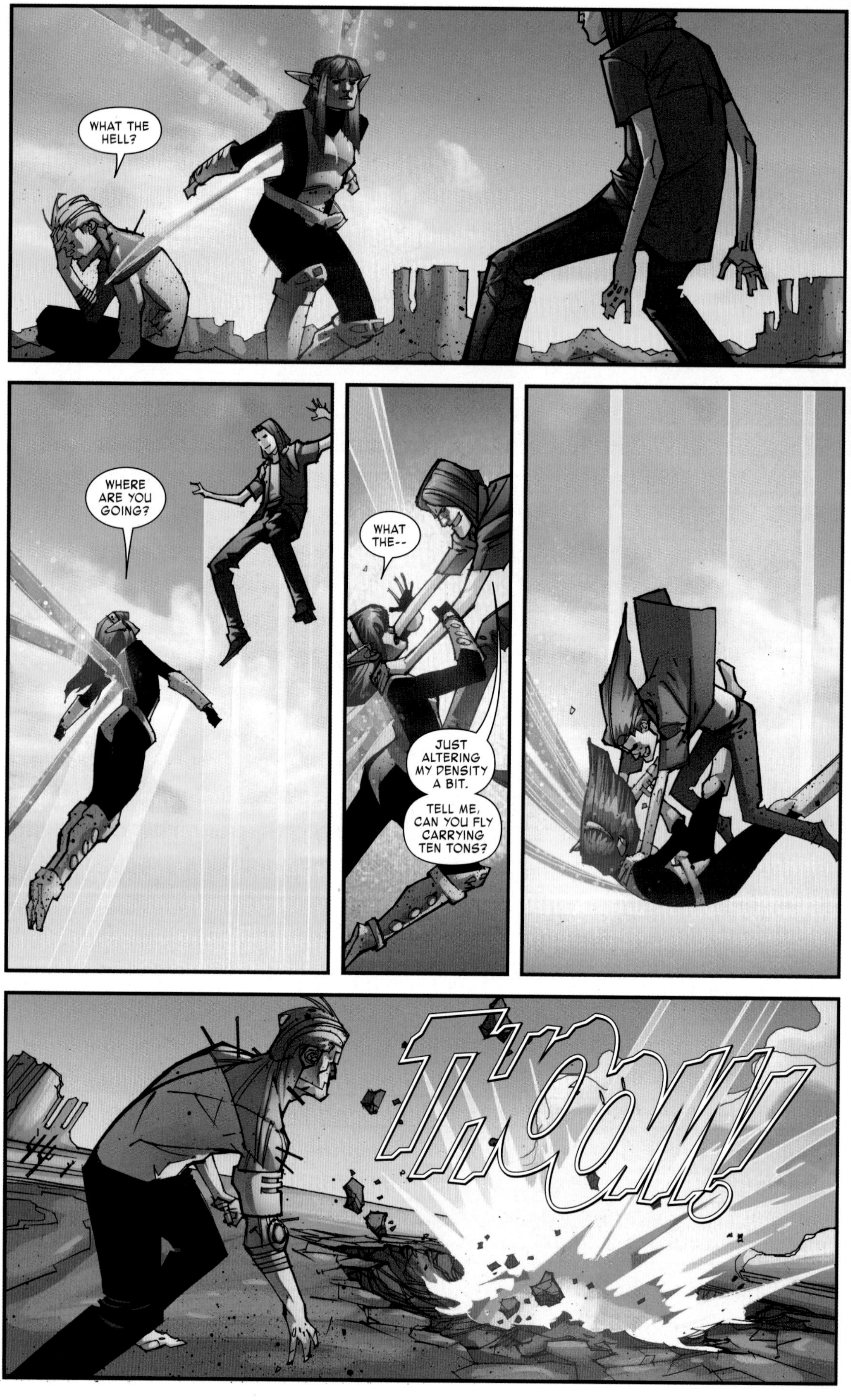
WHAT THE HELL?
WHERE ARE YOU GOING?
WHAT THE--
JUST ALTERING MY DENSITY A BIT.
TELL ME, CAN YOU FLY CARRYING TEN TONS?
THOOM!

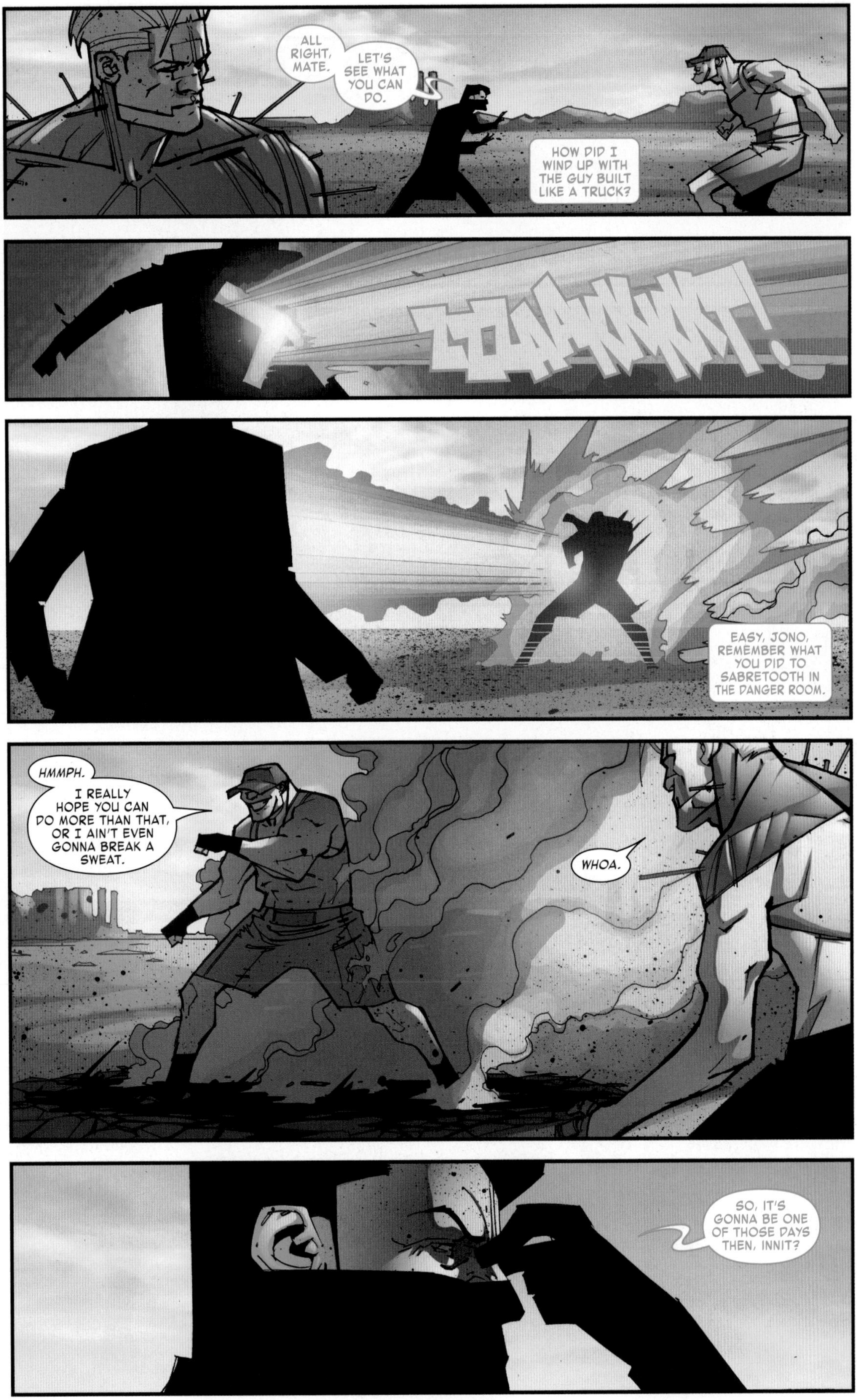
ALL RIGHT, MATE.
LET'S SEE WHAT YOU CAN DO.
HOW DID I WIND UP WITH THE GUY BUILT LIKE A TRUCK?
ZZZAAKKKKT!
EASY, JONO, REMEMBER WHAT YOU DID TO SABRETOOTH IN THE DANGER ROOM.
HMMPH.
I REALLY HOPE YOU CAN DO MORE THAN THAT, OR I AIN'T EVEN GONNA BREAK A SWEAT.
WHOA.
SO, IT'S GONNA BE ONE OF THOSE DAYS THEN, INNIT?

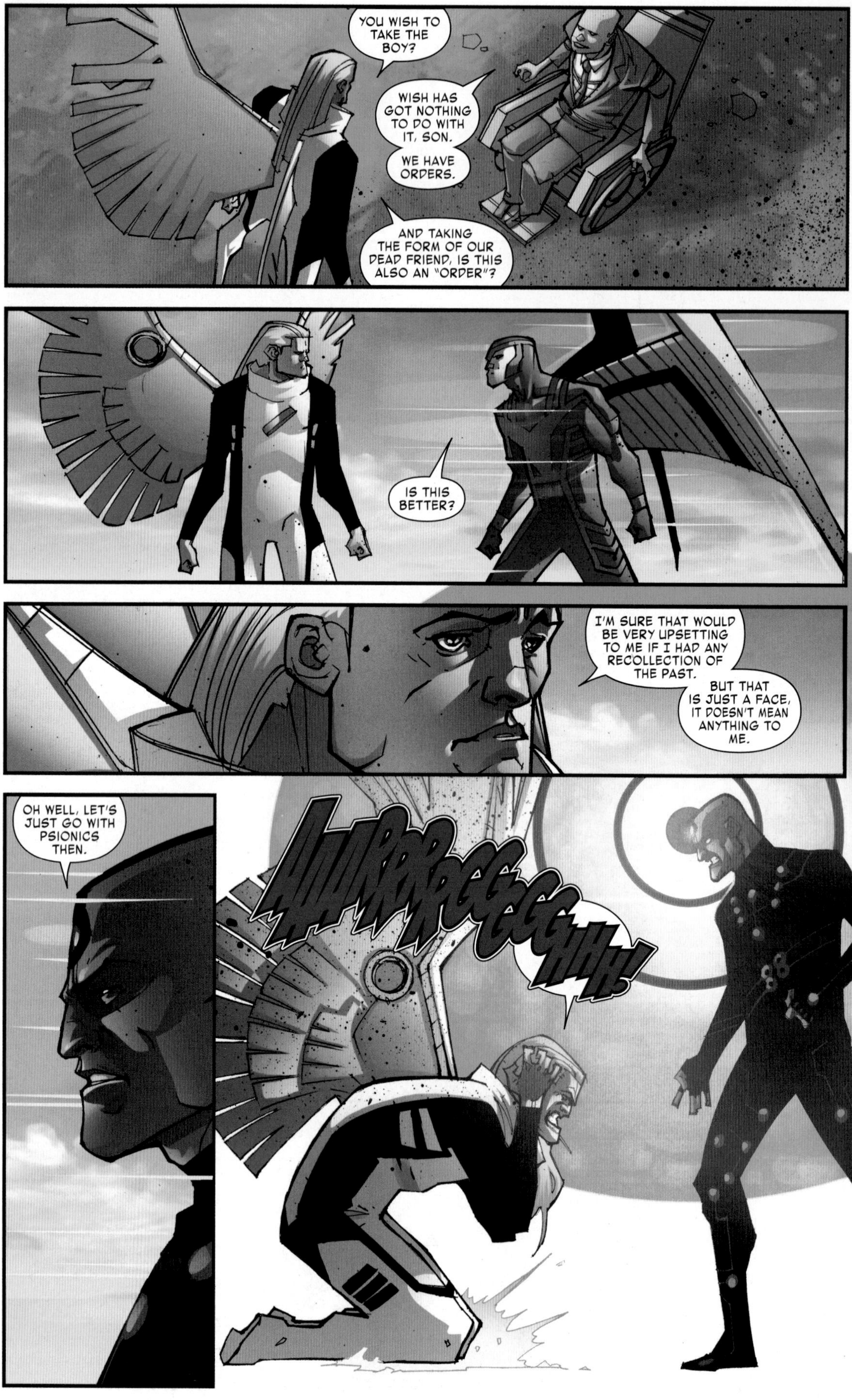
YOU WISH TO TAKE THE BOY?
WISH HAS GOT NOTHING TO DO WITH IT, SON.
WE HAVE ORDERS.
AND TAKING THE FORM OF OUR DEAD FRIEND, IS THIS ALSO AN "ORDER"?
IS THIS BETTER?
I'M SURE THAT WOULD BE VERY UPSETTING TO ME IF I HAD ANY RECOLLECTION OF THE PAST.
BUT THAT IS JUST A FACE, IT DOESN'T MEAN ANYTHING TO ME.
OH WELL, LET'S JUST GO WITH PSIONICS THEN.
HUURRRRGGGGHHH!

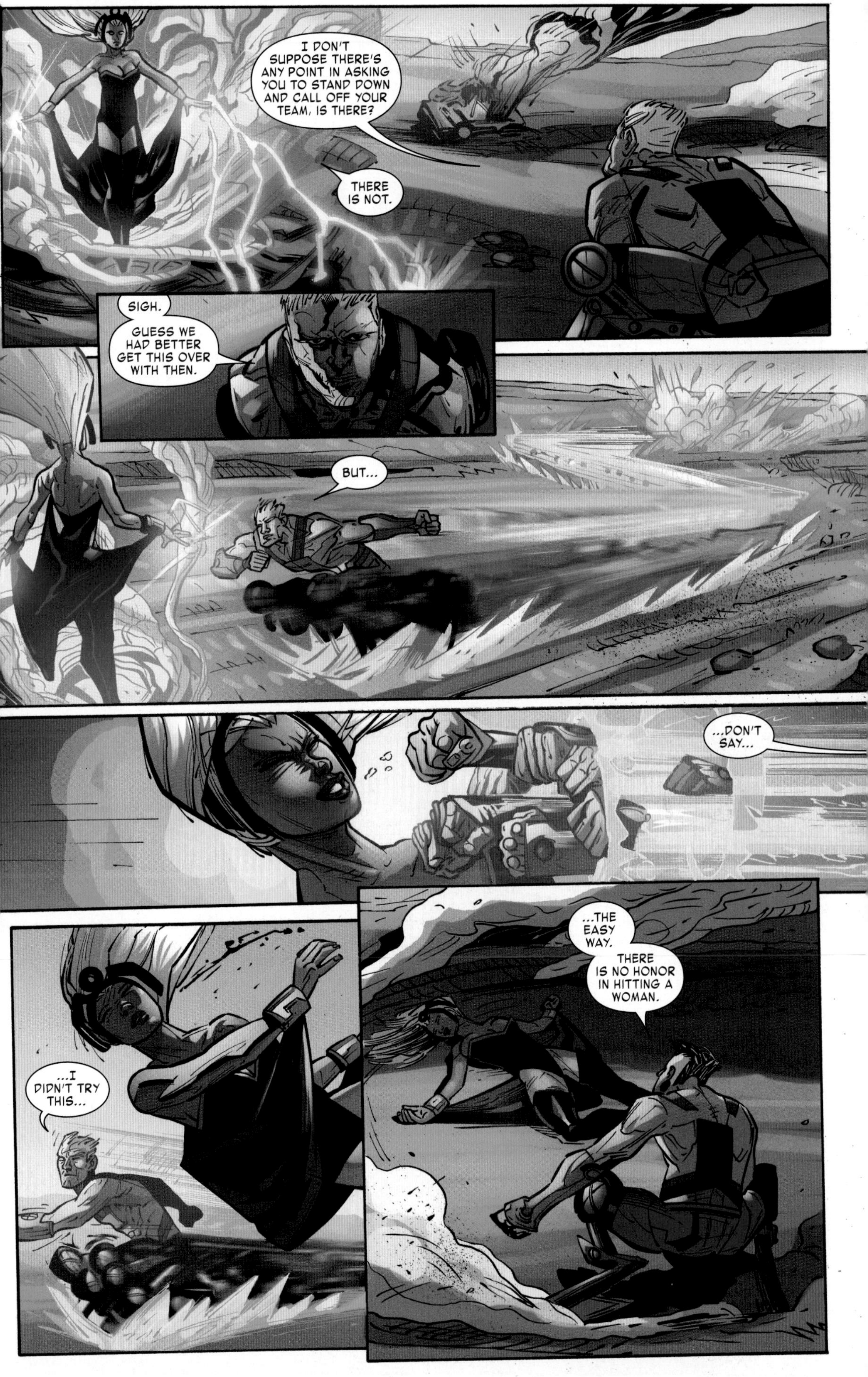
I DON'T SUPPOSE THERE'S ANY POINT IN ASKING YOU TO STAND DOWN AND CALL OFF YOUR TEAM, IS THERE?
THERE IS NOT.
SIGH.
GUESS WE HAD BETTER GET THIS OVER WITH THEN.
BUT...
...DON'T SAY...
...I DIDN'T TRY THIS...
...THE EASY WAY.
THERE IS NO HONOR IN HITTING A WOMAN.

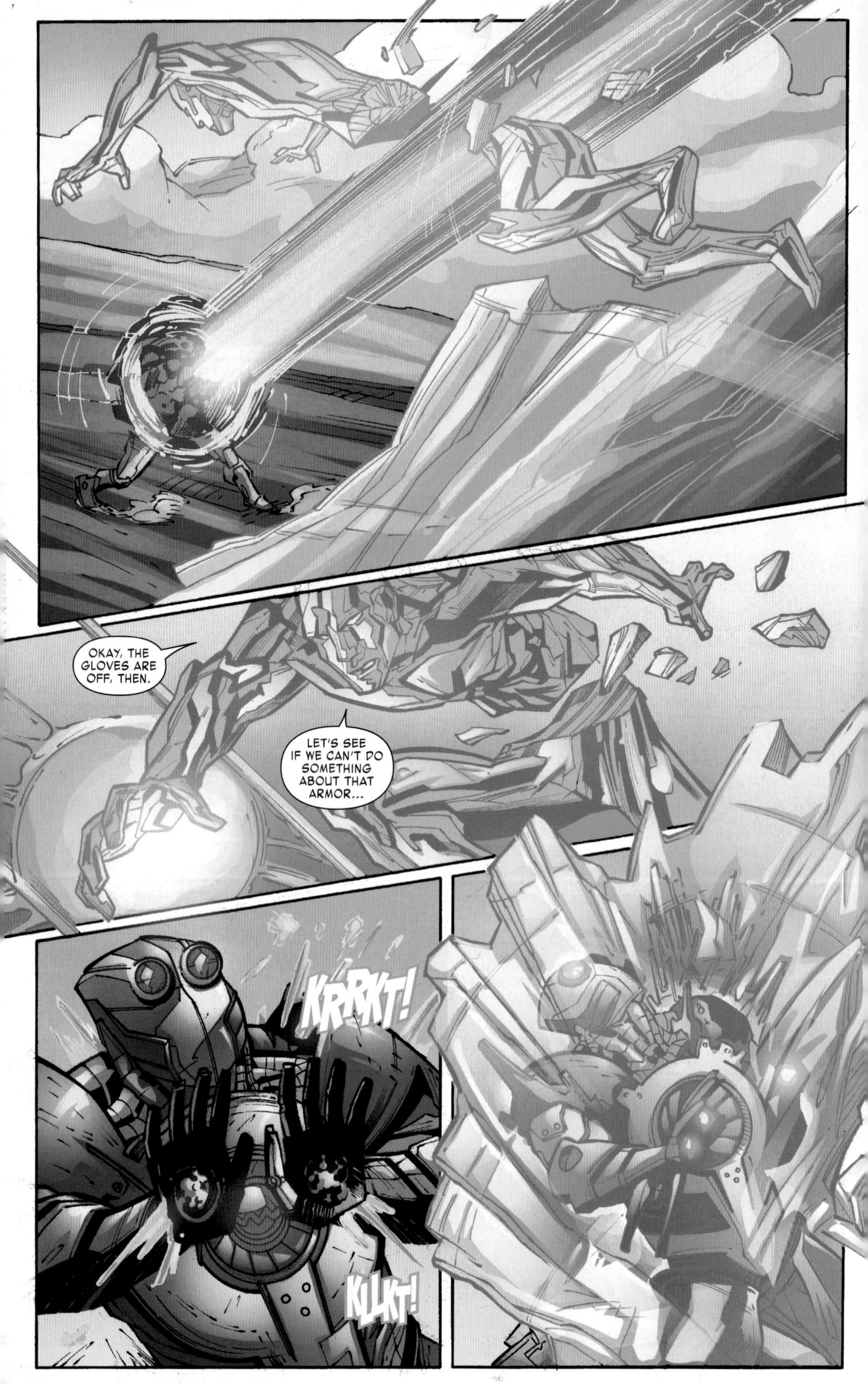
OKAY, THE GLOVES ARE OFF, THEN.
LET'S SEE IF WE CAN'T DO SOMETHING ABOUT THAT ARMOR...
KRRRKT!
KLLKT!

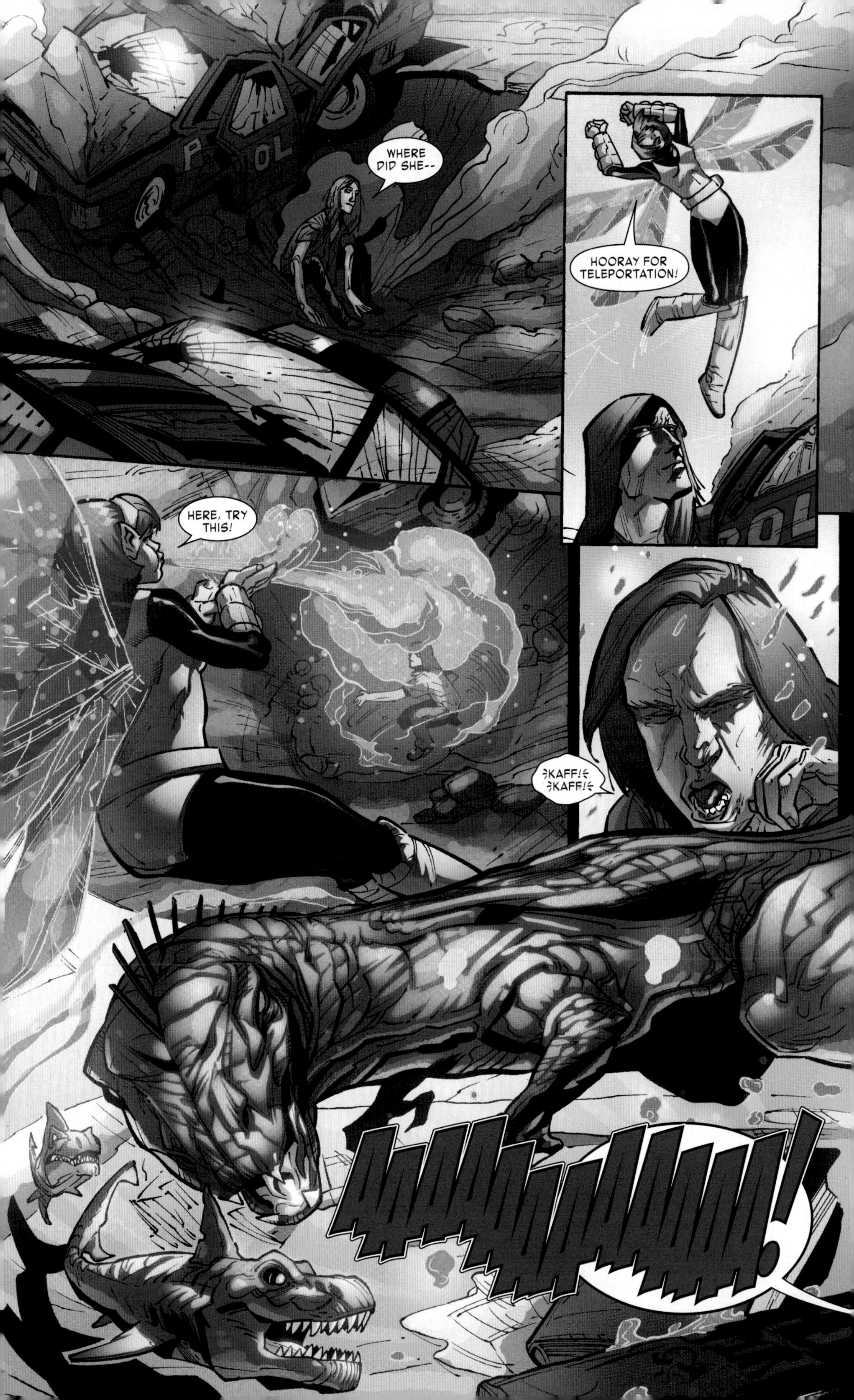
WHERE DID SHE--
HOORAY FOR TELEPORTATION!
HERE, TRY THIS!
KAFF! *KAFF!*

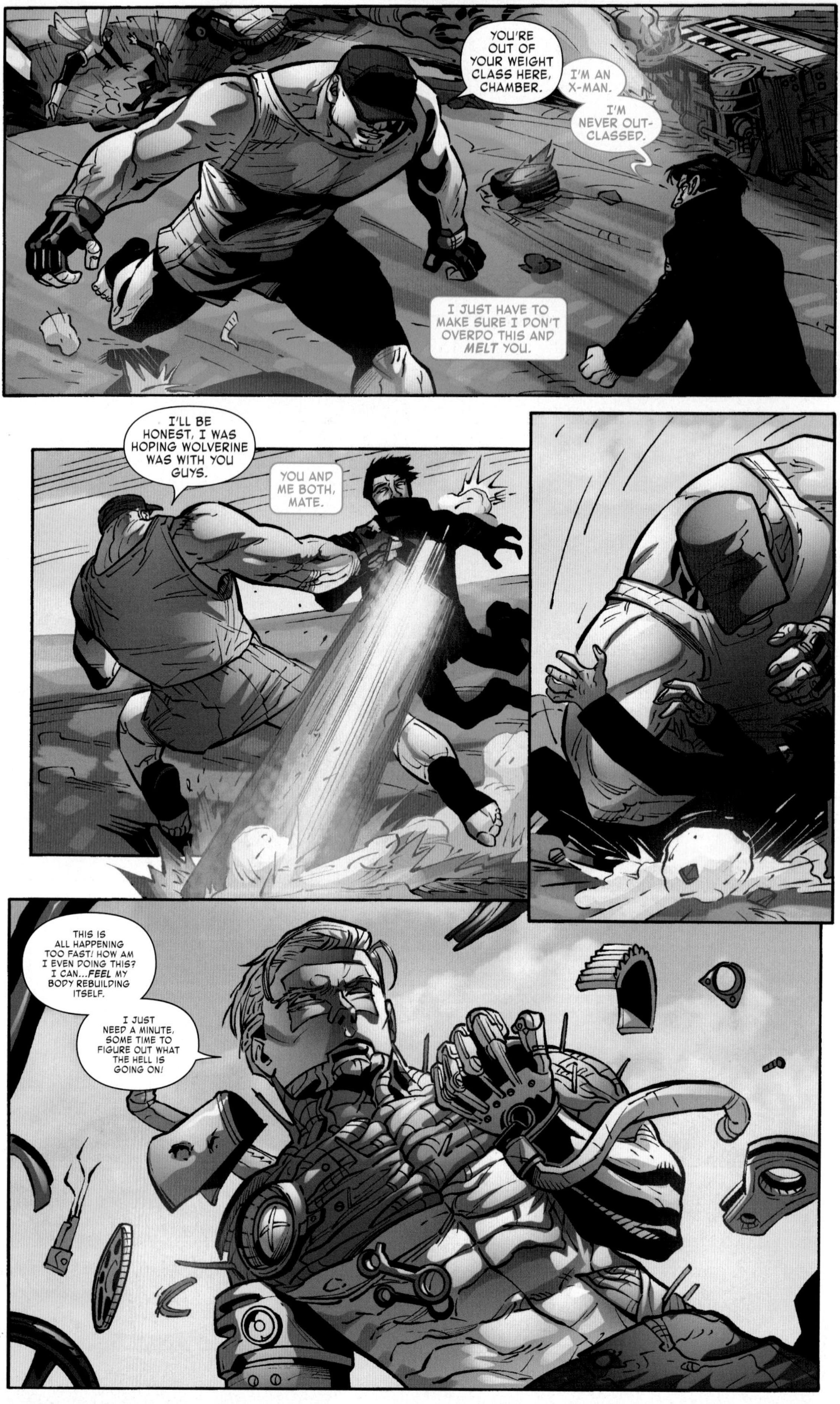
YOU'RE OUT OF YOUR WEIGHT CLASS HERE, CHAMBER.
I'M AN X-MAN.
I'M NEVER OUT-CLASSED.
I JUST HAVE TO MAKE SURE I DON'T OVERDO THIS AND MELT YOU.
I'LL BE HONEST, I WAS HOPING WOLVERINE WAS WITH YOU GUYS.
YOU AND ME BOTH, MATE.
THIS IS ALL HAPPENING TOO FAST! HOW AM I EVEN DOING THIS? I CAN...FEEL MY BODY REBUILDING ITSELF.
I JUST NEED A MINUTE, SOME TIME TO FIGURE OUT WHAT THE HELL IS GOING ON!

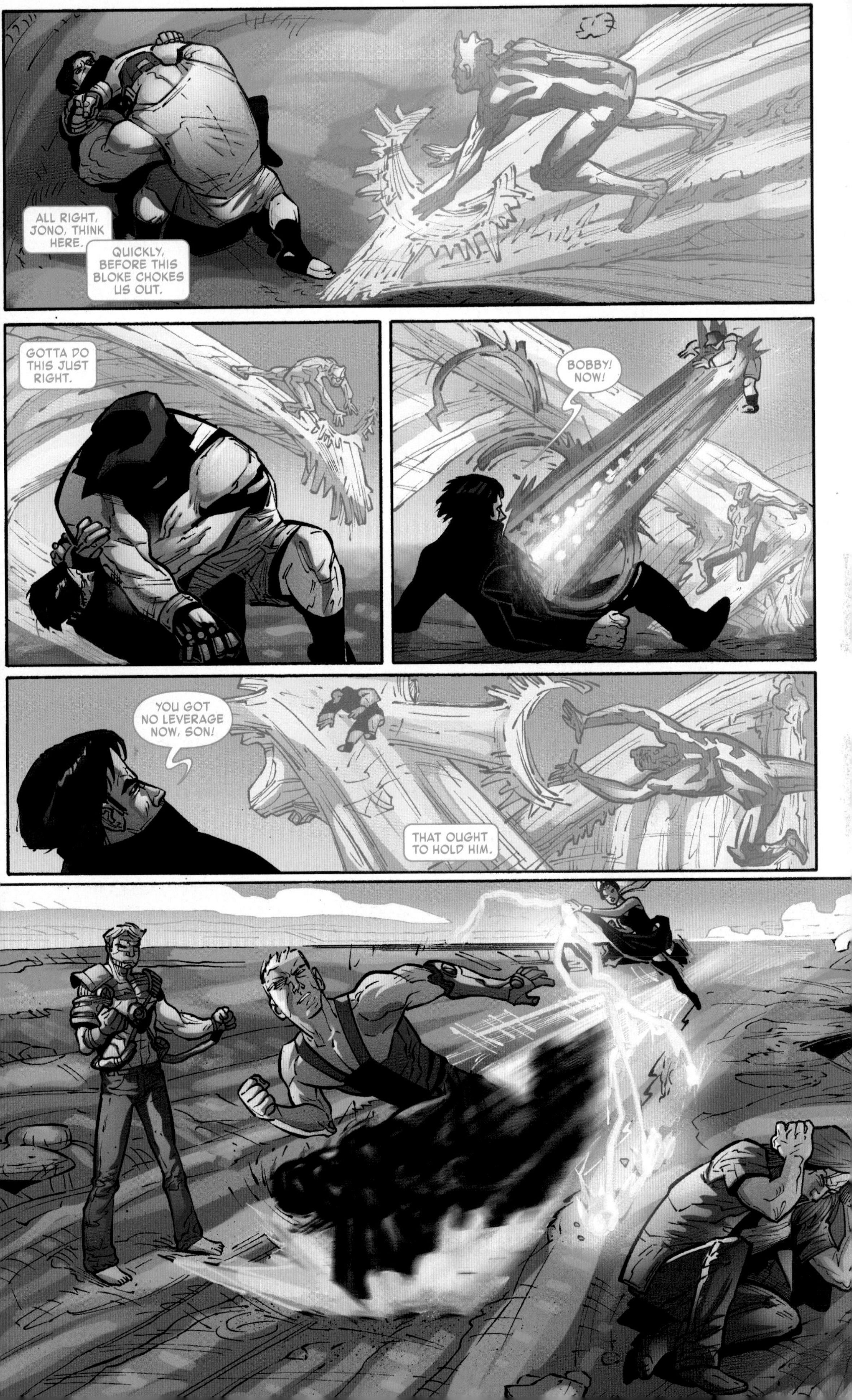
ALL RIGHT, JONO, THINK HERE.
QUICKLY, BEFORE THIS BLOKE CHOKES US OUT.
GOTTA DO THIS JUST RIGHT.
BOBBY! NOW!
YOU GOT NO LEVERAGE NOW, SON!
THAT OUGHT TO HOLD HIM.

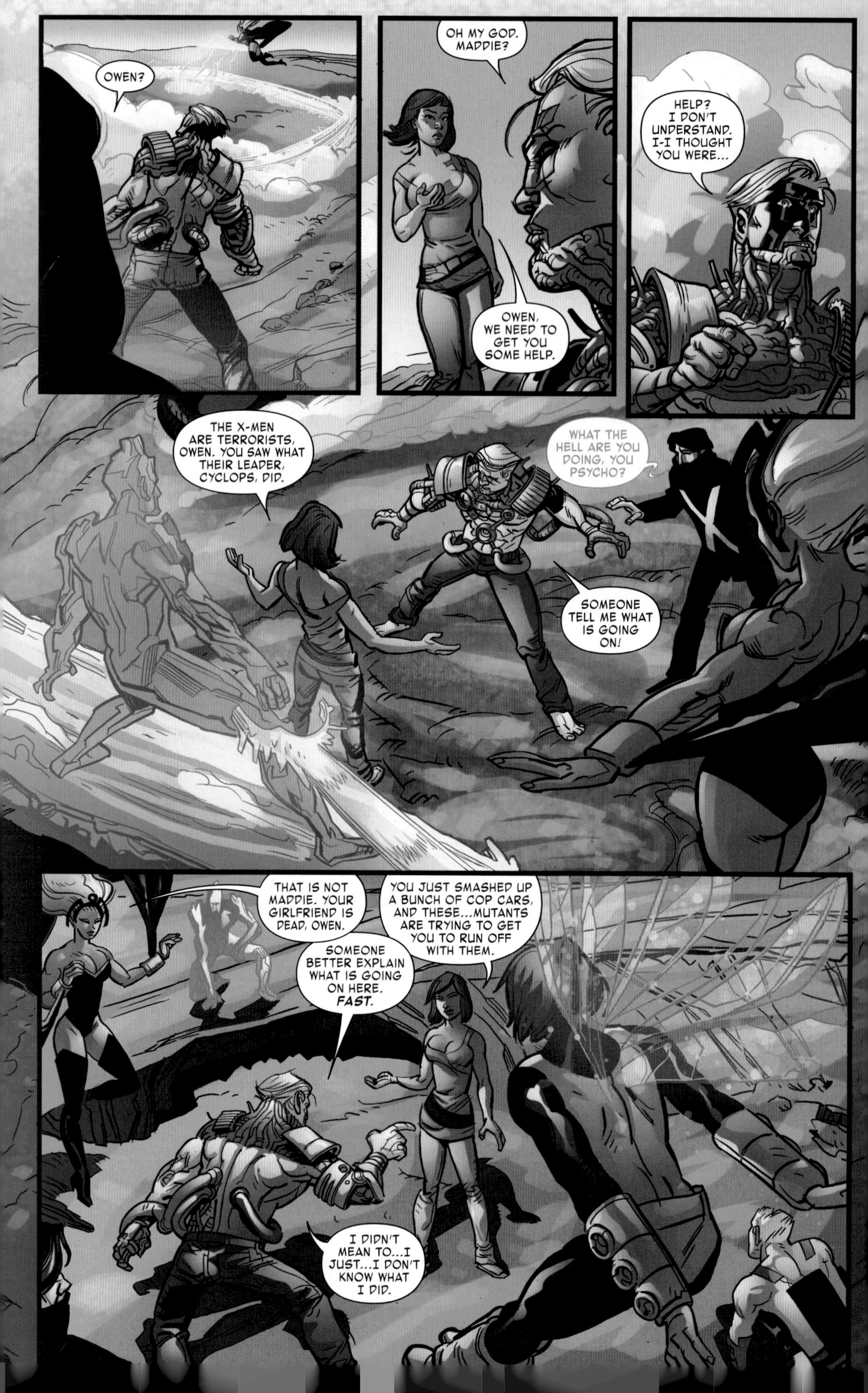
OWEN?
OH MY GOD. MADDIE?
OWEN, WE NEED TO GET YOU SOME HELP.
HELP? I DON'T UNDERSTAND. I-I THOUGHT YOU WERE...
THE X-MEN ARE TERRORISTS, OWEN. YOU SAW WHAT THEIR LEADER, CYCLOPS, DID.
WHAT THE HELL ARE YOU DOING, YOU PSYCHO?
SOMEONE TELL ME WHAT IS GOING ON!
THAT IS NOT MADDIE. YOUR GIRLFRIEND IS DEAD, OWEN.
YOU JUST SMASHED UP A BUNCH OF COP CARS, AND THESE...MUTANTS ARE TRYING TO GET YOU TO RUN OFF WITH THEM.
SOMEONE BETTER EXPLAIN WHAT IS GOING ON HERE. FAST.
I DIDN'T MEAN TO...I JUST...I DON'T KNOW WHAT I DID.

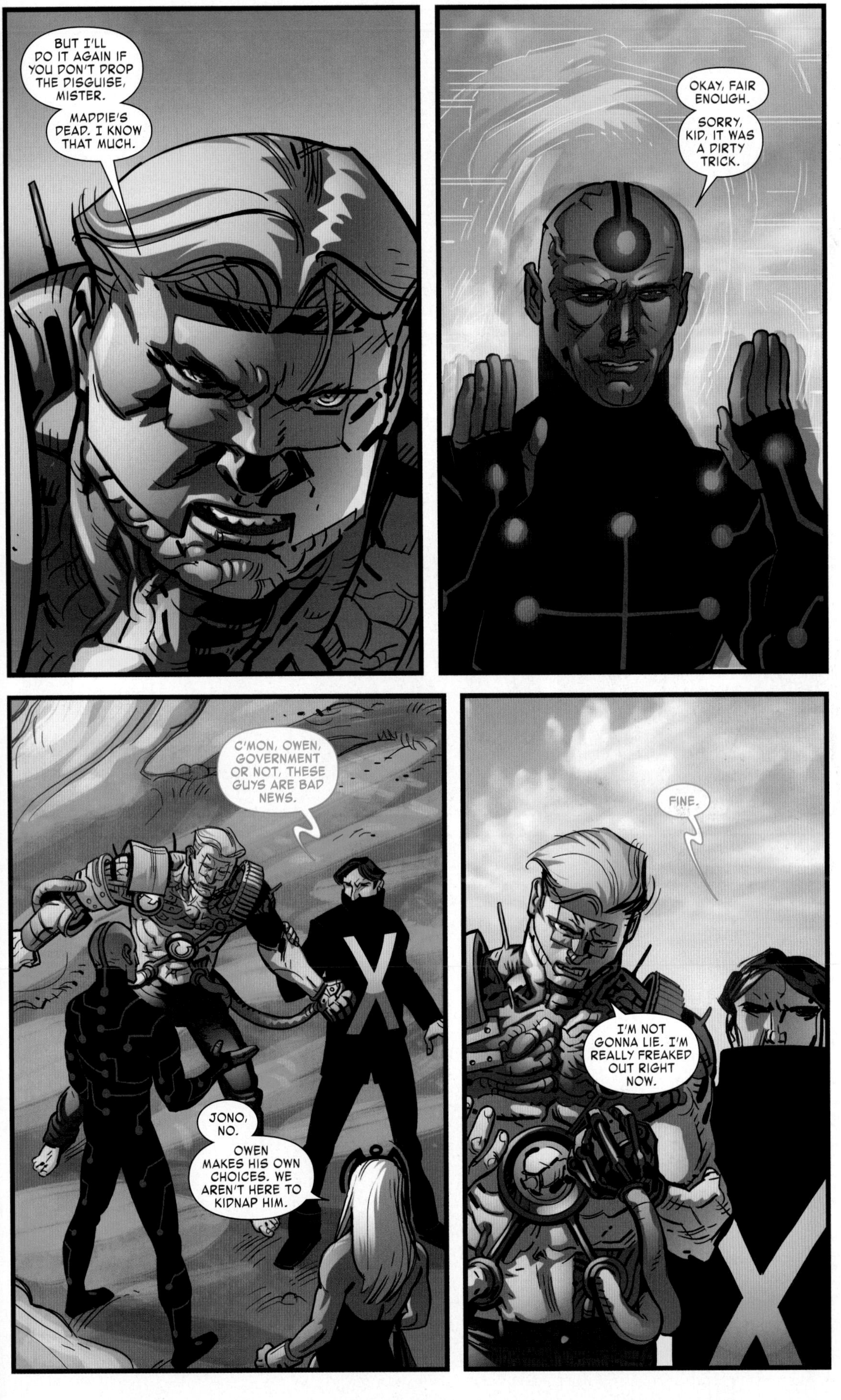
BUT I'LL DO IT AGAIN IF YOU DON'T DROP THE DISGUISE, MISTER.
MADDIE'S DEAD. I KNOW THAT MUCH.
OKAY, FAIR ENOUGH.
SORRY, KID, IT WAS A DIRTY TRICK.
C'MON, OWEN, GOVERNMENT OR NOT, THESE GUYS ARE BAD NEWS.
JONO, NO.
OWEN MAKES HIS OWN CHOICES. WE AREN'T HERE TO KIDNAP HIM.
FINE.
I'M NOT GONNA LIE. I'M REALLY FREAKED OUT RIGHT NOW.

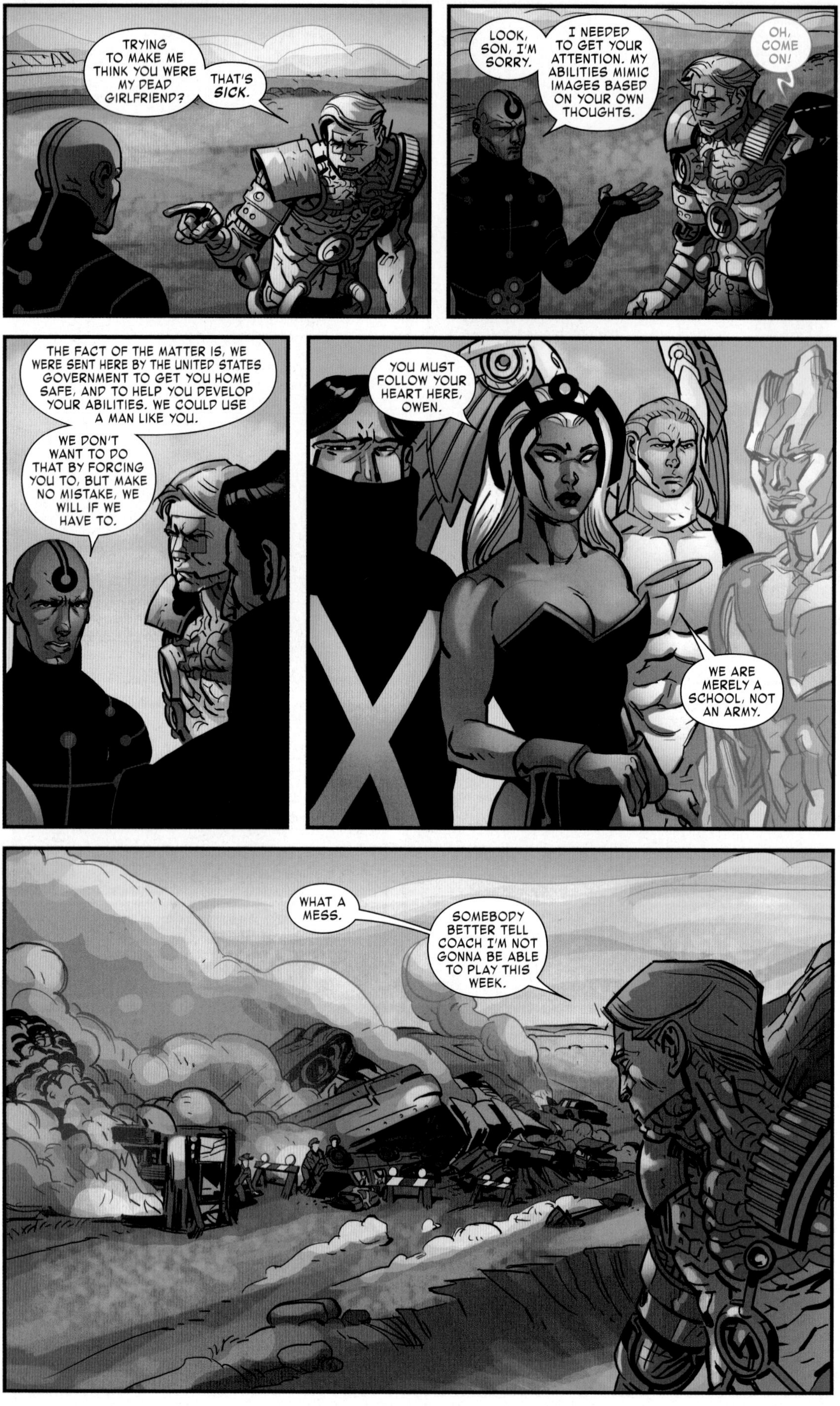
TRYING TO MAKE ME THINK YOU WERE MY DEAD GIRLFRIEND?
THAT'S SICK.
LOOK, SON, I'M SORRY.
I NEEDED TO GET YOUR ATTENTION. MY ABILITIES MIMIC IMAGES BASED ON YOUR OWN THOUGHTS.
OH, COME ON!
THE FACT OF THE MATTER IS, WE WERE SENT HERE BY THE UNITED STATES GOVERNMENT TO GET YOU HOME SAFE, AND TO HELP YOU DEVELOP YOUR ABILITIES. WE COULD USE A MAN LIKE YOU.
WE DON'T WANT TO DO THAT BY FORCING YOU TO, BUT MAKE NO MISTAKE, WE WILL IF WE HAVE TO.
YOU MUST FOLLOW YOUR HEART HERE, OWEN.
WE ARE MERELY A SCHOOL, NOT AN ARMY.
WHAT A MESS.
SOMEBODY BETTER TELL COACH I'M NOT GONNA BE ABLE TO PLAY THIS WEEK.

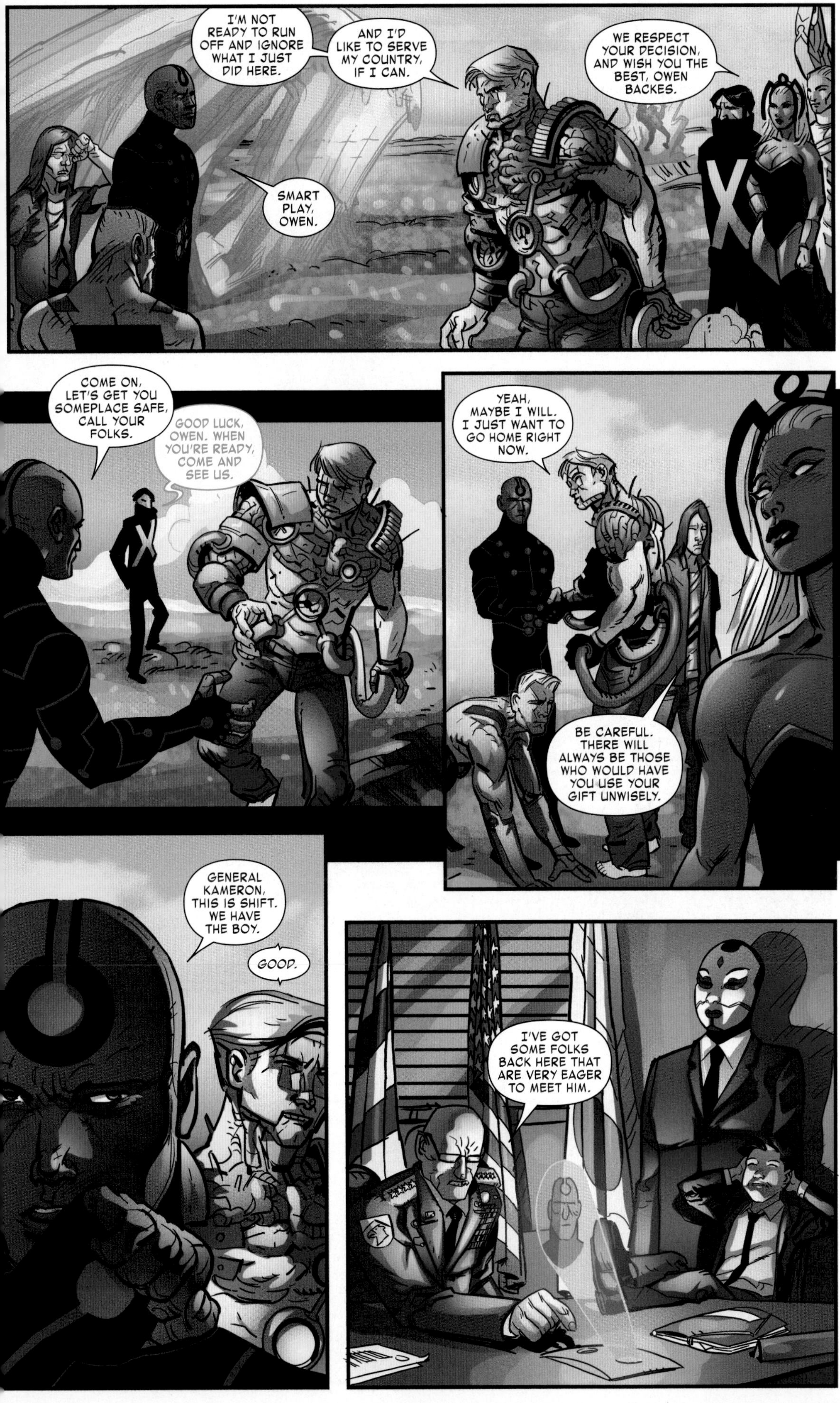
I'M NOT READY TO RUN OFF AND IGNORE WHAT I JUST DID HERE.
AND I'D LIKE TO SERVE MY COUNTRY, IF I CAN.
WE RESPECT YOUR DECISION, AND WISH YOU THE BEST, OWEN BACKES.
SMART PLAY, OWEN.
COME ON, LET'S GET YOU SOMEPLACE SAFE, CALL YOUR FOLKS.
GOOD LUCK, OWEN. WHEN YOU'RE READY, COME AND SEE US.
YEAH, MAYBE I WILL. I JUST WANT TO GO HOME RIGHT NOW.
BE CAREFUL. THERE WILL ALWAYS BE THOSE WHO WOULD HAVE YOU USE YOUR GIFT UNWISELY.
GENERAL KAMERON, THIS IS SHIFT. WE HAVE THE BOY.
GOOD.
I'VE GOT SOME FOLKS BACK HERE THAT ARE VERY EAGER TO MEET HIM.

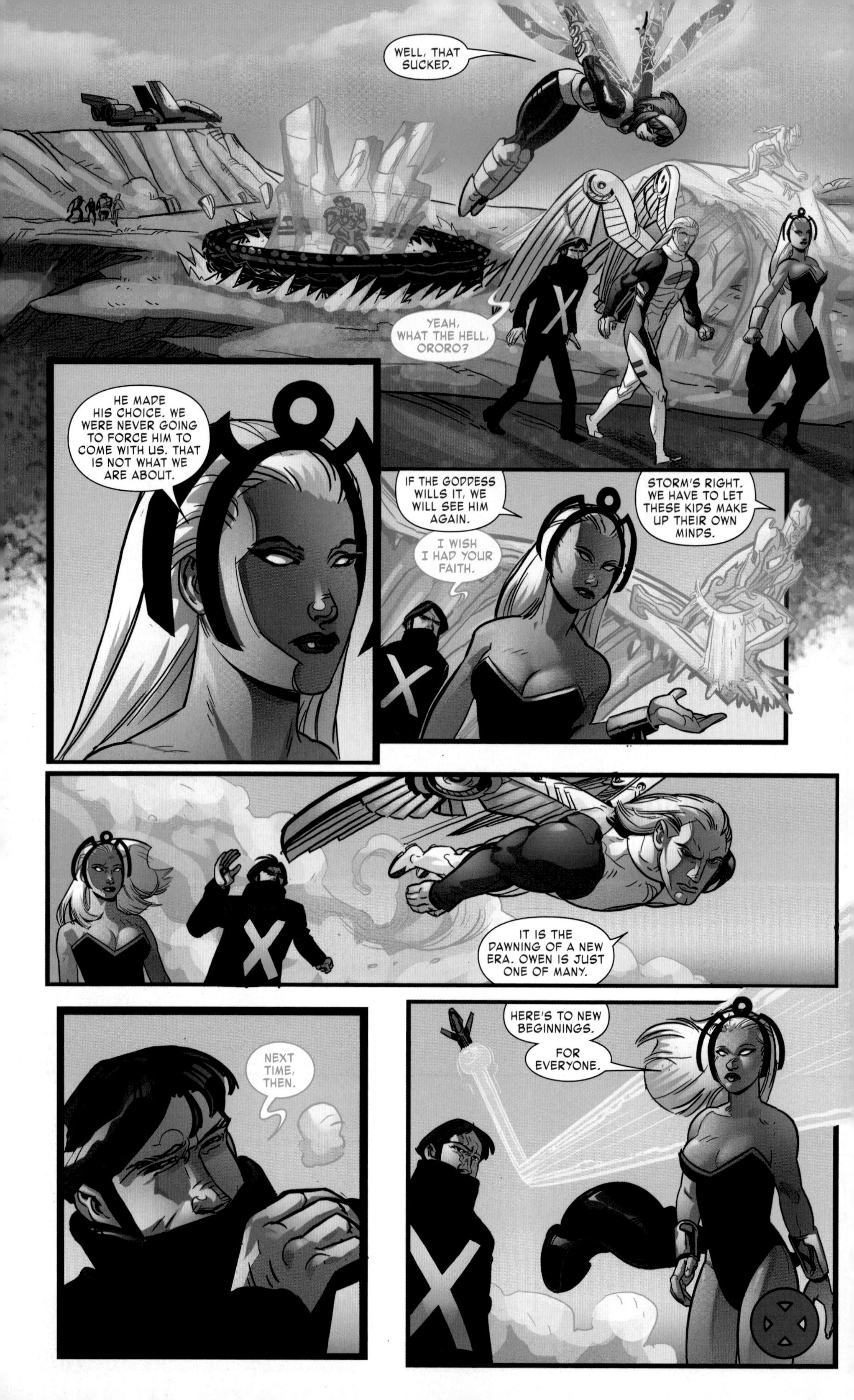
WELL, THAT SUCKED.
YEAH, WHAT THE HELL, ORORO?
HE MADE HIS CHOICE. WE WERE NEVER GOING TO FORCE HIM TO COME WITH US. THAT IS NOT WHAT WE ARE ABOUT.
IF THE GODDESS WILLS IT, WE WILL SEE HIM AGAIN.
I WISH I HAD YOUR FAITH.
STORM'S RIGHT. WE HAVE TO LET THESE KIDS MAKE UP THEIR OWN MINDS.
IT IS THE DAWNING OF A NEW ERA. OWEN IS JUST ONE OF MANY.
NEXT TIME, THEN.
HERE'S TO NEW BEGINNINGS.
FOR EVERYONE.

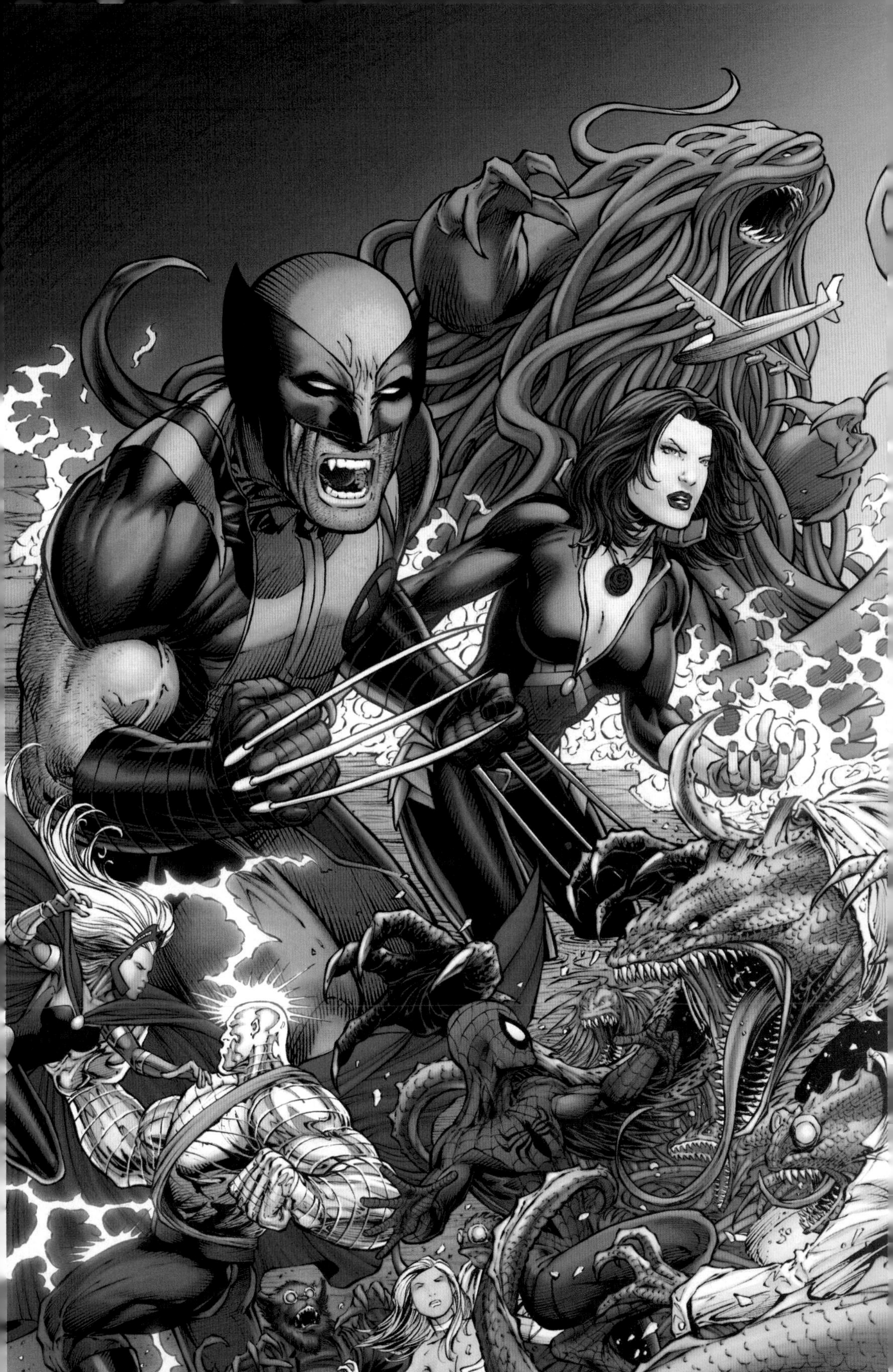

#1 VARIANT BY DALE KEOWN, DANNY MIKI & MORRY HOLLOWELL

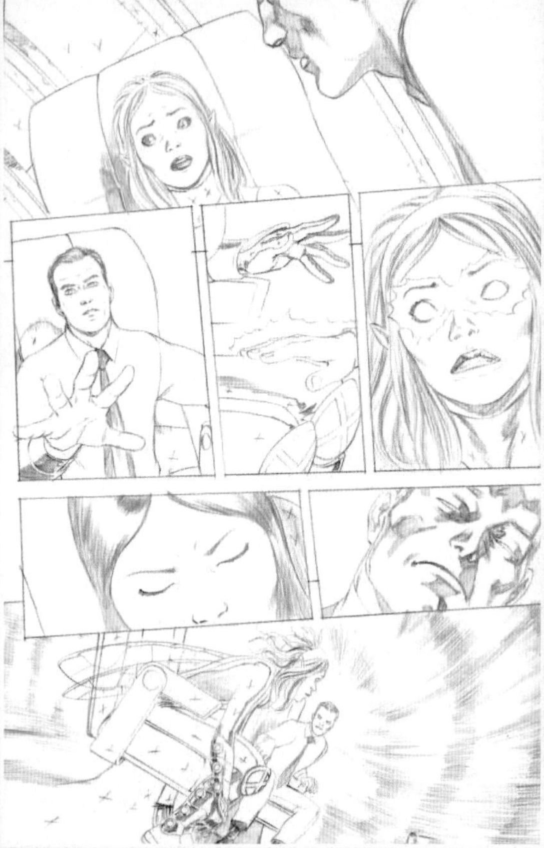

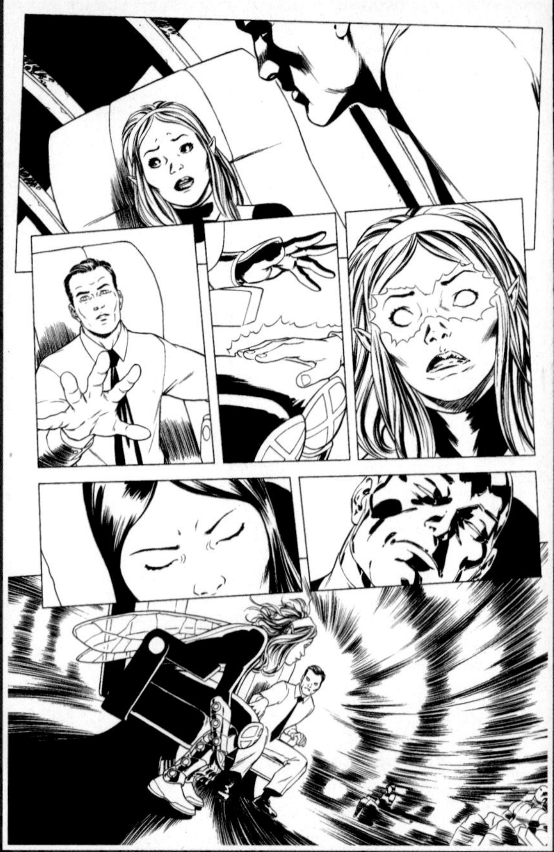

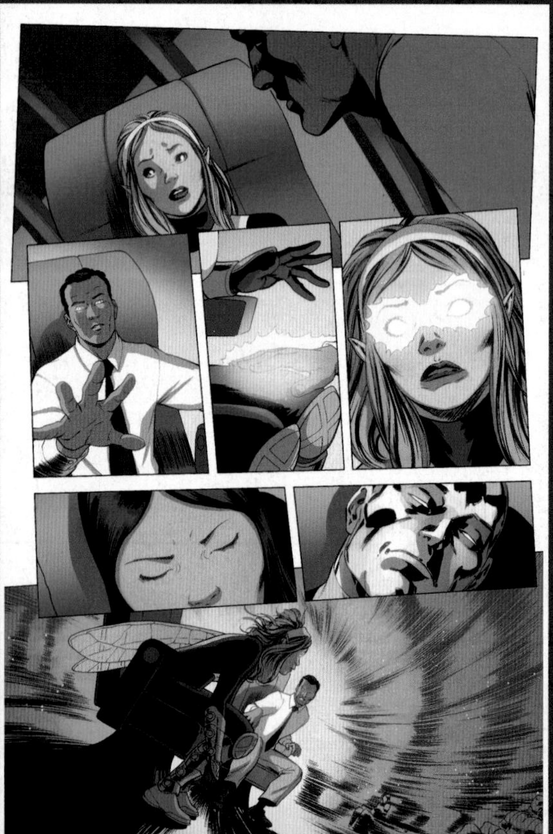

#36 PAGE 15 ART PROCESS BY DAVID LÓPEZ, ÁLVARO LÓPEZ & RACHELLE ROSENBERG

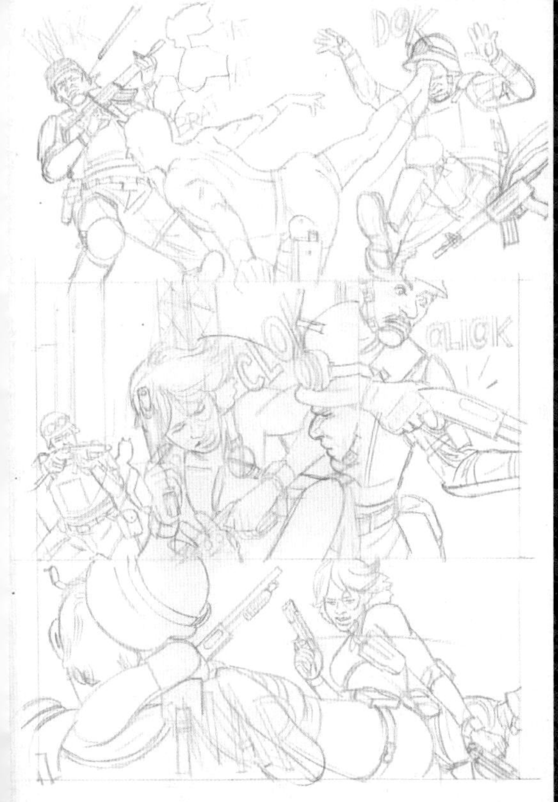
DOK
CLOK

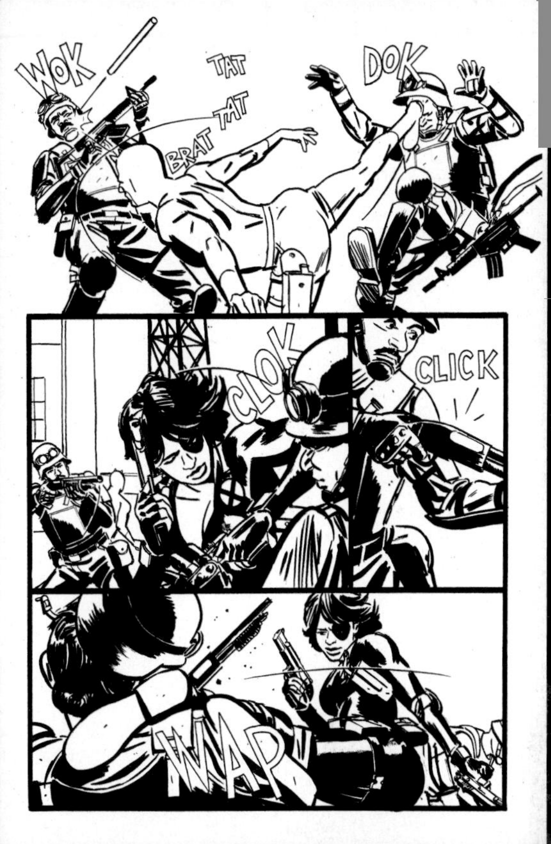
WOK
TAT
TAT
BRAT
DOK
CLOK
CLICK
WAP

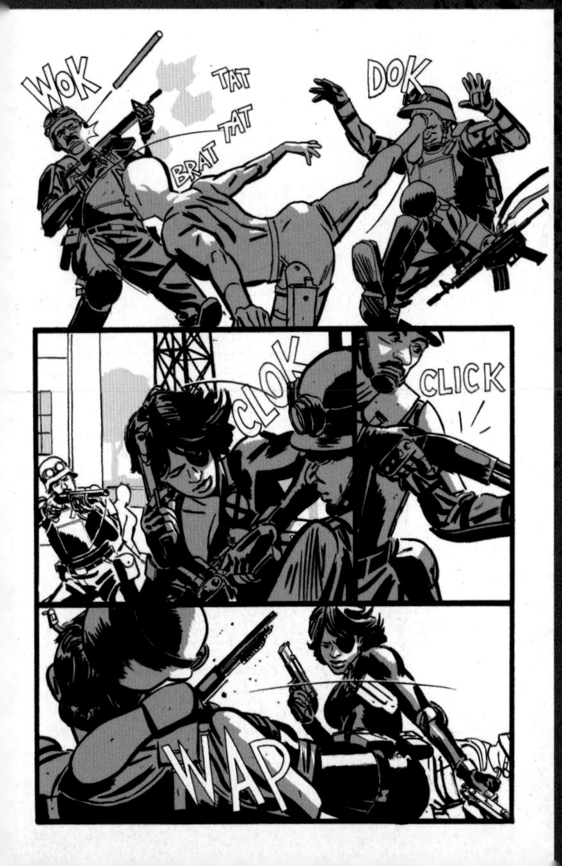
WOK
TAT
TAT
BRAT
DOK
CLOK
CLICK
WAP

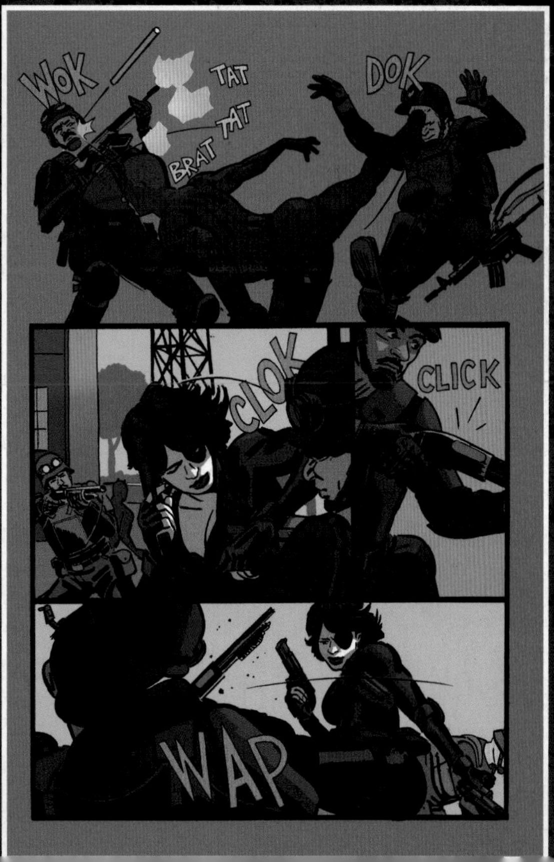
WOK
TAT
TAT
BRAT
DOK
CLOK
CLICK
WAP

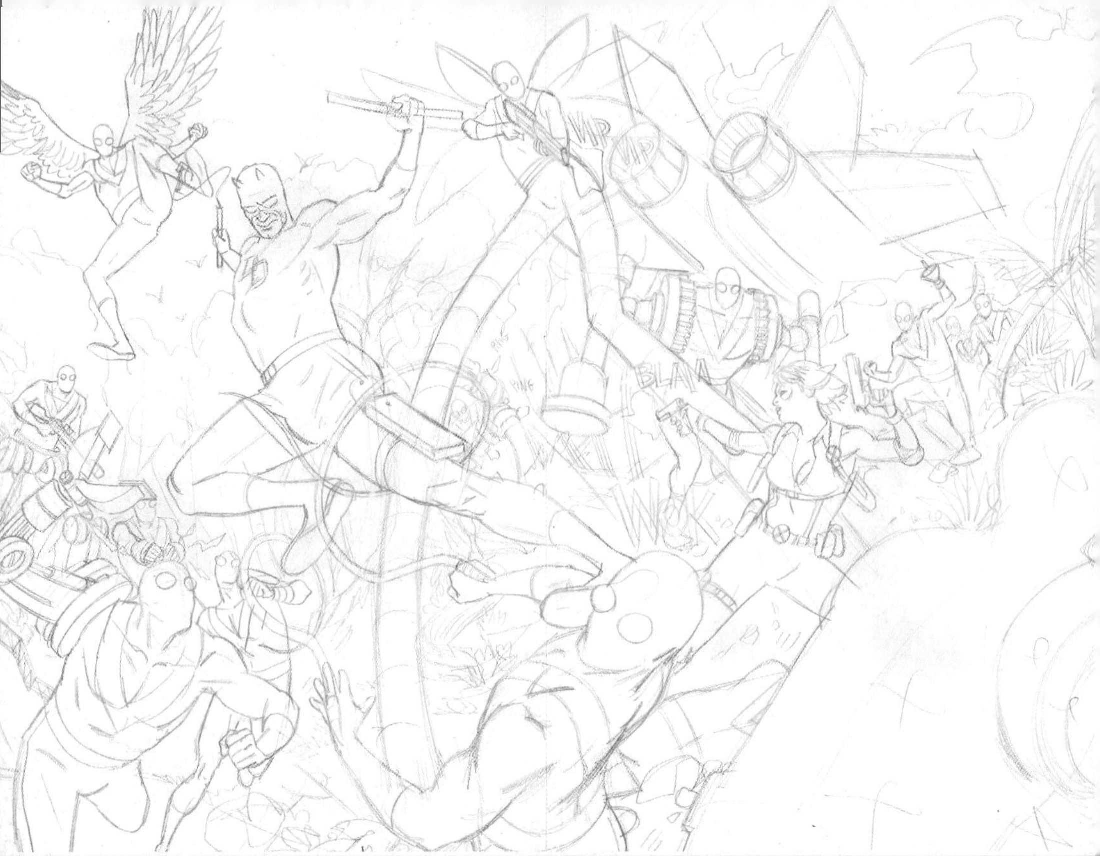
VIP VIP
PING
PING
BLAM
WOK

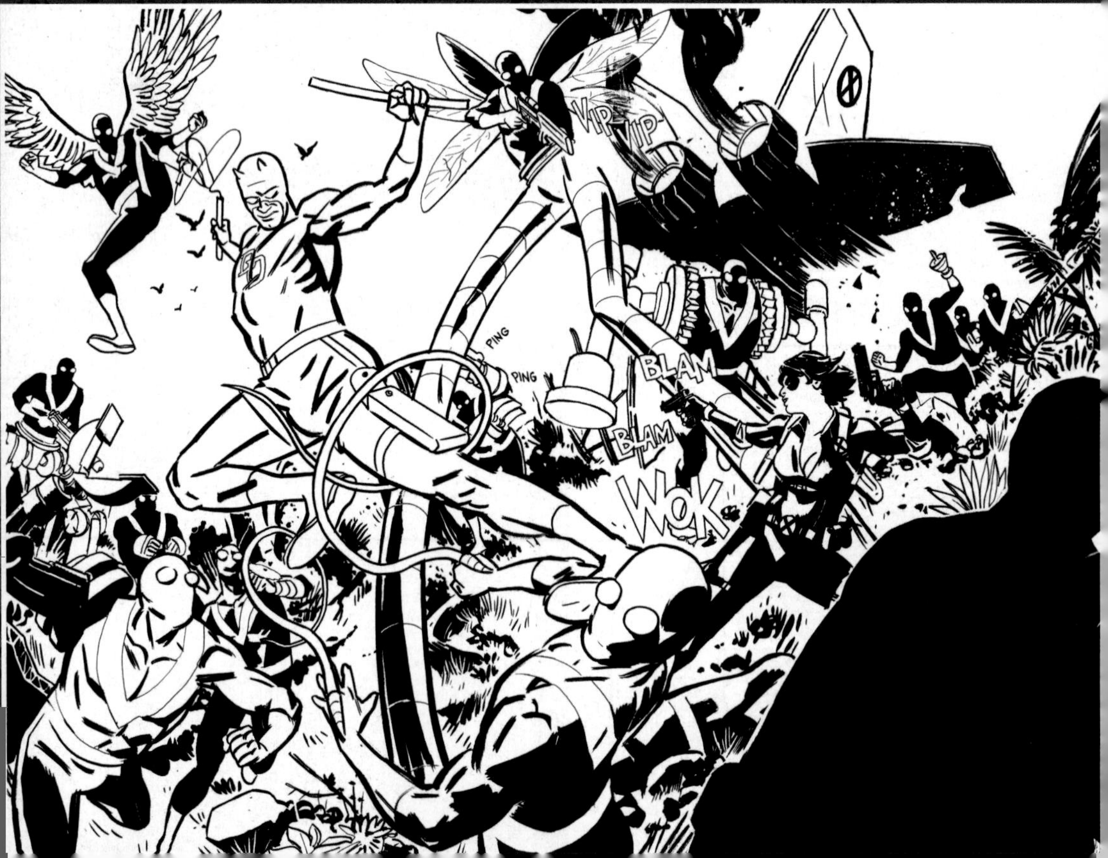
VIP VIP
PING
PING
BLAM
BLAM
WOK

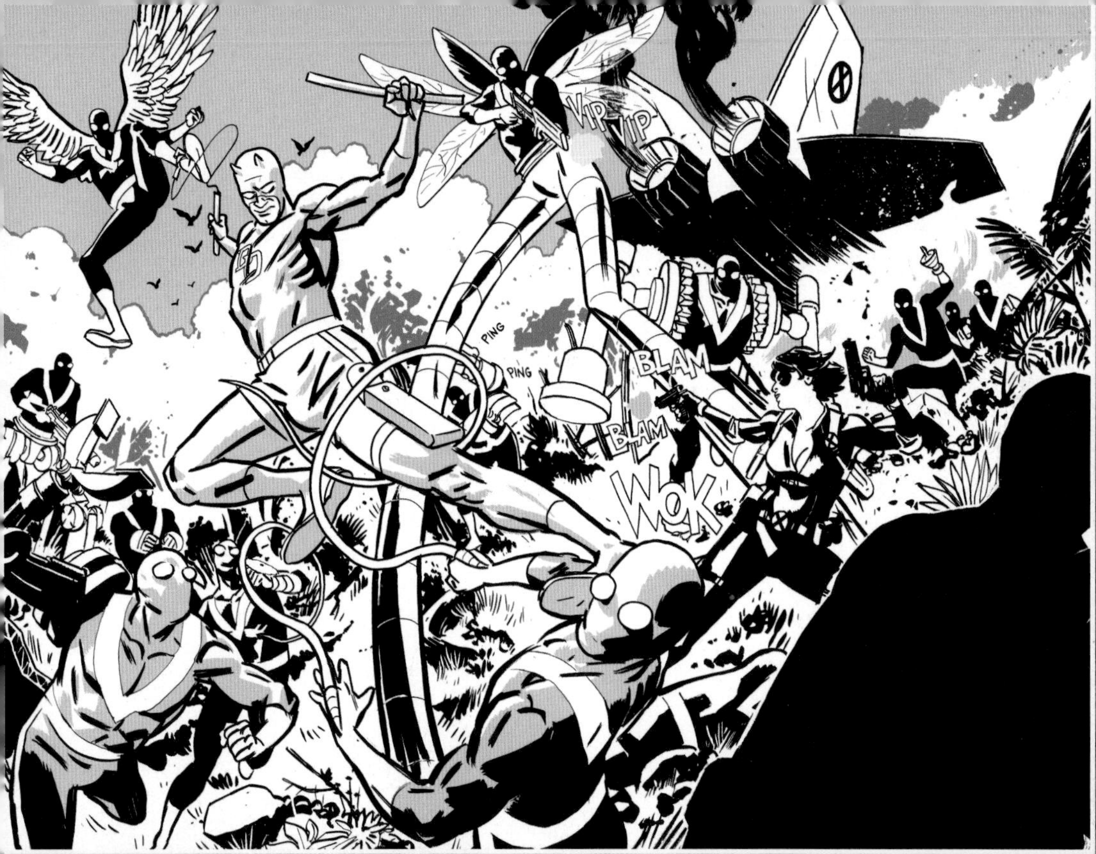
VIP VIP
PING
PING
BLAM
BLAM
WOK

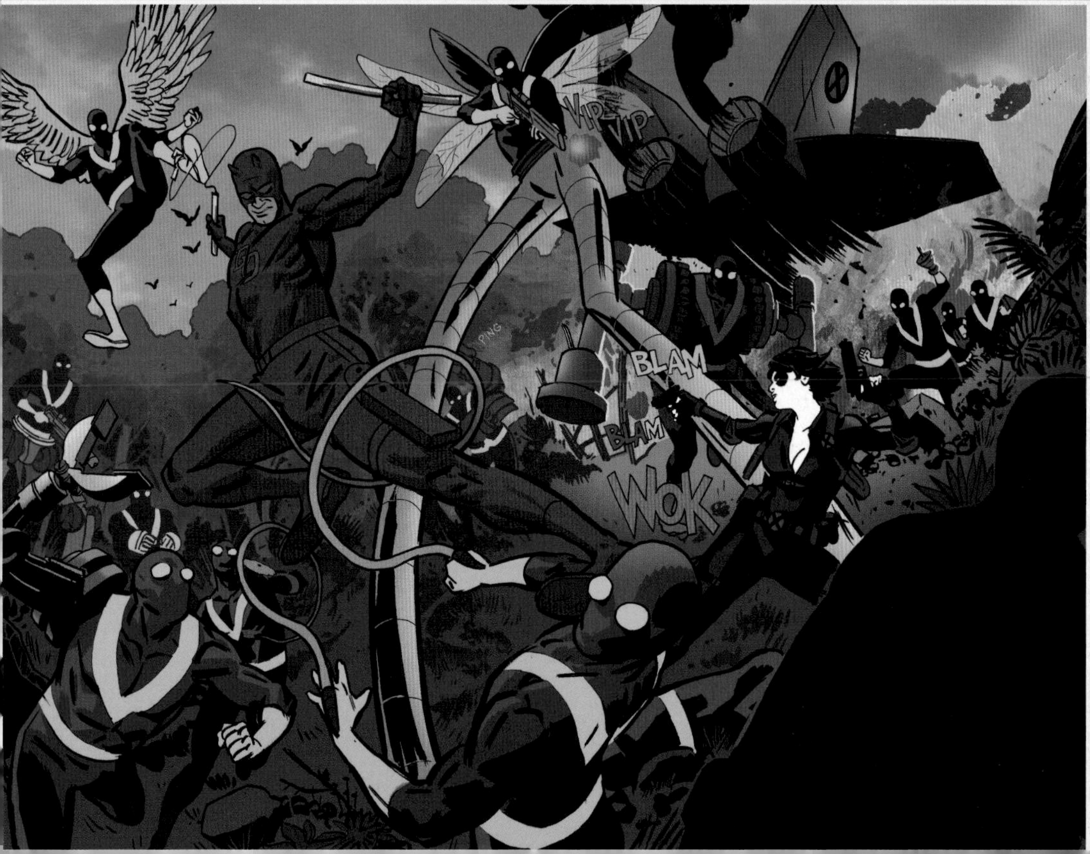
VIP VIP
PING
BLAM
BLAM
WOK

FREEDOM FORCE
CHARACTER SKETCH
BY GUILLERMO MOGORRON

TIN MAN CHARACTER SKETCH
BY JEFTE PALO

TIN MAN